Forth to the Mighty Conflict

(ADDSCO Collection, University of South Alabama Archives)

FORTH TO THE MIGHTY CONFLICT

ALABAMA AND WORLD WAR II

ALLEN CRONENBERG

The University of Alabama Press
Tuscaloosa & London

Library of Congress Cataloging-in-Publication Data

Cronenberg, Allen, 1940–
Forth to the mighty conflict : Alabama and
World War II / Allen Cronenberg.
p.   cm.
Includes bibliographical references and index.
ISBN 0-8173-0737-0
1. World War, 1939–1945—Alabama. 2. Alabama—History—1819–1950. I. Title.
D769.85.A2C76   1994
940.53'761—dc20   94-7603

British Library Cataloguing-in-Publication Data Available

I dedicate this book to my mother,
Virginia Cobb Cronenberg,
who understands the importance of remembering
the wartime experience of the men and women
of her generation,
and to the memory of my father,
A. Thomson Cronenberg (1903–79).

Contents

Preface   ix

One   The Eve of War   1

Two   The United States Goes to War   8

Three   Alabama Goes to War   19

Four   Alabama's Military Camps   36

Five   Producing for Victory   47

Six   Governing Alabama   60

Seven   The War and Society   73

Eight   Prisoners of War   94

Nine   Liberating Europe   109

Ten   Alabama and the War at Sea   125

Eleven   Capturing the Pacific   137

Twelve   The End of the War   161

Appendix   Alabama's War Heroes   167

Notes   175

Bibliography   201

Index   213

Preface

This book is about the profound effects of World War II on Alabama and the contributions the people of the state made to Allied victory over the Axis powers. Initially, it was conceived as an extended essay to commemorate the fiftieth anniversary of Alabama's role in World War II. It was to be written for the Auburn University Center for the Arts and Humanities, which, under the energetic leadership of Leah Rawls Atkins and with a grant from the Alabama Humanities Foundation, launched a year-long public history program entitled "World War II: A Time Remembered." My appointment as scholar in residence at the humanities center in 1991–92 enabled me to complete the research for this manuscript and to begin writing. As the project matured, however, it became clear that the subject of Alabama's role in World War II deserved more than a brief essay.

Although World War II was a watershed event, especially for the American South and West, few regional or state histories of the war's impact exist. This study seeks to fill partially that void. Although monuments to the past—like the patriotic granite tablets and columns standing sentry on the lawns of virtually every county seat in the United States—are important, this book seeks to transcend the mere memorialization of World War II.

The title of this book, *Forth to the Mighty Conflict*, comes from the second verse of a zealous Protestant hymn, "Stand Up, Stand Up, for Jesus." To my mind, World War II assumed something of the character of a crusade. Filled with righteousness, nearly all Americans felt obligated to do their share to vanquish the foes. The nation's sense of purpose and solidarity justified the war's burdens and sacrifices. The mighty conflict did not end in 1945. It is not ended yet. Victory over tyranny and inhumanity abroad hastened the onset of equally momentous moral struggles for equality at home.

This book about Alabama and World War II came about almost accidentally. By birth, I am a North Carolinian who even after more than a quarter century of living in Alabama still retains a strong sense of identity with his home state. Moreover, most of my professional life has centered on European and global history. But a 1984 Independence Day dive on the *Empire Mica*, a British tanker torpedoed by a German submarine during World War II twenty miles off Florida's Cape San Blas in the Gulf of Mexico, aroused my curiosity about the war's impact on the American South. A chance discovery a few years later of a publication issued by the North Carolina Division of Archives and History on that state's role in World War II led me to envision a similar work for the state and people of Alabama.

This project has come to fruition with the support and assistance of many colleagues, friends, and family members. I am particularly indebted to the Auburn University Center for the Arts and Humanities and especially its director, Leah Rawls Atkins, who has achieved remarkable success in developing and taking public humanities programs to eager adult audiences throughout Alabama. Her sensible—and generous—advice invariably pointed me in the direction of indispensable sources. Jay Lamar not only has few peers as copy editor, grammarian, and human thesaurus but she, too, is devoted to promoting the humanities in Alabama. I could always count on Serlester Williams's constant cheerfulness and unflappability in the eye of the storm.

I am also grateful to my colleagues in the History Department who covered my classes during my absence. Gordon Bond, Dean of the College of Liberal Arts, and Tal Henson, Acting Head of the Auburn History Department, tirelessly persevered to obtain my assignment as scholar in residence at Pebble Hill. I profited greatly from the wisdom and experience of Wesley P. Newton, Auburn history professor emeritus, who read the entire manuscript.

Numerous librarians and archivists provided essential assistance in chasing down sources. Gene Geiger, Director of Special Collections in Auburn's Ralph B. Draughon Library, and his staff were always eager to help. Dwayne Cox, Auburn University archivist, drew to my attention several important collections on World War II history. Chapters on the home front could not have been written without materials in the Alabama Department of Archives and History. In particular, I would like to thank Norwood Allen Kerr and other reference archivists for their knowledgeable and thoroughly professional assistance. Librarians at the Linn-Henley Research Library of the Birmingham Public Library and the Aliceville Public Library rendered generous help. Rob Spinner, who has studied World War II's impact on Tennessee, provided information on defense investment in the South. Ray Andrews, Adjutant of the Alabama Department of the American Legion, furnished photographs and biographical sketches of Alabama's Congressional Medal of Honor recipients in World War II. Mike Breland, and his predecessor Gayle Fuller, of the USS *Alabama* Battleship Memorial Park generously provided assistance in recording the role of the battleship in World War II.

Throughout this project, I was aided by dozens of Alabamians—too numerous to mention—who eagerly recounted their experiences in war and at home. I hope this book fairly summarizes their experiences and accords with their remarkably fresh memories of events and circumstances now half a century old.

My wife Frannie and son Tom have been unfailingly constant in their support—and patience—during the last two years. One of my greatest pleasures has been Frannie's enthusiastic interest in Alabama's role in World War II. She seems to think that this topic is an important one. Much to my joy, Tom, who is college-bound and has announced his intention to major in history, has acquired an appreciation for humankind's past.

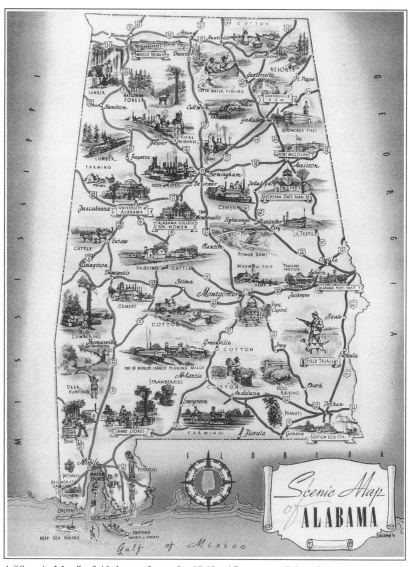

A "Scenic Map" of Alabama from the 1940s. (Courtesy of the Alabama Highway Department)

One

The Eve of War

In the two years before Pearl Harbor, President Franklin D. Roosevelt, with the support of Congress, began to mobilize the nation for war. China's helpless struggle against Japanese aggression in Asia and Germany's blitzkrieg campaign in Europe, culminating in the collapse of France in summer 1940, convinced Roosevelt that the United States had little choice but to prepare for the likelihood of military involvement. Anticipating that the country would require two years to achieve readiness for a global military struggle, the War Department recommended measures to build up a defense infrastructure capable of producing the weapons, munitions, ships, planes, tanks, and other essentials that war would require. Alabama, "the great arsenal of the South," and its nearly three million people were to play an important part in this buildup.[1] The war, in its turn, would play a leading role in shaping the state, initiating or accelerating sweeping changes in many areas of society. It greatly enlarged equality of opportunities with revolutionary implications for race relations and the role of women in society; it accelerated the decline of tenant farming and its replacement by large-scale, mechanized agriculture; it brought about an explosive expansion of industry; it hastened the demise of rural domination and the steady accretion of urban influence; and it expanded educational opportunities through the postwar GI bill of rights.

Conventional wisdom holds that World War II revived the nation's industrial and agricultural output, which eventually surpassed the robust levels of manufacturing and commercial activity of the 1920s. But one of the least appreciated trends of the pre–World War II period was the degree to which the national economy—and Alabama's—had already begun to recover from the Great Depression. The state's steady economic expansion during the four years before 1941 was attested to in late 1941 by W. A. Steadman, president of the Alabama Chamber of Commerce. He reported that fifty-five nondefense industries had opened in Alabama that year, investing $27 million and employing

3,000 Alabamians, while existing industries had spent $78 million in expansion.[2] These investments, however, paled in comparison to defense-related expenditures. In October 1941 the Office of Production Management reckoned that Alabama ranked seventeenth in the nation in defense spending with $600 million in contracts and orders, including $150 million in construction alone. Even agriculture had rebounded. Although cotton was no longer king, its prices recovered to a twelve-year high in the weeks following the attack on Pearl Harbor, selling by late January 1942 for nearly twenty cents a pound, a stark contrast to depression prices of "five-cent cotton."[3]

Warm weather, good transportation systems, extensive rural areas, cheap labor, and a population generally supportive of the armed services made Alabama attractive to both the military, which looked forward to doubling its size, and the private companies that would produce the munitions, outfit the planes, and manufacture the matériel of war. The location of military bases and industrial plants in the state would mean boom times for once-sleepy small towns and a period of busy prosperity unprecedented in Alabama history.

Mobile, particularly, enjoyed an economic boom before the war.[4] With its port facilities and five railroads, the city had excellent transportation. The $4 million Bankhead Tunnel opened in February 1941 and made the city accessible to workers and shoppers from the eastern shore. Although the state docks had opened in 1928, it was 1937 before the state convinced Aluminum Ore Company, a subsidiary of Aluminum Company of America, to lease a site. This $4 million plant became one of the country's three largest aluminum producers. Bauxite for the aluminum industry soon supplanted bananas as Mobile's number-one import.[5] Forest-product companies and chemical industries located plants in Mobile and together represented some $32 million in industrial development in the late 1930s and early 1940s. Thanks to the efforts of the flamboyant and jovial millionaire congressman Frank Boykin, Mobile was chosen over Tampa to become the site of a major facility for bomber modification that at its busiest employed more than 17,000 workers, half of whom were women.[6]

Birmingham, like Mobile, stood to gain economically from the federal government's defense buildup in 1939–41. The Birmingham district possessed coal, iron ore, limestone, and other minerals needed for iron and steel production. Railroads and trucking firms provided excellent transportation for commerce. River barges connected the port of Birmingham on the Warrior River with Mobile. The Birmingham district had 89,000 workers in 1940, and one-third of them labored in mining or iron- and steel-related industries. Although the Tennessee Coal and Iron division of U.S. Steel was the crux of the city's industrial complex, other companies such as Republic Steel Corporation, Sloss-Sheffield Steel and Iron Company, O'Neal Steel Corporation, American Cast Iron Pipe Company (ACIPCO), and Hardie-Tynes Manufacturing Company were heavily involved in arming the United States before the attack on Pearl Harbor.

The city of Montgomery also benefited from the military's buildup. Maxwell Field, on a site selected by the Wright brothers for the country's first flying school during a 1910 visit to the city, began as an Army repair depot during World War I.[7] In the early 1930s the Army transferred its professional school for aviation officers from Langley Field in Virginia to Montgomery. In 1940 Maxwell became the Southeast Air Corps Training Center, and in the following year it also became a large preflight school. At the same time, Montgomery's municipal airport was taken over by the Army, renamed Gunter Field, and converted into a basic flight school. So many pilots, navigators, and bombardiers trained in Montgomery that it was later said that "the road to Tokyo leads through Maxwell Field."[8]

On the eve of the war, more than $6 million was spent adding new barracks, mess halls, and training facilities at Fort McClellan in Anniston.[9] Among the divisions that spent time at McClellan was the Thirty-first, or Dixie Division, which consisted of National Guard components from Alabama and other southeastern states. Following the establishment of the selective service system in autumn 1940, Fort McClellan became an important induction center in the Southeast.

Alabamians worked hard to convince the War Department to build air bases in the state. Congressman Sam Hobbs, Senator Lister Hill, and Dallas County merchants and civic leaders lobbied for Selma's selection as the site for a major aviation training facility. Completed in spring 1941, Craig Field became an advanced single-engine flight school. Camp Rucker, in Dale County, was the result of considerable lobbying by Ozark congressman Henry Steagall.[10] The Wiregrass camp was built on a former Agriculture Department game preserve known as the Bear Farm. In nearby Dothan, Napier Field became a training ground for British, French, and Mexican as well as American aviators.

The construction of an aviation training facility at Tuskegee in 1941 and the formation of the Ninety-ninth Pursuit Squadron commanded by Colonel Benjamin O. Davis, Jr., expanded opportunities for African-American aviators.[11] Prior to 1941, the Army Air Corps did not accept blacks for training as pilots, mechanics, or technical specialists, but mobilization was in full swing and the Air Corps was expanding rapidly. Under the leadership of President Fred D. Patterson, Tuskegee Institute set out to become the center of black aviation in the nation. Since its founding in 1881, Tuskegee Institute had sought to provide for black students the kind of practical education championed by its first president, Booker T. Washington. In 1939 Tuskegee Institute became one of six colleges and two private enterprises to train black aviators under the Civilian Pilot Training Program. In the following year, despite fierce competition from Chicago's Coffey School of Aeronautics, Tuskegee was selected as the only program to offer advanced training to black aviators.[12] Alfred "Chief" Anderson, a pioneer in black aviation, was hired as chief instructor. In order to provide adequate facilities for this program, Tuskegee Institute built an airport, which was named Moton Field.[13]

Under intense pressure from such groups as the National Association for the Advancement of Colored People and the National Airmen's Association of America, and with the encouragement of Eleanor Roosevelt, who visited Tuskegee to express her support, the Army Air Corps agreed to accept black aviators into service. Most proponents of black aviation urged an integrated Air Corps.[14] Instead, the Army established a segregated program at Tuskegee for training black fighter pilots for the Ninety-ninth Pursuit Squadron. The first class of thirteen cadets, including Captain Benjamin O. Davis, Jr., arrived for preflight training in July 1941.[15] Construction of the Tuskegee Army Air Field near the Chehaw community to the north of Tuskegee was under way when war was declared in December.[16] In March 1942 the first five African-Americans to earn their wings as Air Corps pilots graduated from the advanced flight school at Tuskegee.[17]

Military bases brought jobs, money, and prosperity, but they occasionally brought problems as well. Phenix City, long regarded as the sin capital of east Alabama, attracted some of the 50,000 soldiers stationed at Fort Benning in nearby Columbus, Georgia. They hired cabs to take them across the Chattahoochee River to what they called "the western front," where they visited honky-tonks like "Ma" Beachie Howard's, Merryland Bar, Big Apple, and the Dixie Bar. Beer and hard liquors flowed, and high-stakes games of chance were easy to find. Prostitutes could be procured for as little as $2.50, two bucks for their services and four bits for the "accommodations."[18]

Rivaling Phenix City's wild and raucous reputation was Childersburg, where the location of a $46 million DuPont explosives plant had converted a town of about 500 people, with no paved streets and only two policemen, into a boom town. Rumors of bootlegging and prostitution abounded. Investigation into allegations of vice in the area brought reports of, among other things, a dramatic increase in the number of taxicabs, whose "principal business seems to be transporting men to bootlegging joints and to women."[19] Little attention was paid to municipal government. Residents were too busy making money. An often-repeated story claimed that when the mayor stepped down on account of illness, his letter of resignation lay unnoticed on the city clerk's desk for two years.

Other towns experienced tremendous changes as ordnance projects were located in or near them. Job hunters and fortune seekers overran Talladega, seeking employment at the newly constructed Brecon Loading Company, which filled bags with gunpowder for artillery. Housing and sanitation were strained to the limit, and in summer 1941 public health was threatened by the worst outbreak of polio in the state's history. Two ordnance plants were constructed at Huntsville, together costing more than $81 million.[20] The Redstone Ordnance Plant, later known as the Redstone Arsenal, manufactured conventional artillery shells and grenades, and the Huntsville Arsenal produced incendiary material and such highly toxic agents as mustard gas.

In September 1939 Germany's invasion of Poland had prompted President Roosevelt to proclaim a limited state of emergency. Following the collapse of France, Congress authorized the president in late August 1940 to call up the Army Reserves and to federalize the National Guard, creating a force of about half a million men. A little more than a week later, Congress approved a $5 billion defense measure that included, among other things, additional ships for a "two ocean" Navy. Taking an even more radical step, Congress then passed the Selective Training and Service Act, which required all males between the ages of twenty-one and thirty-five to register for a system of military conscription that would induct enough men to create a 1.5 million-member armed force by mid-1941.[21] In writing governors about the duties of the states in the draft system, President Roosevelt pointed out—especially in deference to southern governors—that the law "wisely contemplates that the selective process shall be carried out by the states and the local communities."[22] The president declared 16 October, a Wednesday, as national registration day.

Most Alabamians agreed that democracy was under fire and that strong measures were in order. They supported a strong defense program and increased military aid to Great Britain and to China.[23] The recently established Gallup Poll reported in late September 1940 that 70 percent of southerners believed it was more important to help England than it was to stay out of the war altogether.[24]

In less than two weeks, Alabama governor Frank Dixon and Adjutant General Ben M. Smith created the machinery for the selective service. Approximately 17,000 citizens were appointed to 1,300 boards whose responsibility was to register an anticipated 425,000 eligible males and to supervise the draft.[25] By early June 1941, more than 350,000 Alabamians had registered for the draft. Nationwide, 16 million American men had appeared before selective service boards.[26] Alabama's initial draft quota was set at 39,522 soldiers. The *Negro Year Book*, compiled at Tuskegee Institute and edited for many years by Jessie Parkhurst Guzman, reckoned that only 1.2 percent of white Alabamians called up for induction in 1942 were rejected on educational grounds while more than 19.0 percent of Alabama's black inductees fell short, not surprising in a state that in the late 1930s spent, on average, $840 per white classroom and less than half that amount for each black classroom.[27]

As a stopgap measure before conscription could be fully implemented, National Guard units throughout the United States were expanded and their training intensified. By 1940 the Alabama National Guard had been increased by 900 men to more than 3,800 troops. It eventually furnished 388 active and reserve officers, 3 warrant officers, and 4,985 enlisted men to the Army's Thirty-first Dixie Division. In late March 1939 Colonel Alexander M. Patch, who would later lead the invasions of Guadalcanal and southern France, became senior infantry instructor for the Alabama National Guard. Never before had these guard troops received such high-quality military instruction.[28] On the eve of the war, Brigadier General John C. Persons, president of the First National Bank of Birmingham, succeeded Albert H. Blanding of Florida as the commanding officer of the Dixie Division. Persons later achieved the distinction of being one of only two National Guard commanders to lead their divisions into combat during World War II. Although Persons's troops fought with distinction in the Pacific campaign, the Dixie Division was equally well known as a training division to which numerous units were assigned for additional training before being shipped overseas. The Thirty-first Division took considerable pride in its claim that it trained more recruits during World War II than any other division in the Army.

By summer 1941, fully six months prior to the Japanese attack on Pearl Harbor, Alabama's military bases, defense industries, port facilities, and selective service system were in full tilt and prepared to serve the nation's needs in the event of hostilities.

Two

The United States Goes to War

Months before the attack on Pearl Harbor, an undeclared state of war existed between the United States and the Axis nations. On the high seas, the naval forces of Germany and the United States had fired shots in anger. Although officially a neutral nation, the United States aided Great Britain in many ways. In exchange for British bases in the Americas, President Roosevelt transferred fifty destroyers to the British navy. American warships routinely assisted Allied convoys in the Atlantic. For his part, Adolf Hitler had forbidden German naval forces from initiating an attack at sea on American vessels. But heavy seas, foul weather, and darkness often made it difficult to identify with certainty the nationality of vessels in the Atlantic sea-lanes. Consequently, German U-boats had come perilously close to ramming or torpedoing U.S. destroyers. Under such circumstances, the odds were high that a warlike incident eventually would occur.[1]

In early September 1941 an episode in the Denmark Strait off the coast of Iceland involving the American destroyer *Greer* and a German U-boat brought the two nations to the brink of war. Believing the American destroyer to be part of a British naval and air antisubmarine attack force, the commander of U-652 launched torpedoes at the American warship. The *Greer* took evasive action, and although no harm was done, Roosevelt issued "shoot first" orders and instructed the Navy to fire upon any vessel imperiling maritime traffic.[2] Six weeks later, during the night of 17 October 1941, while escorting a convoy that came under fierce attack by a German U-boat wolfpack in the North Atlantic, the American destroyer *Kearney* was torpedoed. The badly damaged *Kearney*, on which 18 Alabamians served, limped to port, but 11 U.S. sailors were dead, including an Alabamian, Russell Burdick Wade.[3] Just one day away from celebrating his first anniversary in the Navy, the twenty-one-year-old Wade, from the small town of Houston in Winston County, became the first of 4,500 U.S. servicemen from Alabama to lose their lives in the Second World War.[4] Over the next six weeks, undeclared war and additional menacing actions raged in the North Atlantic. The sinking of the destroyer *Reuben James* on 31 October with the loss of 115 lives nearly provoked the United States into dropping its "short of war" policy.[5]

Far to the west, the Pacific Fleet had been stationed at Pearl Harbor since April 1940 to act as a deterrent to Japanese aggression. A smaller Asiatic Fleet was at Manila, thus closer to the Asian mainland but with no vessel larger than a cruiser. General Douglas MacArthur, then serving as adviser to the Philippines, was recalled to active duty and ordered to prepare for the defense of the island commonwealth. To strengthen MacArthur's forces, thirty-five B-17 bombers and various other aircraft were transferred from Oahu to the Philippines in autumn 1941. This move left General Walter C. Short with only a half dozen B-17 Flying Fortresses and a handful of older bombers to defend the Hawaiian Islands. As diplomatic tensions mounted, careful observers regarded war with Japan as highly likely.

In Alabama, the weekend of Japan's surprise attack on Pearl Harbor began like any other. Colder than usual, the people in Mobile were warned that temperatures were likely to dip below freezing. Snow flurries were possible in northern Alabama. Although it was not a big football weekend in the state, Crimson Tide fans were interested in the outcome of the Texas A & M game against Washington State. Coach Frank Thomas's team was lined up to play the Aggies in the Cotton Bowl on New Year's Day, and the 7–0 Aggie victory guaranteed that the Tide would have its hands full. Two of the big bowl games for black colleges were being played that weekend. Many of Tuskegee Institute's fans had gone to Orlando, only to see their team lose to a tough Florida A & M squad in the Orange Blossom Bowl.[6]

Sunday morning newspapers on 7 December 1941 carried headlines about the Russo-Finnish war and about the desperate Russian resistance against the Germans just outside Moscow. There was also mention of deteriorating relations with Japan. Journalists had little hope that Emperor Hirohito's two emissaries who were in Washington that very weekend would agree to concessions that would reduce tensions between Japan and the United States. Newspapers speculated that a secret message that Roosevelt had just sent to the Japanese emperor was a last-ditch effort to avert hostilities in the Far East.[7] After church, people returned home to finish reading their newspapers, fry chicken for dinner, and perhaps go visiting after a nap.

Hollywood was at its height in 1941. Walt Disney's classic animated film, *Fantasia,* had drawn large audiences following its opening in November. On the eve of the Pearl Harbor attack, two of the year's finest films debuted on silver screens across the state. Orson Welles's critically acclaimed *Citizen Kane* was at Birmingham's Empire Theatre.[8] Elsewhere, Alabamians braved the cold to see young and handsome Gary Cooper portray the title character in *Sergeant York.*[9] This was a timely film, which the critics had called propaganda, about a deeply religious mountain man from Tennessee to whom the commandment not to take life was sacred but who had become one of World War I's most decorated heroes. In a less serious vein, Leo Gorcy and the East Side Kids were engaged in a zany *Bowery Blitzkrieg,* while Bing Crosby, Dorothy Lamour, and Bob Hope were on the cinematic road again, this time to Zanzibar.[10]

Black moviegoers who were soon to be called upon to defend democracy and freedom had to purchase their tickets on that "day of infamy" at the side windows of movie box offices. Climbing steep stairs to reach the balconies, African-Americans sat in roped-off "Colored" sections, areas that future Selma attorney J. L. Chestnut, Jr.—at that time a student at Knox Academy, Selma's segregated black high school—and his friends called the Buzzards' Roost.[11]

Television was in its infancy in big cities in 1941. For most Americans, listening to the radio was a popular Sunday activity. Big bands dominated the airwaves. The year 1941 produced several hits that became enduring American favorites, including Glenn Miller's "Chattanooga Choo Choo," which sold a million copies, and Duke Ellington's "Take the 'A' Train." The "sweet swing" sound of the Sammy Kaye orchestra was popular on Sunday afternoons. In the evening, the Jimmy Dorsey band featured two of the nation's favorite vocalists, blonde Helen O'Connell and Buddy Eberle. Jimmy Dorsey's band had no fewer than six of 1941's top ten big-band tunes, including "Amapola," which was the year's top selling recording.[12] Devotees of classical music looked forward to the Philadelphia Philharmonic. Later in the afternoon, Bulldog Drummond would be solving a crime or helping out a "dame" in distress. Jack Benny, the Great Gildersleeve, and Charlie

McCarthy promised many laughs. Instead of dialing in favorite programs on the evening following the attack on Pearl Harbor, most Alabamians gathered around their radios to hear popular newsmen H. V. Kaltenborn and Walter Winchell discuss the few sketchy details about the shocking news from Hawaii.[13]

Many Alabamians remember vividly what they were doing when they first heard the news about Japan's surprise attack. Hoyt M. Warren, a young graduate of Alabama Polytechnic Institute who went on to become a P-51 pilot in a famed reconnaissance squadron in Europe during the war, later reminisced that he and several friends left Mrs. Sadler's guest hotel in Camden just a little before noon on that fateful Sunday to see a movie in nearby Selma.[14] Around one o'clock, as the lights in the Wilby Theater dimmed, a message flickered on the screen: "Flash! Flash! News Bulletin! The Japanese have attacked Pearl Harbor!" Even the madcap high jinks of Bud Abbott and Lou Costello in *Keep 'Em Flyin'* could not keep Warren from realizing that he was destined to play a part in this unfolding war. Perhaps, he thought, he could earn his wings at the new flight school at nearby Craig Field.

Five thousand miles to the west, several Alabamians found themselves in the midst of Japan's attack on Pearl Harbor. Joan Nist, later a professor of education at Auburn University for nearly twenty years, was a high school junior in Hawaii in December 1941. She remembers spending that Saturday night at the home of a girlfriend whose house overlooked Wheeler Field. Just before eight o'clock on that Sunday morning, while getting ready for church, Joan and her friend heard the steady hum of distant planes coming through a narrow pass between the hills. As there had been numerous drills in recent days, the two girls gave little thought to the appearance of so many aircraft. To their horror, these planes began dropping real bombs whose explosions were soon heard. Plumes of smoke rose from the devastated American warships in the harbor. Joan and her friend were especially taken aback when a Japanese plane, apparently mistaking a nearby orange-roofed building for military barracks, broke formation and flew along a ridge toward them, strafing a neighbor's chicken house as it approached.[15] In Honolulu, Montgomerian Anna Busby, a member of the Army Nurse Corps, tended to the wounded who flooded into Tripler General Hospital.[16]

Confusion reigned in the harbor. Initial news accounts greatly underestimated the casualties and damage. Headlines in the *Montgomery Advertiser* claimed "JAPS KILL 350 AMERICANS IN SURPRISE PLANE ATTACK."[17] In reality, the bomb that blew up the forward magazine of the *Arizona* alone killed more than 1,000 sailors. One of those was Luther James Isom, a sailor from Huntsville. Another was Charles Andrew Boyd from outside Dothan. Julius Ellsberry, a mess attendant from Birmingham, was one of nearly 500 sailors who lost their lives on the USS *Oklahoma*, which capsized after being torpedoed. Ellsberry became Jefferson County's first war victim and Alabama's first African-American serviceman killed in combat. The *Birmingham World* hailed Ellsberry as the Crispus Attucks of World War II.[18]

The Pearl Harbor attack was a humiliation in many ways. The intelligence from which Japanese intentions might have been divined was never properly evaluated. Defenses were lax. Following customary practice, many vessels in the Pacific Fleet had returned to Oahu for the weekend so that sailors could enjoy recreation on shore. At the airfields, planes, which had been parked wingtip to wingtip to prevent sabotage, provided sitting-duck targets for Japanese dive-bombers and strafing fighters. Few of the planes on Oahu managed to take to the air. Of six Army fliers decorated for their actions at Pearl Harbor, two had graduated from advanced flight school at Maxwell Field after doing their basic training at Gunter Field. Each destroyed a Japanese plane in a dogfight.[19]

Captain Charles H. McMorris and Lieutenant Joseph H. Willingham were two career naval officers from Alabama who survived Pearl Harbor. McMorris, a Wetumpka native and 1912 graduate of the United States Naval Academy, served as chief of war plans for Admiral Husband E. Kimmel, the commander of U.S. naval forces in the Pacific. Renowned for his analytical brilliance, friends called him Socrates. Convinced that Japan's strategic interest lay in Asia and not in the mid-Pacific, McMorris dismissed any prospect of a Japanese air attack on Pearl Harbor. When asked by Kimmel only ten days earlier what possibility there was that the Japanese would attack Hawaii, McMorris had answered, "None, absolutely none."[20]

Unlike his chief, McMorris was not sacked in the aftermath of the attack. McMorris later commanded the heavy cruiser *San Francisco* in the Battle of Cape Esperance off Guadalcanal in October 1942, for which he received the Navy Cross. He was promoted to admiral and served as chief of staff to Commander in Chief Pacific Fleet Chester Nimitz from July 1943 to September 1945, during which time U.S. forces hopped from island to island across the Pacific.[21]

Joe Willingham of Pell City, who became one of the most celebrated World War II submarine skippers, commanded the *Tautog,* which, during the furious attack on Pearl Harbor, was tied to one of the finger piers at Southeast Loch near Kaneohe Naval Air Station. Willingham had come aboard in 1940 as the submarine's first skipper. Ordered to Pearl Harbor shortly after commissioning, the *Tautog* joined twenty-one other submarines in Rear Admiral Thomas Withers's Pacific submarine fleet. On the eve of Japan's attack, Willingham and the *Tautog* had only recently returned from Midway Island, where they had engaged in maneuvers and deep dives.[22]

At about nine o'clock on the morning of 7 December, when the second wave of Japanese bombers appeared over Oahu, a skeleton crew on the *Tautog* swung into action, firing its .50-caliber machine guns. Directed by Barney Sieglaff, who later succeeded Willingham as the *Tautog*'s skipper, the gunners downed a Japanese plane, which fell into the water not more than fifty yards away. The *Tautog* is credited with being the first U.S. submarine to shoot down a Japanese warplane.

Suffering no damage, the submarine subsequently eased out of Pearl Harbor to scout the Marshall Islands. Willingham's observations of Bikini, Kwajalein, and other islands in that group provided essential intelligence for Admiral William "Bull" Halsey, whose task force of three carriers made the first American retaliatory strike against the Japanese in the Marshall and Gilbert islands on 1 February 1942.

At Pearl Harbor the U.S. fleet lay in tatters. Three battleships were sunk, another capsized, and four more required repairs before they could sail against the enemy. Three cruisers, three destroyers, and numerous smaller vessels had been destroyed by Japanese bombers. Japanese attacks on Pearl Harbor's airfields destroyed about 170 aircraft and damaged 102 others. Nearly 2,400 American servicemen and civilians lost their lives and another 1,000 were wounded in the two waves of attack. The Japanese attackers suffered minimal, and acceptable, losses—49 aircraft and five midget subs.[23]

The surprise attack on Pearl Harbor could have been worse. The

Students at Alabama Polytechnic Institute in Auburn listen to President Roosevelt's address to Congress after Pearl Harbor. (Auburn University Archives)

fleet's three aircraft carriers, quite by chance, were at sea in the Pacific. Admiral Isoroku Yamamoto's plan targeted ships, not harbor facilities and oil storage tanks, which would have taken much longer to replace or repair. Finally, because the harbor is no deeper than forty feet, several warships were quickly raised, repaired, and returned to battle. Nonetheless, the cry "Remember Pearl Harbor" galvanized the American people.

On 8 December President Roosevelt addressed a joint session of Congress, telling the assembled lawmakers that the attack on Pearl Harbor was a day that would live in infamy. Alabama students, such as senior Neal Howard and junior William Robinson of Montgomery's Sidney Lanier High School, listened intently to FDR's speech, which was broadcast over the intercom into cafeterias and classrooms.[24] Pensive students at Alabama Polytechnic Institute in Auburn gathered around a loudspeaker mounted atop an automobile parked beside

Langdon Hall to hear the proceedings in Congress.[25] With one dissenting voice, Congress voted for war against Japan. Three days later, the other Axis powers—Germany and Italy—declared war on the United States. Fearing attacks on continental America, reinforcements rushed to the Atlantic and Pacific coasts. Wild rumors of imminent invasion by German soldiers landing in dirigibles abounded. Alabama National Guard troops of the Thirty-first Dixie Division were ordered from training at Camp Blanding, Florida, to help guard Jacksonville Naval Air Station and Fort McDill in Tampa. The Twenty-seventh Division, a National Guard outfit from New York that was training at Fort McClellan in Anniston, dispatched 600 troops to protect the ordnance plant in Childersburg and 60 troops to secure Wheeler Dam.[26] When fear of invasion subsided, the Twenty-seventh Division received orders to entrain for southern California to await embarkation for the Pacific.[27]

The attack on Pearl Harbor was only the opening move in Japan's unfolding strategy to eliminate American power in the Pacific. Elsewhere, Japanese forces went into action, catching the Americans and British unprepared. Only hours after the attack on Pearl Harbor, two Japanese destroyers shelled Midway Island, where a small U.S. Marine detachment was stationed. This attack was followed by Japanese bombing of American installations at Wake and Guam islands and attacks on British positions at Nauru and Ocean islands. In Southeast Asia, Japanese forces invaded Thailand and, following a naval bombardment, landed on the beaches of British Malaya and drove toward Singapore, which surrendered two months later. In China, Kowloon fell to the Japanese, and on Christmas Day British forces surrendered Hong Kong. As British positions crumbled in the Far East, the Japanese moved against Dutch colonies. Following landings in the Celebes, at Rabaul, and in the Solomons, Japanese armies overran the resource-rich Netherlands East Indies.[28]

The last remaining major obstacle to Japanese domination over the western Pacific and Asia was General Douglas MacArthur's force in the Philippines, and his position looked increasingly untenable. Inexplicably, Japanese bombers from Formosa caught MacArthur by surprise. Most of his Far Eastern Air Force—eighteen of thirty-five Flying Fortresses, fifty-six fighters, and twenty-five other planes—was destroyed on the ground at Clark and Iba fields while its pilots were eating lunch just hours after Japan's attack on Pearl Harbor. By 10 December, when troops from two Japanese task forces from Formosa began landing on Luzon, American air power in the Philippines had been neutralized.[29]

Following the main Japanese landings on 22 December, the American and Filipino defenders fell back rapidly, and Japanese forces entered Manila early in the new year. MacArthur withdrew to the Bataan peninsula, but the situation there grew increasingly hopeless. As supplies dwindled, Americans and Filipinos were soon on half rations. Toward the end of February, President Roosevelt ordered MacArthur to leave the Philippines for Australia. Reluctantly, MacArthur, his wife, son, and close aides boarded four PT boats on the heavily fortified island of Corregidor in Manila Bay. After reaching Mindanao three days later, they took a Flying Fortress to Darwin in Australia, where MacArthur assumed command of forces in the southwest Pacific.

Meanwhile, General Jonathan Wainwright succeeded MacArthur in the Philippines. The condition of Wainwright's "battling bastards of Bataan" continued to deteriorate. Malnourished and riddled with malaria, less than a fourth of the troops on Bataan were capable of fighting. Early in April most of the American troops surrendered to the Japanese, while Wainwright and a remnant of soldiers fell back to the island fortress of Corregidor with its many tunneled passageways. For the next month, Japanese artillery and bombers mercilessly pounded the island. The 11,000 defenders of "The Rock" knew that their days were numbered, but miraculously no one inside the island's tunnels was killed by the bombardment. After a month of nearly continuous shelling, Wainwright—completely without hope and fearful of the carnage he expected the Japanese to inflict upon the nurses, civilians, and soldiers within Malinta Tunnel—ordered the surrender of Corregidor.

Several Alabamians played conspicuous roles in the last days of Corregidor and the organization of Filipino resistance, only to fall prisoner to the Japanese. One was Brigadier General Carl H. Seals, who served as MacArthur's adjutant general in the Philippines. Born in Eufaula, Seals had moved to Birmingham where he became a banker before joining the Army during the First World War. Remaining in the Army following the Versailles Treaty, Seals was eventually posted to the Philippines, where at the time of the Japanese invasion he was in his third tour of duty. Seals, his wife Margaret, and seven nurses were captured by the Japanese in May when their escape plane developed engine problems over Mindanao.[30]

The war in the Philippines, however, had not ended with the defeat at Bataan, MacArthur's departure for Australia, and Wainwright's surrender at Corregidor. The Filipinos continued to wage a guerrilla struggle from the mountains. An American around whom some of the guerrillas coalesced was Captain Joseph Rhett Barker. Growing up in Birmingham in the early days of the depression, Barker developed a fancy for horsemanship. This passion drew him into the Birmingham Sabres, a cavalry unit of the Alabama National Guard. Following a stint as orderly to Alabama's National Guard commander, General John C. Persons, Barker received an appointment to the United States Military Academy at West Point.[31]

Barker was posted to the Philippines in 1938, where he served in the Twenty-sixth Regiment of Philippine Scouts. Infatuated with his new surroundings, the young officer acquired a rudimentary knowledge of Luzon's languages, studied the history of the Philippines, and collected ceramic artifacts of early Chinese settlements in the islands. In his first two years in the Philippines, he had much time for polo and the active social life of a bachelor.

Barker's life of leisure ended in 1941. As war clouds gathered in the Pacific, General MacArthur and his officers hastened their efforts to shape their Filipino allies into an effective fighting force. Captain Barker and the Twenty-sixth Philippine Scouts were among the best-trained soldiers facing General Masaharu Homma's 43,000 Japanese troops who waded ashore at Lingayen Gulf just before Christmas 1941. Pushed back by Homma's Fourteenth Army, they struggled southward through the jungle. Exhausted, they were among the last effective units in Bataan. With surrender imminent, Barker and the remnant of the Twenty-sixth Philippine Scouts made their way into the mountains to join forces with Colonel Claude Thorpe, who established liaison with organized guerrilla resistance in the interior of Luzon.[32]

Following Thorpe's capture and execution by the Japanese, Barker attempted, with little success, to subordinate this group of Philippine nationalists to American military control. By day, the guerrillas hid in the mountains; at night they harassed the enemy in the central plain.

Disguised as a priest, Barker made contact in Manila with the anti-Japanese underground, which in December 1942 produced a crude but effective resistance newspaper, taunting the Japanese and urging Filipinos to resist the occupation of their islands.

Mounting a vigorous campaign to crush these rebels, the Japanese captured Barker during a raid at Makatipu in Rizal Province in January 1943. There was a widespread belief that he had been betrayed. Barker was taken first to Santiago Prison in Manila and then in September to the notorious Bilibid Prison built by the Spaniards in the sixteenth century. Failing to break Barker with torture into betraying his fellow guerrillas, the Japanese executed him in a Chinese cemetery a few miles north of Manila where he and five other prisoners were unceremoniously dumped into an unmarked grave. Never crushed by the Japanese, the guerrilla movement continued to harry the occupiers and played an important role in the liberation of the Philippines when General MacArthur returned in 1944. Virtually unknown until after the war, Barker's courage and zeal were revealed through letters of individuals who knew him, especially in those last months as a war prisoner. Paying tribute after the war to this incredible exploit, General Wainwright attended a Birmingham memorial service in which the Distinguished Service Cross, Silver Cross, and Purple Heart were awarded posthumously to Captain Barker.[33]

In the five months between the attack on Pearl Harbor and the surrender of American forces on Luzon, the Japanese had achieved virtual domination over the western Pacific. Only Australia and India offered possibilities as bastions from which counterattacks against Japan could be launched. Although little real damage was done, Lieutenant Colonel Jimmy Doolittle's raid on Japan in mid-April 1942 boosted American spirits. The sixteen B-25s that took off from the deck of the carrier *Hornet* and flew to Japan demonstrated that with sufficient air and naval power at their disposal the United States and its allies could dislodge the Japanese from their Asian hegemony.

Three

Alabama Goes to War

Alabamians reacted to the news of Pearl Harbor and the opening of war in the Pacific with both relief and dread. Correspondents from *Time* magazine, sampling public sentiments about the attack, summarized the mood of people in Birmingham: "They are deeply resentful of the treachery. Vengeance-bent, confident of victory, dazzled by cataclysm, but with little second thought yet of the cost."[1] What had been feared so long had finally come to pass, although not quite in the way many people had imagined. The nation's attention had largely been riveted upon Europe. The boldness of Japan's daring raid on the Pacific Fleet in Hawaii took the United States by surprise, although those who kept abreast of world events had realized for months that war with the Axis nations was virtually inevitable. But the sense of relief was soon displaced by concern and fear about the future.

Following President Franklin D. Roosevelt's address to a joint session of Congress shortly after noon on 8 December 1941, the United States formally declared war against Japan. There was only one dissenting vote, that of Representative Jeanette Rankin, an isolationist and pacifist from Montana who had voted against war in 1917 and who said that good democracies should never be unanimous, even in making war. Most Americans, however, believed this war was necessary and just. A *Montgomery Advertiser* editorial three days after the attack on Pearl Harbor reflected the generally held view that "the attack has solidified American sentiment as nothing else would have done." The "treacherous attack" on Pearl Harbor, the editorial continued, "serves to squelch forever the specious arguments of those who held that an ordered, happy life was still possible on this planet, even with gangster mobs roaming and pillaging its surface." Indulging in xenophobia, this editorial claimed that Japanese and Germans were "far less admirable than the lowest Indian savages our ancestors exterminated." What lay ahead was "a dirty, unpleasant job, with precious little romance or glamour." Americans, the editorial soberly concluded, would be called upon to make many sacrifices.[2]

Throughout the world crisis leading up to war and in the war itself, most black Alabamians patriotically supported the war against the Axis powers. Nonetheless, African Americans were acutely aware of the irony of the nation's struggle to defend democracy abroad and to oppose nazism's racist doctrines while at home racial segregation remained entrenched. Hugh Hill, editor of the *Talladega Student*, expressed a widely held view when he declared that fellow students at his black college were willing to defend the United States and "precious liberty." But, he added, "We want to defend a nation which gives all her citizens a chance to win bread and cast ballots, we want to defend a nation which gives all her youth a chance to learn and grow."[3] With varying degrees of commitment, Alabamians stood shoulder to shoulder with the rest of the nation in opposing aggression abroad.

Armed with broad public support and at war with Japan, but not yet with Germany, Roosevelt found himself in a dilemma. The president had favored a Germany-first policy. Declaration of U.S. neutrality in Europe's war belied Roosevelt's undisguised support for beleaguered Britain. Roosevelt's quandary was solved by Japan's European allies who themselves had been kept in the dark about Yamamoto's audacious plan to bomb the American fleet in Hawaii. Caught off guard by the events in the Pacific, Germany and Italy declared war on the United States four days after the attack on Pearl Harbor.[4]

Fear of enemy sabotage swept the United States. Paranoia eventually led to wholesale relocation of tens of thousands of Japanese-Americans in the Pacific Coast states. The southeastern states, in contrast, had few identifiable resident aliens. Governor Frank Dixon, however, warned Axis aliens in Alabama that they had until 28 January 1942 to register for an identification certificate. The 1940 census revealed that only 21 of the estimated 127,000 Japanese living in the United States resided in Alabama. Less than twelve hours after the bombing of Pearl Harbor, authorities in Athens, Alabama, arrested a Japanese citizen who was suspected of terrorist intentions. When it was established that the alleged saboteur was a thirty-three-year-old Presbyterian minister from Hokkaido and a guest of Professor J. T. Wright, the director of Trinity School whom he had met at the Union Seminary of Sacred Music in New York, Mr. Matsumoto was released.[5] Elsewhere in Alabama, authorities briefly detained five Germans and one Italian.

Because of its heavy concentration of industry, Birmingham was popularly believed to be the second or third most important city on Germany's list of vital targets. Pittsburgh and possibly New York would be hit first, followed by Birmingham. Even such smaller communities as Huntsville rushed to post guards at their public water works to prevent alien agents from poisoning the local populace. In May 1942 the *Mobile Press Register* announced Federal Bureau of Investigation "Anti-Espionage Classes" for local law-enforcement personnel.[6]

Fear of Axis espionage and sabotage grew more frenzied following the arrest in late June 1942 of two groups of German agents who, along with explosives and a considerable amount of cash, had been put ashore by German submarines. One group landed on a remote stretch of beach just south of Jacksonville, Florida. The second sabotage team paddled to a beach on Long Island, New York. The apprehension of these saboteurs, followed by their highly publicized secret trial and the execution of all except two who cooperated with the FBI, created an atmosphere of distrust toward aliens throughout the United States. Coastal dimouts, urban blackouts, and air-raid drills fanned American paranoia.

Fearing domestic emergencies, President Roosevelt created an Office of Civilian Defense in May 1942. At its head was the popular mayor of New York City, Fiorello H. La Guardia. Civilian defense officials organized local communities to prepare for air raids, sabotage of electrical power systems or water supplies, civilian disorders, and other emergencies. Normally the National Guard would have carried out many of these duties, but it had been federalized. Alabama, along with many other states, created a State Guard, consisting of approximately 2,600 part-time soldiers, that was called out on several occasions to deal with natural catastrophes, labor conflicts, and racial disturbances. To create networks of emergency personnel in local communities, La Guardia oversaw the formation of state civilian defense organizations.

Within a year of its creation, Alabama's civilian defense program could boast of being the leading program in the Southeast and second only to Indiana among all the states.[7] A State Defense Council, headed by Calhoun County's Houston Cole, coordinated state civilian defense activities. In Alabama nearly 80,000 individuals, including 23,000 women, became involved in civilian defense activities or were participating in training programs. The largest number of volunteers were air-raid wardens, followed by Red Cross workers, almost half of whom were women. In addition each community had auxiliary police, auxiliary firemen, emergency personnel, and crews for demolition and clearance. In the aftermath of the Pearl Harbor attack, coastal cities grew jittery. Although New Yorkers shrugged off the fear of attack, tensions ran high in San Francisco, Los Angeles, and other West Coast cities.

Throughout Alabama, local defense councils grew more alert and reviewed plans for catastrophe. Typical of the local civilian defense groups was the Limestone County Defense Council, which met in the office of Athens's mayor, R. H. Richardson, on 11 December to go over plans for providing first aid, emergency policemen, and emergency firemen.[8] To keep an eye on tunnels, bridges, and trestles, the L & N Railroad hired special guards, and Fort McClellan sent soldiers to secure Decatur's bridges over the Tennessee River and to protect the river's dams and locks.

Civilian defense authorities established training courses to teach volunteers about procedures for air-raid warnings and blackouts. To the great disappointment of the state's Saint Patrick's Day celebrants, the first statewide blackout was held on Tuesday, 17 March 1942. Beginning in Mobile and moving northward, every town or city with 5,000 or more residents extinguished all lights, an exercise that was capped with a speech by Governor Dixon.[9] In May 1942 the State Defense Council began distributing sirens and other equipment to local communities.

Dissatisfied with the presumed absence of imaginative and forceful civilian defense leadership at the national level, states and municipalities began taking matters into their own hands. In Birmingham enthusiastic civil defense officials organized an antiterrorist exercise, the goal of which was to capture saboteurs who parachuted at night into their city. Taking up positions in the middle of a Birmingham golf course, sixteen "saboteurs" tried to run past a cordon of a hundred men on the perimeter. Using rules similar to tag football, only twelve of these make-believe terrorists were apprehended. Luckily for Birmingham, no real enemy agents attempted to infiltrate the city.

The ground observer corps watched the skies to give warning against approaching enemy bombers. A Japanese carrier-based attack posed only the remotest threat to the West Coast, and Germany lacked aircraft carriers. Only if Martinique or some other Caribbean possession of Vichy France fell under German control was there the slimmest possibility that the Southeast could be bombed. Nonetheless, ground observers posted themselves along the coasts, binoculars and silhouette charts in hand, to give warning in the event of an air attack.

The Civil Air Patrol was of greater practical utility.[10] Founded by La Guardia in 1941, the CAP transported officials and emergency messages or supplies around the country and flew antisubmarine missions along lengthy and sometimes desolate American shores. Although claims were exaggerated during the war, CAP planes were credited by war's end with destroying two German submarines off the U.S. coast. Even the "yellow bees"—small, unarmed civilian aircraft—had a deterrent effect on German submarine commanders who sounded the alarm and made crash dives. The presence of CAP aircraft along American shores undoubtedly saved many lives and ships.[11]

In the first six months of 1942 German U-boats furiously attacked shipping in American-protected waters, catching the United States ill-prepared. Of the nearly 400 vessels sunk by German submarines in this period, most were torpedoed and shelled along the Atlantic coast and in the Caribbean and the Gulf of Mexico. German submarines attacked with impunity. Of the twenty-one U-boats sunk by enemy action in these months, only six were in American waters.[12] In the spring and summer, flaming hulks of torpedoed ships often illuminated nighttime horizons along Atlantic and Gulf coasts. In the mornings following such attacks, the flotsam and jetsam of wreckage washed ashore. Bathers on Florida beaches witnessed attacks in broad daylight.[13]

This successful U-boat campaign in the western Atlantic forced the United States, in mid-May 1942, to declare the eastern seaboard a military zone and to order a coastal dimout for the Carolinas, Georgia, and Florida. There was widespread fear that coastal illumination served to silhouette ships on the horizon, making them easy targets for German torpedoes. Although the Navy wanted to impose restrictions on nighttime illumination on the coasts weeks earlier, the tourist trade and the fishing industry had fought such steps.

Amazed to find coastal towns and cities such as Miami illuminated as in peacetime, German U-boat commanders confided to their logs their surprise over the slackness of American efforts to protect shipping.

Erich Würdemann, commander of one of the first two German submarines to operate in the Gulf of Mexico, concluded his log by observing
that "we apparently took the enemy quite by surprise and found him
unprepared."[14] This future Knight's Cross winner expressed disbelief
that systematic surveillance either at sea or in the air was lacking, that
merchant ships continued to travel singly and not in convoys even after
the sinkings began, that ships failed to zigzag to present a more difficult
target, and that navigational aids and shorelights shone brilliantly as
though the United States was not at war.

Attacks by German submarines in the Gulf of Mexico early in May
1942 forced the Army to extend the coastal dimout from the Florida
panhandle to Texas.[15] Dimout restrictions applied to all lighting within
ten miles of the sea and for any town with a population of 5,000 within
thirty miles of the Atlantic or Gulf of Mexico.[16] Floodlights and adver-
tising signs were forbidden, streetlights were dimmed, windows facing
the sea had to be curtained, and the top half of automobile headlights
were blacked out with paint or tape.[17] Perhaps to the relief of parents
with teenagers, bonfires and automobiles on the beaches were strictly
prohibited. Near the Gulf coast, neither the crack of the baseball bat on
sultry spring nights nor the roar of football games on crisp fall nights
was to be heard.

Faced with daily news reports of Allied shipping being sunk by
German U-boats off the American coasts, yachtsmen and fishermen
volunteered to patrol offshore as naval pickets, but the Navy thought
these volunteer sailors were more likely to foul up things than to help
matters. However, mounting political pressure to take drastic steps to
curtail the U-boat threat forced the Navy in late June to sanction the use
of civilian craft to patrol coastal waters in what was popularly known as
the Hooligan Navy.[18] Civilian commodores were given appropriate
temporary rank in the Coast Guard Reserves, and their vessels were
equipped with radios and weapons.

Southern congressmen and businessmen urged the Navy to build
thousands of small, fast craft as submarine hunters for the Gulf. Leaders
in the languishing pleasure-boat industry, such as Andrew Jackson
Higgins in New Orleans and Paul Prigg in Miami, supported this
project, realizing it would stimulate demand for boats that they could
build easily.[19] Promoted by oil millionaire Joe Danciger of Fort Worth,

this proposal gained the backing of several members of Alabama's congressional delegation, including Representatives Frank Boykin and Joe Starnes and Senator John Bankhead, Jr. As a member of the House Merchant Marine and Fisheries Committee, which funded the Maritime Commission, Boykin had a great deal of clout on Capitol Hill on maritime matters.[20] Boykin called these fast boats "aqua bombers." Louisiana's senator Joseph Ellender was also a prime mover, and Vice-President Henry Wallace, whom many southerners ordinarily viewed with suspicion, listened attentively—and patiently—to Boykin's schemes. The Navy evaded taking action on these proposals, preferring to leave the task of chasing submarines to Coast Guard cutters, destroyers, and aircraft. Picket vessels manned by civilians, however, were stationed in the Gulf of Mexico, but they had little deterrent effect and were regarded by German U-boat commanders as negligible factors.

Other volunteer organizations contributed to the war effort. Red Cross workers played many vital roles during the war. They produced "comfort kits" that were distributed to British civilians who had taken refuge in bomb shelters. Red Cross workers also produced tens of millions of surgical dressings and other bandages. The Birmingham chapter made 4,000,000 such dressings on a production line at the public library.[21]

The Red Cross also recruited nurses for the Army and the Navy, and its Nurse's Aid Corps did volunteer work in hospitals, freeing trained nurses to carry out urgent medical duties. Red Cross blood drives took on added importance, and local communities took great pride in exceeding their quotas. In rural areas, white and black county farm agents promoted Red Cross blood drives. Large towns had Red Cross motor corps that stood ready to transport equipment, supplies, and personnel on a moment's notice. Servicemen and servicewomen were especially grateful for Red Cross canteens and traveler's-aid services operated at military installations, railroad terminals, and bus stations.

In wartime, when normal avenues of communication were disrupted, the Red Cross assisted individuals in communicating with relatives and friends in other countries. Its international network and its credibility as a genuinely humanitarian organization enabled it to serve as intermediary for prisoners of war and to assist displaced persons. Prisoners of war and their families corresponded through Red Cross channels that were also used to send packages of food and clothing to prisoners.[22] In addition, Red Cross officials inspected POW camps to assure compliance with the Geneva convention's directives regarding treatment of war prisoners.[23]

Civilians contributed to the war effort in numerous other ways. The Alabama Extension Service, Boy Scouts, Salvation Army, and Junior Red Cross conducted salvage drives and carried out a "war on waste." Urged to save fats and grease, which could be made into explosives, households earned red ration points by bringing household fats to their butchers.[24] Even slivers of soap bars were collected.

Every community collected tin cans and scrap metals. Children enjoyed helping their parents with this task, which required removing the labels from tin cans, cutting out both ends, and then applying the full force of their Tom Brown or Pol-Parrot shoes to smash the cans flat. In Ozark, school principal and superintendent Emma P. Flowers organized the "junior army" to collect everything from rusting plow points to coat hangers, a drive capped by a "scrap metal parade."[25] Rubber was collected ostensibly—though the technology to do so was lacking—to make tires from old hot-water bottles and rubber bands. In 1943 the Negro County Farm Bureau, administered by Tuskegee Institute, sponsored a series of "victory mass meetings," which attracted overflow crowds of black Alabamians, to encourage participation in blood drives and salvage campaigns.[26]

Towns with military installations established servicemen's clubs and, later, United Service Organizations facilities. By March 1942 nineteen USO clubs and units entertained servicemen in Alabama towns.[27] Montgomery, whose Soldiers' Center was the first civilian-run servicemen's club in the United States, was among the most active cities. The Soldiers' Center was subsequently transformed into the Army-Navy USO Club, whose hostess was the congenial and motherly Vera Ruth Gomillion Prentiss. Called Millie by her husband, she was known as Willy-Nilly to thousands of servicemen who passed through Montgomery, many of whom wrote her postcards and letters from the front lines. An unknown but grateful soldier who passed through Montgomery during the war described her as "a sort of hostess, manager, chum, chief cook and bottlewasher [who] draws the line at scrubbing—and can SHE draw a line."[28]

The USO facilities at 119 Commerce Street in Montgomery in-cluded a music room, poolroom, kitchen, patio, office, and two mice named Harry and Johnny. The club curfew was 11 P.M., and alcohol was strictly forbidden. Patrons could always count on getting an "Original Salvation Army World War I Doughnut" and a cup of coffee.[29] Some of the nation's finest bands played for dances sponsored by the center and Maxwell Field that were closely chaperoned by Millie and other Mont-gomery matrons. Guy Lombardo and his Royal Canadians performed in August 1942 at a formal dance held at Hangar Six for the cadets and their partners. In late 1942 Captain Glenn Miller led the Maxwell Field band, which performed a half-hour concert broadcast by radio through-out Alabama on Christmas Eve.[30] Celebrities, including film and radio stars Bob Hope and Lorraine Day, also visited the Montgomery club.

Then, as now, Montgomery was very civic minded, especially when it came to the hometown folks in uniform. To keep in touch with Montgomery service personnel, radio station WSFA sponsored a news-letter entitled *Letters from Home*, which was sent to hundreds and, later, thousands of Montgomerians in military service. Mailed on Fridays, the 126 issues of *Letters from Home* contained stories about servicemen and servicewomen visiting homefolks and about engagements, weddings, births, deaths, football scores, and other items of local and state news.[31] In turn, the newsletter inspired thousands of letters, postcards, and V-mail from appreciative Montgomerians in service who eagerly antici-pated mail call whether they were on a beach in Sicily, under the palms of Saipan, in a hospital in Sussex, or—as retired Auburn history profes-sor Wesley P. Newton remembers—in a foxhole hacked out of frozen ground in Germany.[32]

Other towns provided similarly warm receptions for servicemen and servicewomen stationed in their communities. Ozark, for example, had a first-class USO operation for white troops at nearby Camp Rucker in its Community House, originally built by the National Youth Ad-ministration during the New Deal but refurbished as a USO club complete with swimming pool. Black soldiers, however, lacked ad-equate recreational facilities until March 1944, when the Army pro-vided $45,000 for that purpose.[33]

Selma was particularly active in providing for the recreational and social needs of the soldiers stationed at nearby Craig Field. Citizens such

Montgomery Colored USO Club, 215 Monroe Street. (State Defense Council photograph, Alabama Department of Archives and History)

as Paul Grist, the popular director of the local YMCA, and Mayor Lucien Burns founded a club for servicemen even before a USO branch was established. The city opened its "white" swimming pool first to the workers constructing Craig Field and later to the cadets. The town sponsored dances as well as basketball and softball leagues for aviators stationed at the nearby airfield.

Unlike many towns where recreational facilities for African-American servicemen did not exist early in the war, Selma had its Dallas County Colored Community Center. This facility had been completed in 1939 as a Works Project Administration undertaking. Serving as the social hub for African-American soldiers and the local community, this center housed a USO club and served as the headquarters for black Selma's war bond, Community Chest, and Red Cross drives.

Various charitable organizations raised relief funds for use abroad and in the United States. In Alabama four community-relief programs existed prior to 1942, but by war's end there were twenty-six such organizations. One of the most important local relief efforts was the Alabama War Chest, initiated by Governor Dixon in the last year of his administration to mitigate some of the distress and hardships at home and abroad. This charitable organization served as a model for President Roosevelt's efforts to spur voluntary war relief efforts. Through the efforts of its president, Montgomerian Haygood Patterson, local defense councils, prominent business leaders, and civic groups, the Alabama War Chest raised nearly $4 million, about half of which was donated for USO operations.[34] The War Chest also supported British, Greek, Russian, Chinese, Dutch, and Polish relief organizations. Alabamians contributed generously to the Red Cross War Relief Fund, which provided badly needed assistance to refugees and others whose lives had been disrupted by the war. Private social clubs, such as the Elks

Ladies of Anniston's First Methodist Church serving punch at USO club. (State Defense Council photograph, courtesy of Alabama Department of Archives and History)

Lodge of Montgomery, sent cigarettes to hometown servicemen in foreign POW camps.

When it came to purchasing war bonds, Alabama claimed a distinction achieved by no other state. In each of the seven war bond drives conducted during World War II, every Alabama county reached its quota. Writing to Governor Chauncey Sparks in July 1945, Ed Leigh McMillan, chairman of Alabama's War Finance Committee, pointed out: "Alabama has a proud War Bond record; the record of no other state in the Union equals ours. We have made every call: every county has made its every quota in every War Loan Campaign. In every campaign we have been within the top seven states in the sale of E-bonds."[35] The success of the war bond campaign was due in no small measure to the efforts of the Alabama Extension Service, whose white and black home-demonstration agents organized the sale of war bonds and stamps.[36] Alabama maintained its record in the eighth war loan effort, launched in October 1945 to pay for winding down the war and for the GI benefits that had been promised to the returning veterans.

The war loan campaigns encouraged towns, counties, and even large businesses to set fund-raising goals, which, if met, permitted them to designate and to name what their funds purchased. Madison County prided itself on being the first Alabama county to sell enough war bonds—$446,000—to purchase a B-24 Liberator bomber.[37] During the third war loan drive in September 1943 the African-American community of Birmingham and Jefferson County set a goal of $300,000 to pay for a bomber to be named for "a Negro hero of this crisis." A committee of prominent black businessmen and civic leaders, headed by Birmingham tycoon Arthur G. Gaston, urged black residents of Jefferson County to contribute at least $2 to this fund. In this way, the black citizens of Birmingham would "serve millions of men who are in a death struggle at this very moment to save our democracy, to save our nation and secure freedom and protection for all the peoples of the earth who are inclined towards good government, citizenship, religion and human rights."[38] This was a stirring, patriotic, and high-minded commitment from a community that was, for the most part, excluded from the democracy that its own children were helping to defend. Exceeding their goal, contributors purchased a Liberator bomber, which they named *Julius Ellsberry* in honor of Alabama's first black serviceman killed in the war.[39] This aircraft, as well as *The Spirit of Tuskegee Institute,* also purchased by black participation in the war loan campaign, were dedicated on 6 October 1943 at the Bechtel-McCone-Parsons aircraft modification plant in Birmingham. Americans were besieged with requests to purchase war bonds. Not to do so was tantamount to lack of patriotism. The purchase of war bonds not only helped pay for the war but, by taking currency out of circulation, also promoted the Treasury Department's policy of keeping inflation in check.[40] Available in large and small denominations, war bonds could be purchased by rich and poor alike.

Because consumer goods were in short supply anyway, Americans had little choice but to save for the future. With the diversion of industrial production to war goods, rationing became a fact of life. Although it disrupted and inconvenienced life on the home front, rationing was approved by Americans as necessary and fair. Tires and gasoline were among the earliest items in short supply. France's collapse in summer 1940 disrupted the West African rubber trade, but more important were Japan's conquests of the Dutch East Indies and Malaya, which together supplied about 90 percent of the world's raw rubber.

Begun in early 1942, tire rationing lasted for the duration of the war. Alabama's allotment from March through May 1942 totaled 1,366 tires. Limestone County got 24 tires and 26 inner tubes during the month of January 1942.[41] Rationing forced many stores to cut back on home delivery. The Gish Fish Company of Athens reluctantly announced that it could no longer deliver to "anybody, anywhere, anytime." The War Production Board's decision to curtail the delivery of rubber to the manufacturers of girdles and other foundation garments evoked storms of protest, causing a rare reversal of policy in January 1942.[42]

In view of the fact that in the early 1940s the United States was wholly self-sufficient in petroleum, the rationing of gasoline aroused controversy. The *Montgomery Advertiser* castigated Secretary of Interior Harold Ickes as a veritable Scrooge for proposing gasoline rationing in late 1941, calling the need for such a policy a "figment of Mr. Ickes' imagination."[43] Two important factors, however, forced the United States to tighten the spigot. A dramatic upswing in automobile sales in the late 1930s, further evidence that the depression was receding, put more cars on the road.[44] Also, petroleum exports soared in the early

1940s. To meet Great Britain's urgent energy needs, President Roosevelt put at London's disposal fifty tankers normally used to deliver 250,000 barrels of oil to East Coast refineries.

Further complicating matters was the appearance of German submarines in the western Atlantic. Because approximately 95 percent of the petroleum refined on the Atlantic seaboard arrived by tanker, German U-boats posed a grave threat to oil supplies.[45] The arrival of five German submarines off the East Coast in early 1942, and the subsequent waves of submarines that followed in the spring and summer, seriously disrupted tanker traffic and gave rise to proposals for oil pipelines from Texas to the East Coast. In March 1942 alone, German and Italian submarines sank twenty-nine tankers and damaged seven more in the Atlantic and Caribbean. In early May the *Munger T. Ball* became the first tanker to be sunk in the Gulf of Mexico.[46] By the middle of that month, gasoline supplies were so interrupted that motorists in the Atlantic Coast states and in the South were standing in line for gasoline ration cards. As one historian put it, anyone who had a twelve-cylinder Packard and three gallons of gasoline per week was in for "the grimmest of realities."[47] With top speed on the open road put at thirty-five miles an hour to conserve fuel, most drivers had to learn to be patient.

Car pooling was a practical way to save both gasoline and tires. Sponsored by Governor Dixon and Birmingham mayor Cooper Green, the "Alabama Plan" evolved into a national movement to promote ride sharing. Bumper stickers reading "I WANTA RIDE" were widely distributed.[48] "Thumbing rides" remained a respectable way for young men to travel. It became downright unpatriotic to speed past a hitchhiker in uniform without stopping to give him a lift.

Life during the war was filled with many minor hardships and inconveniences. Housewives and especially working women found their lives more complicated because the chores of obtaining and preparing food, as well as doing the laundry and cleaning—even if they worked full-time outside the home—still fell upon their shoulders.[49] Shopping for essentials often proved frustrating. Some goods were in short supply because of panic buying or hoarding. Axis conquest and disruption of trade led to rationing of other goods. The Emergency Price Control Act signed by President Roosevelt in late January 1942 authorized the Office of Price Administration to establish a system for rationing scarce consumables. Subsequently, War Ration Book One with stamps for sugar and coffee was issued to Americans at elementary schools in early May 1942. Two weeks later, automobile owners in the eastern United States received stamps for the purchase of limited quantities of gasoline. More complicated point rationing books for other commodities, including meats and fats, were issued a year later.[50]

As early as the Monday following the attack on Pearl Harbor, shoppers had descended upon grocery stores to stock up on sugar. They had learned from experience in the First World War or knew from hearsay that sugar would be requisitioned to manufacture ethyl alcohol for the production of explosives. Even before rationing was introduced in April 1942, sugar prices had risen by 33 percent. Merchants were allotted one pound of sugar for each dollar of gross sales in their stores, and households received sugar coupons according to the size of the family.

Not only were fewer pies to be baked, but local Coca-Cola bottlers cut production, threatening the social life of some Alabamians. White middle-class women of the South served so much of the soft drink that their gatherings were called "Coca-Cola parties." A Limestone County newspaper said that it looked as though the popular soda pop was about to become a complete casualty of the war and that the "men and women of the South are in for one of the severest blows since Appomattox."[51] Sugar rationing did more to put a crimp in bootlegging than all the tent revivals in Alabama. Presumably law-enforcement personnel and temperance organizations welcomed this development as proof that sometimes sows' ears did produce silk stockings.[52] Americans told the Gallup Poll that they missed sugar more than any other rationed good.[53]

For a brief period from late 1942 into early 1943, coffee was rationed, largely because of the disruption of the Caribbean trade by German U-boats. Each American over the age of fifteen was entitled to one pound of coffee every five weeks. By July 1943 conditions in the Caribbean stabilized and rationing of coffee ended. But beginning in May 1943 meat rationing started, necessitated by increased demand. For one thing, military mess halls were serving good cuts of beef and pork several times a week to hundreds of thousands of servicemen and servicewomen, some of whom had never seen meats other than chicken necks or chitlins on their tables. Also, working Americans enjoyed higher wages, enabling them to patronize butchers more often than previously. Because one cut of meat was not the same as another, rationing was more complicated for meat than for sugar or coffee.

Men were not as likely to understand the rationing system as the women who tucked the coupons and ration books into their purses and went to do battle at the market. Most Americans—about two-thirds—supported rationing.[54] Nonetheless, black market activity was common. In its more benign form, neighborhood merchants were loathe to turn down longtime customers, but unscrupulous and greedy black marketeers could make huge illegal profits. Advertisements urged women to take the "home front pledge" to pay no more than top legal prices and to accept no rationed goods without surrendering ration stamps. In this way, women could "rout the forces of selfishness" and help wipe out the chiselers, war profiteers, and black marketeers.[55]

Rationing remained one of the most direct ways the war touched the lives of virtually all Americans. One of the jokes of the day asked, "What was the first thing Noah grabbed before he got on the Ark?" Answer: "His ration book!"

Millions of Americans responded to shortages by planting small victory gardens, a movement popularized in the First World War. For many small-town Americans—if they could spare the gas and tires—curb markets provided another source of fresh vegetables and fruits in season. With pressure cookers and Ball jars, housewives canned and preserved for the winter months. Americans also became acquainted with new commercial ways of processing and preserving foods. Spam, dehydrated soups, and frozen foods were novelties. People were urged to take vitamin pills, a recent innovation, to ensure their health.

Most durable items were in short supply during the war. Metal shortages meant fewer bicycles and toy trains under Christmas trees. Households had to do without new pots and pans, as well as stoves and refrigerators. The automobile industry survived by making military vehicles for the war. Shoes were rationed because leather was requisitioned to make boots for soldiers. The war and its shortages affected clothing styles. Designers created pants without cuffs and jackets with narrower lapels. Long dresses gave way to shorter skirts. Frayed jackets, trousers, and sweaters were rehabilitated. Patches covered threadbare elbows and knees. Replaced by nylon hose, silk stockings became a thing of the past. Old stockings that no amount of fingernail polish could rescue were turned into parachutes and powder bags. Military clothing and airplanes consumed great quantities of the new miracle fabrics—rayon and nylon. Nonetheless, cotton fabrics—used to make canvas for tents and storage bags for the military—were harder to find. Even time was rationed or, more precisely, rearranged. Believing that it would save a half-million kilowatts of electricity each day, daylight saving time was introduced in February 1942. The national effort to keep thermostats set no higher than sixty-five degrees during winter days and even lower at night was not as great a sacrifice for Alabamians as for other Americans.

For the most part Alabamians endured these minor inconveniences and sufferings with equanimity and forbearance. Occasionally there were complaints from the well-to-do that the poor were using up all the tires riding around in cheap, secondhand cars. But that sort of petty sniping was not unique to wartime. Alabamians understood that their small sacrifices were making important contributions to the war effort.

Four

Alabama's Military Camps

Federalization of the National Guard and implementation of the draft expanded the armed forces to more than 1.5 million troops by summer 1941. New military bases were needed. Cheap land and mild winters favored the American South for military training. By early 1942 Alabama's military bases and airfields hummed with activity.

Only Texas and California played roles as significant as Alabama's in training aviators for the Army Air Corps. By late 1941 Maxwell and Gunter fields in Montgomery, the Tuskegee Army Air Field, Craig Field in Selma, and Napier Field outside Dothan were in operation. Civilian flight schools, such as the Alabama Institute of Aeronautics at Tuscaloosa, also trained military aviators.[1] As facilities grew cramped, additional bases were established. In spring 1942, land was cleared for a basic flying school near Courtland in Lawrence County just south of the Tennessee River. Training of B-24 crews shifted to Courtland when B-29s arrived at Maxwell. The height of flight training was reached in May 1943 when there were fifty-six flight schools throughout the United States, not to mention hundreds of touch-and-go landing strips, several of which were located in Alabama. By the end of the war, more than 100,000 aviation cadets had gone through training at Maxwell Field alone.

Foreign cadets learned to fly in Alabama as well. Most of the 12,500 British aviators and many of the 4,110 French airmen who earned their wings in the United States passed through either Maxwell or Gunter fields. More than 800 Brazilian and nearly 450 Mexican cadets received their wings in American schools. In 1945 flight training of Mexican aviators was transferred from Foster Field, Texas, to Napier Field. Chinese students, too, came to Alabama.[2]

Maxwell Field and particularly the Air Corps Tactical School, which was located in Montgomery until its dissolution early in the war, molded much of the leadership of the Army Air Forces in World

War II. More than 320 general officers, including the 3 four-star generals in the AAF and 11 of its 13 three-star generals, were Maxwell graduates.[3] Curtis LeMay, whose innovations in tactics were so crucial to the air war in World War II, was a member of the 1939–40 class of the tactical school.

The escalating crisis and ultimately the outbreak of war created unprecedented demands for instructors to train pilots and bombardiers. In May 1942 the Central Instructors School opened at Maxwell, although it moved in the following year to Randolph Field, Texas. In spring 1943 Maxwell received its first contingent of 156 "dough girls" from the Women's Army Auxiliary Corps, later called the Women's Army Corps (WAC), who served as radio and telephone operators, photo technicians, and stenographers. An additional 24 Wacs arrived at Gunter Field. In 1943 Maxwell's main runway was extended to nearly a mile in length, and flight training for four-engine aircraft got under way. During the first year more than 2,000 pilots were trained to fly B-24s. In 1945 runways were again lengthened by 2,000 feet to accommodate B-29 Superfortresses, which were soon to be seen—and heard— flying over Montgomery. More than 700 B-29 crews trained at Maxwell Field and at the auxiliary field at Anniston.

Flying required mental alertness, emotional stability, and physical stamina on the part of aviators. Army psychologists at Maxwell were interested in the intellectual and psychomotor capabilities of pilots and other crew members. They developed psychomotor tests to evaluate steadiness, balance, equilibrium, reaction time, ability to think clearly under stressful situations, and other traits that influenced flying skill. During this testing the important yardstick known as "stanines" (STANdard NINE), which measured abilities on a scale from one to nine, was incorporated into psychological testing.[4]

It was not unusual to spot well-known personalities, such as Glenn Miller and movie idol Lieutenant James Stewart, at Maxwell or at Gunter Field.[5] President Roosevelt himself toured Maxwell during the war. Because foreign aviators—including more than 8,000 British cadets—trained in Montgomery, numerous Allied dignitaries visited Alabama. Escorted by General George C. Marshall, British Foreign Secretary Anthony Eden and Field Marshal Sir John Dill inspected Maxwell Field. Somewhat later, Britain's wartime ambassador to the United

States, Lord Halifax, accompanied by Lady Halifax, made a visit to the state that included stops at Maxwell Field, Tuskegee Institute, and Alabama Polytechnic Institute.[6]

Fifty miles to the west of Montgomery on Highway 80, Craig Field—named for Selma native Lieutenant Bruce K. Craig, a flight engineer killed in a California air crash during the test of a Lend-Lease bomber—was in full swing by late 1941.[7] At that time, Craig Field was the country's most spacious flying field. Eventually 2,000 military personnel and 1,400 civilian employees worked at the base, training the hundreds of cadets in each class who received advanced instruction in single-engine planes. In the early years of the war, British cadets—many of them graduates of the basic phase of flight training at Gunter Field and Cochran Field in Macon, Georgia—also passed through Craig Field.

Although an important mercantile center for the Black Belt counties, Selma remained a small town in the 1940s. Local residents hailed the completion of the Edmund Pettus Bridge across the Alabama River in 1940. During the construction of the airfield and in the early months of its operation, severe housing shortages in Selma were solved by the entrepreneurial spirit—tempered by humanitarian concern—of the many residents of the town who housed cadets in their homes.

At the Tuskegee Army Air Field, the first thirteen African-American aviation cadets—including Benjamin O. Davis, Jr., the son of the Army's only black general—began training in August 1941. By 1946 when the field was deactivated, thirty-four classes had graduated from the flight program at Tuskegee. In the first two years training was limited to single-engine fighters. In 1943 training in twin-engine bombers began. Of the nearly 1,000 black pilots who learned to fly at Tuskegee, half were stationed overseas, and most were assigned to one of three black units. The Ninety-ninth Pursuit Squadron was the earliest black outfit. The squadron first saw combat over North Africa in 1943 and later over Sicily and Anzio.[8] In 1944 the 100th, 301st, and 302d squadrons left Selfridge Field, Michigan, to join the Ninety-ninth in Italy. This newly created 332d Fighter Group, which was an all-black, Tuskegee-trained unit commanded by Colonel Benjamin O. Davis, Jr., was assigned to the Twelfth Air Force. In June the pilots switched over to P-47s and a month later to P-51s. Stationed at Ramitelli,

Twenty-five of the thirty-three original pilots of the Ninety-Ninth Pursuit Squadron, Tuskegee Army Air Field, August 1942. Benjamin O. Davis, Jr., is seated in the center of the front row. Herbert Carter is at the far left, front row. (Courtesy of Colonel Herbert Carter)

in Italy, and transferred to the Fifteenth Fighter Command, the 332d Fighter Group escorted bombers of the Fifteenth Air Force in the Mediterranean and over France, Austria, and Germany.[9] A third African-American outfit was the 477th Composite Group whose twin-engine bombers were mostly crewed by graduates of Tuskegee Army Air Field. Created late in the war, the 477th did not go overseas during World War II.

Although the quality of instruction at Tuskegee Army Air Field was solid and its graduates were as competent and distinguished as students from other flight schools, many African-American leaders thought it had been a mistake to create a separate training facility for black aviators. They preferred a truly integrated Army Air Forces, with commanding officers and crews selected on the basis of competence and skill without regard to skin color.

At Tuskegee several episodes involving racial tensions and disturbances led to strained relations between whites and blacks on the base and in town. One episode erupted when the post exchange restaurant for whites refused service to two black airmen of the Ninety-ninth

Pursuit Squadron. These airmen had recently arrived from Chanute Field, Illinois, where they had not encountered such overt segregation.[10] In another incident, a black military policeman from the airfield and white police officers from the town of Tuskegee struggled for custody over a black airman who had been arrested in town for disorderly conduct. The police summoned reinforcements from the all-white Highway Patrol who forcibly seized the airman and beat the MP so severely that he required hospitalization.

Alarmed about what he called the "Negro soldier situation in Alabama," Governor Frank Dixon protested the stationing of "armed Negro troops" at airfields throughout the Southeast.[11] Major General John P. Smith, commander of the Fourth Army Corps in Atlanta, was unsympathetic to Dixon's attitude about black servicemen. In a letter to the governor, Smith testily reproached those who did not honor all soldiers regardless of their race:

> Incidents have occurred recently which have led the War Department to believe that the Negro in the uniform of the United States Army has not always received the equitable treatment which is due him by virtue of the fact that he is a soldier. The cumulative effect of these incidents has had a deleterious effect on morale in camps where there are numbers of Negro troops.[12]

Unpersuaded by this view, state officials continued to criticize the stationing of black servicemen on Alabama bases.

A 1944 episode involving attempts by black airmen at Maxwell Field to use the post exchange and officers' club set aside for whites produced a storm of protest from Governor Chauncey Sparks and other white leaders. From Birmingham, Commissioner of Public Safety Eugene "Bull" Connor complained to President Franklin Roosevelt that if there were "terror, bloodshed and calamity in this state" it would be the fault of the president.[13]

Despite racial tensions and other obstacles, hundreds of African-American airmen—most of them trained at Tuskegee Army Air Field—became outstanding pilots, navigators, bombardiers, and mechanics. For Benjamin O. Davis, Jr., the first black cadet to graduate from West Point in the twentieth century, flying over the green trees and dark streams in that first summer at Tuskegee "was more exhilarating than anything I could have imagined." But there was no regret when—as commander of the Ninety-ninth Pursuit Squadron—he was ordered to leave for North Africa.[14] For the black airmen of Tuskegee, Alabama had been a bittersweet experience.

At Mobile's Brookley Field, built on the site of the municipal airport on marshy land adjacent to the bay, the U.S. Army Air Forces operated a major supply depot and performed bomber modification. The Southeast Army Air Depot stocked supplies and aircraft parts for the entire southeastern United States, Puerto Rico, and the Caribbean. It was the only Army Air Forces depot in the country with access to an ocean terminal. The Mobile Air Service Command performed aircraft repair, maintenance, and modification. From around the world, B-24 and B-29 bombers were flown to Brookley Field for work on engines or airframes.[15]

Because of serious labor shortages in the Mobile area, the War Manpower Commission conducted frequent recruitment drives among women in Mobile and surrounding communities. With approximately one-third of working-age men in the military, it was imperative for women to join the work force. In encouraging women to apply for jobs in industry, the War Manpower Commission appealed to their patriotism as well as to pecuniary instincts. The Mobile Air Service Command paid trainees $90 monthly, and salaries of full-time employees began at $125 a month.[16] For a population accustomed to depression wages or to unemployment, these were handsome sums. At its peak in 1943 Brookley Field employed more than 17,000 civilian employees, about half of whom were women, making this facility the largest employer of women in the state. Starting with 23 female workers in January 1942, the number of women employed at Brookley Field had risen to 2,300 by September.[17]

In addition to clerical tasks, women were hired for technical jobs, some of which required specialized training and the use of lathes and other equipment. By 1942 women were disassembling and reassembling engines, doing plating, and serving as mechanics' helpers and inspectors. Regarded by many as superior to men in manual dexterity, women were therefore thought to be well suited to such delicate tasks as rewinding electrical motors and to work in confined spaces. Women who might be dubious about their own mechanical skills were told that if they "could operate a sewing machine, open a can of tomatoes, take a vacuum cleaner half apart or make emergency repairs on the refrigerator" they were ideal candidates "to help defeat the Axis."[18] In an effort to relieve the labor shortage, a contingent of Wacs was sent to Brookley Field in early 1944.

The *Birmingham News* reported that Brookley Field had become "the nation's proving ground" for vocational training.[19] It also pioneered the employment of handicapped persons. Eleven blind trainees hired in 1943 proved so successful that paraplegics, individuals with artificial limbs, and persons with hearing impairments were employed. In a daring move for its time, Brookley Field hired pregnant women. This program demonstrated that individuals with physical "disabilities" could become valuable employees.

Fort McClellan at Anniston, the state's oldest infantry encampment, served as a major reception center for inductees into the Army. Two weeks after the attack on Pearl Harbor, the post garrison—New York's Twenty-seventh National Guard Division—shipped out for the Pacific. Fort McClellan was converted into a replacement training center.[20] Inductees arrived for intensive eight-week indoctrination courses before being assigned to combat or other specialized training. In 1943, as more servicemen were needed overseas, the Army revamped its training program. The training period was extended to seventeen weeks, and everything from indoctrination of raw recruits to combat training was carried out at the fort.[21]

Every effort was made at Fort McClellan to provide realistic preparation for war. Infiltration courses and mock villages for simulated street fighting were created to teach tactics. With artillery shells bursting overhead, recruits crouched in foxholes as heavy tanks rumbled above. By 1944 this was the full extent of training received by recruits before their baptisms of fire on battlefields in Europe or the Pacific.

During the war the number of officers, enlisted personnel, and civilian workers at Fort McClellan grew from 1,000 to 3,500. After August 1943 these included two WAC units, one white and one black, to assist in office work as well as the daily operations of the post. By 1943 about 30,000 soldiers were on post undergoing training during the seventeen-week cycles. Celebrities and entertainers—such as boxing champ Joe Louis, who was born in Chambers County—performed at the camp.

In 1942 the Army activated its second African-American division, the Ninety-second, at Fort McClellan. Approximately 6,500 troops in this division trained at the fort. Commanded by Major General Edward M. Almond, the Ninety-second Division joined General Mark Clark's Fifth Army in Italy in September 1944. There it participated in the storming of the Arno line to the west of the Apennine mountains.[22]

Camp Rucker in the Wiregrass region was Alabama's other large infantry training facility. First called the "Ozark Triangular Division Camp," it was renamed in January 1942 for Edmund Rucker, a Confederate general originally from Tennessee.[23] This camp was designed to train approximately 30,000 troops during each seventeen-week cycle. Between 1942 and late 1944, four divisions were stationed at Camp Rucker. The first was the recently activated Eighty-first Division from the Carolinas and Georgia. Few infantry divisions went through as many bloody campaigns in the Pacific as this "Wildcat" Division. Following action on Angaur Island, the Eighty-first was sent to Peleliu to relieve the battered First Marine Division. It later fought at Okinawa. Subsequently, the Thirty-fifth, Ninety-eighth, and Sixty-sixth infantry divisions went through Camp Rucker.[24] In November 1944 the camp

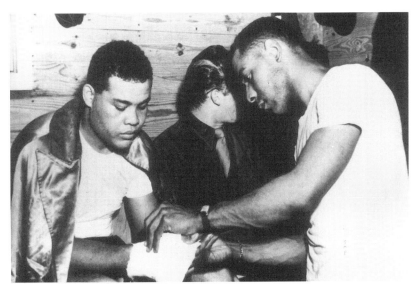

Heavyweight champion Joe Louis, native of Chambers County, puts on an exhibition at Camp Rucker. (Courtesy of Val L. McGee)

Mail Call, Camp Rucker. (Courtesy of Val L. McGee)

was reorganized as a five-regiment infantry replacement training center whose mission was to give crash training to raw recruits before they were sent to the front.

In addition to aviation and infantry training, Alabama was at the forefront of training for chemical warfare. Appropriations for an upgraded Army Chemical Warfare Service not only resulted in the establishment of the Huntsville Arsenal but also led to the construction of Camp Sibert outside Gadsden. As distasteful as chemical warfare was to soldiers, politicians, and the public, the War Department and Congress determined the Army should be prepared to defend against chemical attacks and to wage chemical warfare as a retaliatory response.

By 1941 the Army had run out of space at its Edgewood, Maryland, arsenal to expand training and production for chemical warfare. At the urging of Major General William N. Porter, the new head of the Chemical Warfare Service, a 35,000-acre site near Gadsden was purchased in May 1942.[25] The installation was named Camp Sibert to honor Major General William Sibert, an Etowah County native who oversaw the construction of the Panama Canal and organized the Chemical Warfare Service.

Despite deplorable conditions, replacement training was moved from Edgewood to the Gadsden camp in summer 1942. Because permanent housing did not yet exist, arriving troops lived in "Tent City" and were given a spade or shovel to help with construction, which torrential rains from December 1942 to April 1943 delayed. Despite two minor racial incidents that briefly disrupted training, black soldiers accounted for about 17 percent of all troops trained at Camp Sibert.[26]

Camp Sibert boasted outstanding training facilities. The Chemical Warfare Service had never before possessed enough land to conduct virtually any simulated attack imaginable. Troops were trained on an obstacle course with live machine-gun fire, a jungle course, and a city street layout. Full-scale models of bomb bays and wings made it possible for ground crews to acquire experience in handling and loading chemical bombs as well as installing chemical spray equipment under aircraft wings. A six-square-mile toxic-gas war zone allowed the Army to train in a realistic setting. In addition to conducting simulated exercises, chemical-warfare trainees also learned how to decontaminate entire towns as well as clothing and other personal gear. Portable field laboratories made it possible to run analytical tests very quickly to identify toxic agents used in mock attacks so that decontamination procedures could be put swiftly into effect.

Requirements for chemical-warfare training peaked in 1943. By then, Allied victory appeared certain, which led the Chemical Warfare Service to curtail plans for completing Camp Sibert. Considering that the base was activated for only a year and a half and had cost $18 million, Camp Sibert was one of the Army's most expensive World War II undertakings.[27]

Throughout the war, thousands of soldiers and officers passed through training in camps and airfields in Alabama. Some of these installations closed permanently or were converted to civilian uses after the Axis powers surrendered. But several, notably Maxwell Field, Gunter Field, Fort McClellan, and Camp Rucker (renamed Fort Rucker after World War II), remain active today even though their roles have, in many cases, adapted to new military requirements and organizational changes, such as the beginning of an independent United States Air Force in 1947. Harkening back to the 1930s and the precedent of the Air Corps Tactical School, Maxwell Field became the center for advanced professional study when the Air University was founded in

1946. Fort McClellan, in addition to training military police, succeeded Camp Sibert after World War II in training for chemical warfare. Camp Rucker, the only military training installation established in Alabama during World War II that effected a permanent and dramatic transformation of the surrounding community, survived by becoming the Army's most important helicopter training facility.

Five

Producing for Victory

A s German armies overran the Low Countries and France in spring and summer 1940, the War Department revealed to an incredulous Congress that the United States lacked the ordnance to fight a major war. The press called it a "popgun defense."[1] Among other shortcomings, the United States Army would be unable to provide effective artillery support for ground troops. The French 75s, which remained from the last war and which were mostly still horse-drawn, were obsolete. The forty-eight new 105-mm artillery pieces authorized by Congress had not yet been produced. In its entire arsenal the Army had four recent-vintage 155-mm guns and no modern 8-inch howitzers. Enemy planes flying at high altitudes would have little to fear from American antiaircraft guns. The United States had 400 lightweight tanks compared with Germany's 3,000, many of which were thought to be the heavy 80-ton type.

On the eve of war, the Army had four ordnance plants for artillery and one ordnance facility for chemical warfare. Private armament production had languished in the 1920s and 1930s. Frantically attempting to overcome two decades of isolationist neglect and the effects of the depression, the Ordnance Department began constructing new munitions plants and awarding contracts to private manufacturing firms for the production of desperately needed armaments. Over a frenzied eighteen-month span in 1940–41, the Ordnance Department opened seventeen plants and planned thirty-two more.[2] Dozens of private firms received contracts for the production of munitions. Simultaneously, the Chemical Warfare Service added new arsenals to manufacture chemical weapons. The National Resources Planning Board estimated that 60 percent of the defense expenditures in Alabama was spent on munitions.[3] Half a dozen ordnance plants and arsenals opened in Alabama, and numerous private firms won munitions contracts. The Gadsden Ordnance Plant, managed by Landsdowne Steel and Iron Company, was the only government-owned facility that forged and machined artillery shells.[4] The Ordnance Department also awarded contracts to several Birmingham steel companies for the manufacture of shells and bombs.

Birmingham produced approximately 75 percent of the munitions, steel, and other war materials manufactured in the Southeastern Ordnance District. O'Neal Steel, founded by Kirkman O'Neal, the grandson and son of Alabama governors, employed 1,300 laborers working around the clock to produce general-purpose bombs.[5] By war's end, O'Neal Steel was turning out bombs in half the time of its competitors. Stockham Valves and Fittings produced 4.5 million 75-mm shells and millions of grenades. U.S. Steel's Tennessee Coal and Iron division discovered how to reduce the weight of a 155-mm shell by nineteen pounds, thus saving tons of steel for other purposes. TCI's Birmingham plant manufactured nearly 5 million 155-mm shells. Fired from a range of approximately one kilometer, these shells could pierce a seven-foot concrete pillbox wall.[6] By October 1944 Conners Steel had produced 2 million bomb casings. The vastly increased production of munitions required additional storage capacity. In 1941 the Army constructed the Anniston Ordnance Depot to store ammunition and to repair vehicles, artillery, and small arms. In 1943 the Chrysler Corporation began managing this facility, which had 7,700 civilian employees on its payroll working three shifts around the clock.[7] A small backup storage depot was located at Theodore in south Alabama, and Montgomery became a holding and reconsignment point for ordnance.

The coming of the war and the construction of ordnance plants and other defense industries transformed several Alabama towns and cities into booming centers of manufacture and commerce. A War Department decision to locate an ordnance plant or an airplane modification facility or a Maritime Commission contract to build dozens of Liberty ships meant thousands of jobs on construction sites and assembly lines. No town in Alabama experienced more dramatic, permanent change from the construction of military plants than Huntsville.

On the eve of the war, Huntsville was a peaceful county seat of 13,000 residents in the Tennessee Valley. The chamber of commerce had billed Huntsville as the "biggest town on earth for its size."[8] It served as the mercantile center for the surrounding agricultural community, which survived by planting corn, cotton, and peanuts and raising a little livestock. In 1939 its seventeen manufacturing establishments employed a total of 133 workers. By 1944 there were 17,000 manufacturing jobs, including more than 11,000 civilians employed at Huntsville's two arsenals and the ordnance depot.[9]

Huntsville's first motel, the Maple Grove, was built the year the war started, and its first streamlined train—the *Tennessean*—glided to a stop in the Southern Railway terminal. Three years later airline service arrived, linking Huntsville with major aviation hubs. Pennsylvania Central Airline—later known as Capital Airlines—inaugurated the first regularly scheduled DC-3 service when its *City of Huntsville* landed in November 1944. Subsequently Waterman, Eastern, and Southern airways joined PCA at the Huntsville–Madison County airport. The most famous building in town was the Hotel Russel Erskine, named for the president of Studebaker, who, it was thought, intended to invest a lot of money in Huntsville but who changed his mind.

Huntsville's adventure with the modern world of science and technology began in early July 1941. The announcement that the Chemical Warfare Service intended to build a manufacturing plant in Madison County caused both jubilation and anxiety.[10] For the people of the Pond Beat and Mullins Flat areas, where the arsenal was to be built, it meant moving immediately. Even that was a mixed blessing. Elnora Ragland at Alabama A & M University remembers that her father, Theodore Roosevelt Clay—a sharecropper with a fifth-grade education—was not at all unhappy. Dreaming that his children would not have to go through what he had experienced during the depression, he looked forward to an opportunity to move into town, where his brood could attend better schools.[11] Clay's dreams were fulfilled, and eight of his nine children earned graduate degrees at college.

Several factors favored Huntsville's selection for a chemical-warfare arsenal and depot. There was an abundance of Tennessee Valley Authority electricity, and the transportation network was good. In addition, land was cheap and sparsely settled. Huntsville immediately began to attract construction workers and, later, chemical-warfare employees. More than 35,000 acres were acquired by the federal government. Limited production began in autumn 1942.[12] A storage facility, known as the Huntsville Chemical Warfare Depot (later called the Gulf Chemical Warfare Depot) was built nearby. More than 600 employees worked

at this depot, which was one of five regional facilities across the country
that stored highly toxic or inflammable ordnance. At a site to the south
of the Huntsville Arsenal, the Army constructed another facility—the
Redstone Ordnance Plant—to produce conventional ordnance.[13]

The Huntsville Arsenal consisted of three plants, two of them
carbon copies of each other: if Huntsville were bombed, it was hoped
that at least one of the plants might survive.[14] The arsenal manufactured
various toxic agents and gases that had previously been produced at the
Chemical Warfare Service's Edgewood Arsenal. Mustard gas, the item
produced in the largest quantity, was piped to the filling plants where it
was loaded into mortar shells, land mines, bombs, and spray tanks.[15]
The Huntsville Arsenal also produced daily about thirty tons of phosgene for bombs and rockets. A colorless liquid that smells like freshly
mown hay, phosgene had been introduced by the Germans in World
War I. Also used by the Allies in the Great War, this gas had caused
approximately 80 percent of all wartime casualties resulting from
chemical agents. Had chemical warfare been introduced into World
War II, phosgene would have been the primary chemical weapon of the
United States. Lewisite, another very toxic agent, was also produced,
but its volatility as a gas and the fact that the British discovered a way to
cause it to break down led the Chemical Warfare Service to abandon its
manufacture.[16]

The Huntsville Arsenal also manufactured incendiary materials,
including smoke grenades, bombs, and canisters. Virtually all of the two
million floating smoke pots that concealed Allied troop landings in
amphibious operations were assembled in Huntsville. A plant at the
Wilson Dam TVA facility in the Muscle Shoals area was the single
largest source of white phosphorous, which was an important smoke
and incendiary agent.[17]

Production and loading of toxic and incendiary agents were hazardous undertakings. Fires were the greatest fear. On one occasion while
making yellow smoke bombs, eleven fires broke out in a span of only
two hours. In all accidents, nine lives were lost at the arsenal. The
handling of toxic agents or working in the presence of toxic gases
required special precautions. Employees who handled mustard gas, for
example, wore gas masks and saturated their clothing with a substance
that absorbed the gas to prevent it from coming into contact with the

skin. Careless workers received painful chemical burns. John L. McDaniel, who gave up his job as a high school science teacher for a better-paying job at the arsenal making mustard gas, still had scars on his wrists many years after the war.[18] Eye and respiratory irritations were common. Employees were often seen on Huntsville streets with green or yellow skin, depending on the type and color of the smoke pots or bombs they had been filling. At the end of their shifts, many workers showered in kerosene to remove toxic substances. Despite the dangers and the inconveniences, thousands of job seekers flocked into Huntsville hoping to obtain jobs that paid more than six dollars a day.[19]

Huntsville's leaders, like leaders in other communities that flourished during the war, worried about the effects of peace on their industries. The winding down of the war brought layoffs at the arsenals. Business leaders, especially Fitzgerald Hall whose Nashville, Chattanooga and Saint Louis Railway had experienced a 600 percent increase in business during the war years, came together in 1944 to devise a strategy for postwar Huntsville.[20] These individuals hoped to capitalize on the federal government's plan to give top priority to local governments when it came to disposing of defense properties. Initially, Huntsville sought to attract private manufacturing firms, but those efforts had a shaky start. A 1945 project—the "Fred Project"—that studied propellants for the JB-2, a buzz-bomb similar to Germany's V-1, foreshadowed the future of Huntsville.[21] A 1949 decision to centralize all military rocket research, culminating in the establishment of the Ordnance Rocket Center at Huntsville's Redstone Arsenal, launched the city into an exciting future.[22]

No Alabama county was affected by the war in a more profound but transitory way than Talladega County. As many as 25,000 workers descended upon the Coosa River Valley in east-central Alabama to construct the $90 million Alabama Ordnance Works at Childersburg and the Coosa River Ordnance Plant at nearby Talladega. At the height of the war, more than 14,000 employees worked around the clock at the two facilities. Managed by the Du Pont Company, the Childersburg plant produced smokeless powder and 5 million pounds of trinitrotoluene (TNT) per month. About 30 percent of TNT produced in Childersburg was transported by convoy to Russia. The Alabama Ordnance Works site also housed a top secret operation. An ammonia plant, surrounded by a link fence, stood in an isolated area of the site. In reality, this facility produced some of the heavy water used in the Manhattan Project's development of the atomic bomb. The Coosa River Ordnance Plant, which was operated by the Brecon Loading Company, a subsidiary of Coca-Cola, loaded explosives into powder bags or shells.[23]

Unparalleled economic opportunities sprang up, but so did nearly intractable social problems. Job seekers, hunting work in construction and later in the plants themselves, inundated these communities. The population of Childersburg soared from 500 in 1940 to approximately 9,000 toward the end of the war. Commuters from Birmingham and nearby small towns clogged unpaved roads to and from the Childersburg plant. Traffic was so heavy that it was impossible to pave the roads. When it rained, farmers sat on tractors waiting to earn money by pulling unfortunate cars out of ditches. The narrow road between Birmingham and Childersburg, traveled by thousands of workers daily, was known as "suicide strip." So many employees lived in Birmingham that a special commuter train service was begun.[24]

Employment at the ordnance plants peaked in 1943 as it became apparent war's end was within sight. Area businessmen as well as representatives from the Birmingham business community and the Alabama Chamber of Commerce began looking at ways to convert the Childersburg plant into peacetime industries. Coosa River Newsprint, later Kimberly-Clark, as well as Beaunit and Olin Matherson, located industries on the premises of the powder plant.[25]

Alabama's blast furnaces, foundries, and rolling mills, particularly in the Birmingham area, produced vital metals. Tennessee Coal and Iron, a subsidiary of U.S. Steel, was the South's largest steel producer. TCI not only made armor plating for warships but also produced what it regarded as "the best helmet in the world."[26] Its Gulf Shipbuilding subsidiary in Chickasaw was one of two important shipbuilding firms in the Mobile area. Sheffield's Reynolds Metals and Gadsden's Republic Steel were other important steel producers. Ingalls Iron Works, which had plants in Birmingham and Pittsburgh as well as shipyards in Decatur and Pascagoula, Mississippi, made structural steel and plate for ships.

The Pullman-Standard Car Manufacturing Company turned out a freight car every ten minutes for the vital transportation industry.

American Cast Iron Pipe Company, or ACIPCO, made pipe, much of which went into military encampments. Alabama Byproducts Company manufactured many coal derivatives for the War Department. Its 3,500 employees made tar for runways and highways; benzol for tanks, planes, and trucks; and Toluol for explosives. Alabama Power Company strained to produce electricity for Birmingham's increased industrial production. Between 1940 and 1942, consumption of electricity in Jefferson County jumped by 42 percent.[27]

Alabama played key roles in the aircraft industry. The state produced much of the aluminum used in the manufacture of warplanes. The Aluminum Company of America plant at the state docks in Mobile and the Reynolds Metals plant at Listerhill consumed thousands of tons of bauxite daily to produce this desperately needed metal.[28] Finished aircraft were flown to Alabama to undergo alterations and repairs at two major modification plants, which employed tens of thousands of Alabama workers. In addition to the Mobile Air Service Command operated by the Army Air Corps at Brookley Field, the privately owned Bechtel-McCone-Parsons Company in Birmingham modified more than 5,000 airplanes, mostly B-24 Liberators and B-29 Superfortresses.[29]

Alabama was also a principal producer of warships and merchant vessels. Having flourished during the First World War, the shipbuilding industry had fallen on hard times in the depression. The threat of war in the early 1940s revived the flagging prospects of shipbuilding in Mobile, Decatur, and Pascagoula, Mississippi, where hundreds of south Alabamians found employment during the war. Birmingham's steel industry as well as its machinery fabricators benefited, too, from surging orders for merchant vessels and warships.

Alabama Drydock and Shipbuilding, or ADDSCO, won contracts from the United States Maritime Commission for 20 Liberty ships and 102 huge—22,400 tons—T-2 tankers.[30] In addition, ADDSCO repaired or converted 2,800 vessels for the Army, Navy, War Shipping Administration, and private companies.[31] Gulf Shipbuilding Company at Chickasaw, just above Mobile, launched 7 Fletcher class destroyers, 29 minesweepers, 30 tankers, and one landing-ship dock as well as cargo vessels. At the peak of activity during the war, ADDSCO and Gulf Shipbuilding's 40,000 welders, machinists, electricians, and other workers were producing a ship a week.[32] At its Decatur and Pascagoula shipyards, Ingalls Iron Works produced 20 cargo ships and several smaller vessels for the Navy.

Other companies built parts of ships for the Navy. Birmingham's Stockham Valves and Fittings cast steel fittings for warships.[33] At its modern plant in east Birmingham, O'Neal Steel manufactured gun platforms and deckhouses for destroyers.[34] Another Birmingham firm, Hardie-Tynes Manufacturing Company, built nearly all the precision motors and high-pressure compressors used aboard warships and submarines.[35] Continental Gin, an important maker of industrial machinery in Birmingham, earned a coveted "E" award for products it made for the Navy.

The state docks and the port of Mobile—fifteenth busiest in the nation—played an important role in the shipment of vital wartime goods. New stevedore companies and ship chandlers served the needs of the burgeoning harbor. After his New Orleans company failed during the depression, Angus Cooper moved to Mobile and opened a stevedoring business in competition with a native firm, T. Smith, founded by Terrence Smith in the 1840s.[36] Both firms flourished during the war. To help move T. Smith's huge derricks, Crescent Towing and Salvage Company was established in 1942. Mobile's homegrown Waterman Steamship Line, whose principal routes were to Latin America, prospered in wartime.

William March Campbell, a senior Waterman vice-president who lived in Mobile, was also an author of considerable merit. Writing under the name William March, he drew upon personal experiences in France as a Marine sergeant in World War I to produce a powerful novel, *Company K*, which, like *All Quiet on the Western Front*, depicts the impact of war upon the individual soldier.[37] In another acclaimed novel, *The Bad Seed*, Campbell grappled with the problem of evil and innocence seemingly coexisting in the human soul—a theme the events of the modern world illuminated all too well.

Foot soldiers in World War II not only appreciated their rifles and their guns but were also partial to warm underwear and dry socks. Alabama factories worked night and day to provide creature comforts for the men on the battlefields. Doubling its labor force, the Gardiner-Waring Company in Florence worked around the clock manufacturing cotton underwear, much of it sold to quartermasters of the military

SS Touchet *under construction at ADDSCO in October 1943. Two months later the vessel became the last victim of German U-boat attacks in the Gulf of Mexico. (ADDSCO Collection, University of South Alabama Archives)*

Female welders in Mobile. (ADDSCO Collection, University of South Alabama Archives)

services. Avondale Mills in Sylacauga increased production by 50 percent to meet the demand for osnaburg used for sandbags, denim for fatigues, and ticking for Army mattresses. At the Goodyear Mills plant in Decatur, workers manufactured heavy duck and canvas for military use.[38]

Agriculture was as important to the Allied cause as industry and manufacturing. Alabama's two extension services were placed on a war footing in January 1942.[39] The directors, Paul O. Davis at Auburn and J. R. Otis at Tuskegee, urged farmers to increase production to feed Americans and their allies. Although the industrial and service sectors of the economy had been gaining at the expense of agriculture since World War I, nearly 50 percent of Alabama's population still lived on the quarter million farms in the state.[40]

The state's extension services urged farmers to plant more acres, diversify their crops, and take advantage of new agricultural technology. This was not new advice. From the days of the boll weevil, the extension services recognized that Alabama farmers were overly dependent on cotton. Farm agents emphasized livestock, dairying, fresh and canned vegetables, and peanuts for oils, which were in short supply during the war. The war provided new avenues for education about better ways of farming. Indeed, improved farming was now a patriotic responsibility.[41]

Cotton remained the main cash crop, but it continued to lose ground. Corn and legumes had bumper harvests in 1941, and the state produced a record number of cattle.[42] Joe Poole, the state commissioner of agriculture and industries, urged Alabama farmers to plant more peanuts and soybeans. The 1943 goal was to increase peanut production by 50 percent and soybean harvests by 66 percent. Poole also urged the cultivation of kudzu to be used for hay, to build soil, and to hold down erosion. Little did he realize that kudzu's most important function in the postwar South would be to prop up telephone poles, or that Japanese investors would one day buy kudzu farms to make teas from the leaves of the tenacious vine. Some new products did not catch on, such as "Alayam" made from sweet potatoes. Its developers at the Alabama Experiment Station in Auburn found ways to make other products from sweet potatoes, including breakfast foods, taffy, cookies, spreads, and garnishes. The easy-to-prepare frozen foods, such as the Birds Eye brand that was available in many grocery stores in the early 1940s, appealed to consumers, particularly to busy women who were working at jobs outside the home. Improvements in freezing and chilling diversified the marketing of farm products, paving the way for poultry processing plants and cold storage facilities for eggs.[43]

Research suggested that crop yields could be increased by applying chemical fertilizers and by using chemical pesticides and herbicides to control diseases and pests. Wartime, however, delayed the commercialization of agricultural chemistry. Artificial fertilizers were not widely available because the explosives industry consumed most of the nitrogen. Chemical insecticides, especially the recently developed DDT, appeared to hold great promise for agriculture.[44] For the moment, however, the Army and the postwar military occupation forces had a virtual monopoly on DDT insecticide, which killed lice and thus effectively halted the spread of typhus in war-torn areas of Europe and the Pacific.

In the meantime, farmers began experimenting with mechanization not only to increase yields but, more important, to substitute machines for scarce labor. A tractor revolution that got under way during World War II flourished in the immediate postwar period. Experiments demonstrated that a large tractor could do the work of ten mules whose annual maintenance costs were three times greater than that of the tractor. Innovative farmers shifted increasingly to mechanization, and in 1946 the McLemore brothers of Montgomery harvested an experimental crop of cotton that was planted, cultivated, and picked entirely by machine.[45]

Agricultural research yielded important information for the military. Studies of different types of grasses improved ground covers for airfields. The United States Department of Agriculture's tillage laboratory at Alabama Polytechnic Institute studied the relationship between tread design of heavy vehicles and different types of soil. Scientists Arthur W. Cooper and F. A. Kummer contracted with the Army Ordnance Proving Ground at Aberdeen, Maryland, to apply their knowledge of tread design to military vehicles.[46]

Alabama's forest products industry, which ranked third in the nation in production, flourished in wartime. The military building boom of 1940–42 placed tremendous demands on lumber production. American forests also supplied the needs of the nation's allies. Plywood and other new wood products revolutionized construction techniques. Producers such as the W. T. Smith Lumber Company at Chapman in Butler County, one of Alabama's largest lumbering and sawmill operations, struggled to increase output. One of the company's owners, Earl McGowin, represented the southern lumber industry on the Defense Advisory Commission. Working closely with timber growers in the Southeast, McGowin helped coordinate production and wartime demand. The scarcity of labor, caused by the military draft and traditional low wages in lumbering, was a crisis for the forest products industry. After 1943 the timber industry in the Southeast relied heavily upon Axis prisoners of war to fell trees and operate sawmills.[47]

Alabama's ordnance plants, manufacturing, and shipbuilding industries, as well as agriculture and lumber businesses, set new records for production in the war years. Judged by workers and wages, shipbuilding emerged as the second-largest manufacturing sector in the Alabama economy by 1944. Similarly, ordnance manufacturing, which did not exist prior to World War II, was the sixth-ranking industry in the state by 1944.[48] Layoffs at ordnance works and shipyards in that year, however, pointed to the evaporation of the wartime prosperity and to a trying transition to a peacetime economy. Alabama had made important contributions to the war effort, and its businesses and workers had prospered as never before. The challenge now was to find ways to capitalize on the remarkable expansion of wartime growth and to continue the transformation of Alabama into a prosperous state with an economy balanced between industry and agriculture. Only thus could Alabama absorb returning veterans and, at the same time, preserve newly gained opportunities for women, blacks, and tenant farmers.

Six

Governing Alabama

For the most part, politics in Alabama have turned on local issues, but the Great Depression and World War II brought national politics to center stage. Although the Alabama electorate continued to vote for Franklin D. Roosevelt and to send Democratic congressmen to Washington, the state's recovery from the depths of depression by the early 1940s greatly diminished support for the president and his New Deal. Wartime measures that increased the power of Washington at the expense of the states caused a further erosion of FDR's popularity. In particular, many privileged and powerful Alabamians resented federal policies—prompted largely by wartime labor shortages, but also influenced by a sense of fair play—that fostered greater economic opportunities for women and blacks through such agencies as the Fair Employment Practices Committee. The critics regarded these measures as an unwarranted intrusion into states' rights and a shackling of free enterprise. Tensions that would come to a head with the Dixiecrat revolt in the 1948 election appeared during these years. The outbreak of war, however, spurred a sense of patriotism and national unity that, except for the hotly contested senatorial race between New Dealer Lister Hill and his opponent, conservative Birmingham attorney James A. Simpson, squelched much of the vocal criticism of the Roosevelt presidency.[1]

Alabama's two wartime governors, Frank Dixon and Chauncey Sparks, stood in the conservative wing of the Democratic party, which had dominated state politics in the decades following Reconstruction. Hostile to the New Deal and suspicious of Roosevelt, they represented the interests of the Big Mules—the Birmingham industrialists and Black Belt planters. For the duration of the war, neither Dixon or Sparks risked waging a divisive political struggle against the national Democrats. Privately, however, Dixon and Sparks conducted a spirited campaign against the federal government's labor and racial policies.[2]

For a twentieth-century Alabama politician, Frank Murray Dixon's

Outgoing Governor Frank Dixon (left) at the inauguration of Chauncey Sparks (right) in 1942. (Alabama Chamber of Commerce photograph, Alabama Department of Archives and History)

early life had been an unusual, and cosmopolitan, odyssey. The son of a Baptist preacher with North Carolina roots, Dixon was born in Oakland, California, on 25 July 1892 but soon moved to tidewater Virginia. He received an extraordinarily fine education. After a year of prep school at Phillips Exeter Academy and graduation from a Washington, D.C., high school, he briefly studied at Columbia University before earning a law degree from the University of Virginia. Looking for a rapidly growing city in which to build a law practice, Dixon chose Birmingham over Kansas City, Missouri. A chance meeting on a train with Magic City attorney Hugh Morrow led Dixon in 1916 to the law offices of Francis S. White, a successful attorney and prominent figure in Democratic party circles. White offered the young graduate a desk but no pay. Dixon took the job, but the fifty dollars monthly allowance from his father did not provide many luxuries for the struggling lawyer.[3]

When the United States entered World War I in 1917, Dixon volunteered for military service. After being commissioned a second lieutenant in the coast artillery, he flew as an aerial observer with a French escadrille until German gunfire brought his plane down over Soissons. Dixon escaped with his life but lost his right leg in the crash. France's Third Republic bestowed the Croix de Guerre with palms and Chevalier of the Legion of Honor upon him for his bravery and sacrifices. After his discharge, Dixon returned to Birmingham where he practiced law for the next two decades.[4]

Frank Dixon possessed a keen intellect that accompanied his polished education and cosmopolitan experiences. While no less a pragmatist than other twentieth-century governors, Dixon formulated an elitist philosophy of government. Suspicious of democracy, he could be described as a technocrat, believing implicitly that industrialists, bankers, and other professionals were endowed with superior talents to govern. To Dixon, industrialization and education furnished the keys to solving the problems of Alabama and the South. He championed lengthening the school year and fought for the creation of a retirement system for educators, which the legislature authorized in 1939.[5]

Dixon's first foray into gubernatorial politics produced disappointment but valuable experience. In 1934 the young Birmingham lawyer lost to a popular former governor, Bibb Graves, for the Democratic party's gubernatorial nomination. Four years later Dixon ran again. His 1938 campaign emphasized the need to professionalize state government. Dixon was appalled by the spoils system—epitomized by the Bibb Graves machine—that permeated state government. Believing that state employees should be hired and promoted on the basis of professional qualifications and abilities, Dixon favored a merit system that rewarded competence and not cronyism. He advocated reform in the penal system and argued that paroles should be granted on evidence of rehabilitation rather than favoritism. Hoping to bring greater efficiency to government, he proposed streamlining agencies and reducing their number. By a slender plurality, Dixon defeated Chauncey Sparks in the primary, and Sparks's decision not to force a runoff handed him the election.[6]

Astonishingly, the legislature enacted most of Dixon's reforms into law in 1939 with little opposition. The creation of the departments of revenue and finance out of a hodgepodge of agencies established greater fiscal order and accountability. A budget act promised fiscal integrity by forbidding the state to incur a deficit. Dixon's overhaul of state government was the most important general reform of Alabama's 1901 constitution and, with few modifications, has remained intact to the present.[7]

Earl McGowin skillfully steered Dixon's program through the state legislature. Compared to most other state politicians, McGowin, like Dixon, was cut from a different bolt of cloth. Born in Brewton but raised in the Piney Woods town of Chapman where his father owned a sawmill, McGowin graduated from the University of Alabama. With a Phi Beta Kappa key on his watch fob, he studied at Oxford University on a Rhodes scholarship. Except for a stint in the Navy during World War II, McGowin sat in the legislature from the 1930s until 1950, after which he served as conservation director. Efforts to persuade him to make a run for governor were unavailing. With characteristic good humor he dismissed such suggestions, saying: "I don't chew tobacco, don't wear overalls and do wear a mustache, which, I am reliably informed, is usually fatal to gubernatorial aspirants. . . . I neither yodel nor sing hillbilly tunes but . . . I've studied in England and talk with an Oxford accent."[8] If that did not sink his chances with the electorate for higher political office, McGowin could also have pointed out that he enjoyed banging out jazz tunes on a piano and had a lively interest in ornithology.

McGowin and the governor shared a breadth of education, experience, and vision that was unique in twentieth-century Alabama politics. Both had traveled widely and had lived outside the South, giving each a broad perspective on national and international trends. While McGowin approached politics as a gentlemanly art, the governor tended to look upon politics as a serious commitment to ideology and principle.

Dixon believed that some southern institutions were anachronisms that inevitably must give way. Alabama's future, Dixon was convinced, lay in modern industry rather than agriculture, especially the tenant farming system, which he regarded as a curse. In a speech delivered in Birmingham in 1940, Dixon argued the necessity of greater industrialization. Compared with the sharecropper's average annual income of $73, industrial workers earned $865. In contrast to the regional average income of $314 per capita, workers nationwide took home annual incomes of $600. While the southern states contained 28 percent of the nation's population, they contributed only 12 percent of the country's income tax revenues. Babies, Dixon lamented, were the South's "bumper crop." As a result, Alabama had a third more children to feed, clothe, and educate than the national average.[9]

Governor Dixon asked in his important Birmingham speech how Alabama could tackle the pressing problems of health, education, roads, and pensions when state and local governments together collected less than $30 per capita annually—compared with the national average of more than $50. If Alabama and the Southeast failed, Dixon warned, hard-working people would emigrate from the region or would increasingly turn to desperate, demagogic solutions.

As war approached, Governor Dixon saw an opportunity to assist local communities in attracting new industry, defense contracts, and military facilities. Skilled at organization, his administration quickly moved to implement the selective service system, to create boards to supervise rationing, to establish a State Guard to take the place of the federalized National Guard, and to make preparations for civilian defense. As he achieved these tasks almost effortlessly, Dixon's administrative abilities belied the charges made against him in the 1934 gubernatorial campaign that he was a "theorist" with no administrative talent.

By 1942, the first year of American participation in the global war and the year the voters chose his successor, Governor Dixon grew increasingly concerned over the steady expansion of federal power, especially in the areas of employment and race relations. He was acutely aware of the tendency toward centralization of power that accompanied periods of economic despair and war. Having regarded the New Deal with considerable misgiving because of the expansion of federal powers, Dixon became more apprehensive as the United States geared up for what undoubtedly would be a war of long duration. In a speech delivered in December 1942 to the New York Southern Society, Dixon lashed out at the Fair Employment Practices Committee, which, he argued, took powers away from the states and made it impossible for employers to reject job applicants on the basis of race.[10] Dixon, however, was not an advocate of pure laissez-faire economics. Conceding in this 1942 speech that unregulated free enterprise had led to abuses, Dixon acknowledged that some regulation by government was justified. "There are those," he argued, "who would go back to the old system of free enterprise without needed restraints, the abuses of which beyond any question brought on the needed social reforms of the New Deal." Nonetheless, Dixon believed FDR's executive order creating the Fair Employment Practices Committee went too far in usurping the rights of the states.

In the final analysis, it was the racial issue more than the states' rights question—although the two were intertwined—that roused Dixon's ire against the Roosevelt administration. Several episodes highlighted the race issue in Alabama. Friction in Tuskegee between the black flight school and the town's white power structure frequently surfaced. At Maxwell Field, attempts by black aviators to eat, to socialize, and to shop in the post exchange and in clubs set aside—initially by law and later by tradition—for whites created tensions. A melee in the Mobile shipyards following the hiring of black workers to build Liberty ships generated animosities. More important, however, were the efforts to eliminate the poll tax as a requirement for voting in Alabama.

Frank Dixon's views on the racial question reflected the tensions that typically tugged and pushed at southerners who regarded themselves as progressives. Many people expected him to be a staunch racist. His uncle Thomas Dixon had written *The Clansman*, a pro–Ku Klux Klan novel that was turned into the film *The Birth of the Nation*.[11] But Frank Dixon disavowed the Klan. He had supported Al Smith's candidacy against Herbert Hoover in the 1928 presidential election and lined up behind the national Democrats who organized the Roosevelt campaign in Alabama in 1932. Grover C. Hall, a leading opponent of the Klan in the state and the editor of the *Montgomery Advertiser*, and other progressive Alabamians championed Dixon in those years.[12]

The 1940 presidential campaign drove a wedge between Dixon and the national Democrats.[13] FDR's decision to run for a third term dashed the presidential aspirations of Alabama's William Bankhead, speaker of the U.S. House of Representatives and a Dixon favorite. Roosevelt's choice of arch-liberal Henry A. Wallace as his running mate punctured Dixon's hopes that the president would at least select Bankhead as the vice-presidential candidate. Increasingly, New Deal Democrats fell into disfavor at the Montgomery capitol as Dixon grew more hostile to the federal government's racial, labor, and states' rights policies.

Dixon particularly bristled at efforts to abolish the poll tax. Vigorously opposing the enfranchisement of blacks in the near future, Dixon defended the poll tax as a legitimate voting requirement. Admittedly, the poll tax effectively disenfranchised poor whites, but for Dixon as for many conservatives, the poll tax was the last line of defense in preventing blacks from voting. Post–Civil War amendments to the U.S. Constitution notwithstanding, Dixon argued that the states were free to establish whatever voting requirements they chose—including poll taxes.

Dixon, however, did not completely rule out the possibility of removing the impediments to voting by blacks. But, like Guizot, a French politician on the eve of the 1848 revolution, he regarded the enfranchisement of the lower classes as appropriate only if they would enrich themselves. Taking a position that was not out of step with many moderate southerners of that era, Dixon contended that improvement in economic status and education of blacks should precede voting rights. Perhaps patronizingly, Dixon took the position that blacks had indeed made considerable strides in education and employment in recent decades: "In the main, the Negro race has, in a few generations, made more progress than any race on earth in a comparable period of years. The level of education, of health, of morality, of decency, of economic security, has risen to a remarkable degree." [14] Dixon continued to believe in the half-century-old doctrine of "separate but equal."

When congressmen began talking about legislation to abolish the poll tax nationwide, Dixon was infuriated.[15] Believing that crackpot theorists and bureaucrats in Washington were bent on forcing equal-opportunity doctrines down southern throats, Dixon strongly hinted that southern Democrats might go it alone and form their own party. These threats foreshadowed efforts by some Birmingham Democrats in 1944 to create a third party and later Dixon's own pivotal role in founding the Dixiecrat party in 1948.[16]

These issues, however, were not injected into the 1942 gubernatorial campaign, which was not expected to be a particularly exciting race. Although Dixon had been a popular reforming governor, under Alabama law he could not succeed himself, nor did he wish to do so. The Democratic party primary was scheduled for May, and the victor was a shoo-in for the November election. Republicans were expected to dutifully hold a convention to select a candidate for what would be a lost cause. The *Montgomery Advertiser*'s leading political analyst, Atticus Mullin, prophesied that "this would be the least interesting State campaign in history."[17]

Most political observers believed Bibb Graves would easily clinch the Democratic nomination. The "Little Colonel" had served as governor twice before, in 1926 and again in 1934. The Graves machine forged a powerful political coalition that included educators, veterans, organized labor, and the Ku Klux Klan. Alabamians remembered Bibb Graves as the governor who had built more roads in the state than any previous governor. Having allied himself with the New Deal in the thirties, Graves's reputation as a progressive and as an FDR loyalist was considered unbeatable by most observers. Graves had two liabilities— his age and his health. Recent bouts with kidney stones stirred doubts about his ability to run a strenuous race and to live through another term as governor.[18]

Conservative Democrats were determined not to let the election go to Graves by default. The obvious choice was Chauncey Sparks, the "Bourbon from Barbour," who had run second in the 1938 gubernatorial contest. Although conventional wisdom in Alabama accorded runners-up the victory four years later, Sparks was regarded as a political lightweight. Some of the Big Mules turned to Chris Sherlock who, although he had been highway director during Graves's second term, was held in high esteem by the conservatives. Most political insiders regarded Sherlock as a more attractive candidate than Sparks. In any case, he might play the role of spoiler, splitting the Graves vote and handing the election to Sparks.[19]

A handful of colorful, if eccentric and unlikely, candidates entered the fray as well. Henry J. Carwile, campaigning as the poor man's candidate, crisscrossed the state in a red, white, and blue Model T Ford. An aged Birmingham furniture salesman campaigned on the populist promise of allocating sixty dollars a month for senior citizens, and an Ozark dentist vowed to raise educational standards in the state.

Although his announcement at a political rally in Fort Payne in northern Alabama attracted little attention at the time, towering James E. Folsom, an insurance agent from Cullman, tossed his hat into the ring. The country club set dismissed Folsom as a rube.[20] Born in Coffee

County in the Wiregrass in 1908, his father died from poison whiskey when "Big Jim" was only eleven. After briefly attending the University of Alabama and Howard College, Folsom became a drifter. Like a character in a novel, he went to sea and hopped freight trains. These ventures were followed by brief stints with the Works Project Administration in Marshall County and later with New Deal agencies in Washington. In 1936 and 1938 he tried unsuccessfully to defeat the Third District's popular congressman, Henry Steagall of Ozark.[21] After the failure of his 1938 campaign, Folsom moved to Cullman, which, with its yeoman farmers and its historical reluctance to enter the Civil War, was the antithesis of the Black Belt and the Big Mules.

The 1942 gubernatorial campaign proved more tumultuous than anyone had anticipated. Suddenly falling ill, Graves was hospitalized at Johns Hopkins in Baltimore in January 1942. In the aftermath of the attack on Pearl Harbor, state politics took a backseat, and Graves's illness was momentarily forgotten while he quietly convalesced in Florida. His unforeseen death in March 1942 catapulted Sparks into the front rank and dealt a harsh blow to New Dealers in Alabama.[22]

Although Sparks clung to his wide lead, Folsom's strong showing shocked even the closest of political observers. Borrowing heavily from the techniques of fellow populist politicians, Big Jim hired local bands to attract crowds and warm them for his own folksy style of oratory that combined humor with frontal attacks on the greed and corruption of special interests. To finance the campaign, Folsom supporters passed buckets for donations from the crowds. Although Sparks won the Democratic nomination without a runoff, Folsom's 26 percent of the votes surprised the pundits. If tradition held, Folsom—as the runner-up in 1942—could count on his strength in the Wiregrass and in northern Alabama to win the election in 1946.[23]

Like Frank Dixon before him, Chauncey Sparks performed the normal gubernatorial duties while, at the same time, overseeing the wartime responsibilities of selective service, rationing, and civil defense. The booming wartime economy handed the governor an enviable opportunity to increase expenditures and state services without having to hike taxes. The legislature doubled appropriations for education and increased the school year to eight months.[24]

During the Second World War state expenditures rose from $72 million annually to approximately $85 million, an increase of about 17 percent. Approximately one-third of the state's disbursements, or $28 million, was spent on education in 1944.[25] The second largest expenditure, reaching almost 20 percent, financed the construction and maintenance of roads. Payments to counties and cities of their share of taxes collected by the state constituted the third largest disbursement—about 17 percent—of state funds. Excluding funds spent on correctional institutions, approximately 9 percent of the state's expenditures were in the areas of health and human resources—the public health system, Children's Bureau, hospitals and institutions for the handicapped, Social Security, Department of Public Welfare, old-age pensions amounting to $10 a month, and pensions for Alabama's six living Confederate veterans.[26]

The state was on solid financial footing. Revenues comfortably exceeded expenditures, producing in 1942 a surplus of approximately $10 million.[27] Various state taxes provided approximately three-fourths of the state's revenues. The gasoline tax of six cents per gallon generated the most revenue, or about a fourth of the state's total income. This tax was followed in importance by the general sales, income, property, and tobacco taxes. Rising salaries from expanding defense and industrial activity led to higher receipts from the general sales tax and income tax. More Alabamians paid state income taxes at the maximum rate of 5 percent and more companies were liable for the state's 3 percent tax on corporate net profits than ever before. Of the nontax sources of revenue, federal grants provided the largest, followed by revenue from the alcohol-beverage control system that had been created during the Dixon administration.

Alabama's poll tax generated passionate disagreement. The revenue it produced was minuscule. The state budget's surplus in 1942 was twenty-two times greater than the revenue produced by the poll tax. Contributing less than half a million dollars annually, the purpose of the tax was abundantly clear—to thwart democracy. Because the tax was cumulative, thousands of poor whites and blacks were prevented from exercising the ballot. Proposals to abandon the poll tax were greeted with fire storms of protests.

In 1944 the U.S. Supreme Court handed down a decision that threatened the way southern states elected their governments. In *Smith*

v. *Allwright* the court ruled that Texas's white-only Democratic party primary was unconstitutional.[28] Because party rules in Alabama, except in a few areas such as Macon County, also excluded registered black voters from participating in Democratic primaries, it was only a matter of time before the white-only primary in Alabama and in the rest of the South would be dismantled.

In maneuvering to find ways to prevent blacks from influencing state politics, the legislature passed the Boswell amendment in May 1945. This act required proof of literacy to register for the vote and gave arbitrary—and unappealable—authority to registrars to determine who was qualified to exercise the franchise. After a 1946 referendum, the Boswell amendment became law and for the next two decades perpetuated nearly exclusively white primaries and elections.[29]

Alabama's influence in national politics during World War II was unparalleled in the history of the state. Several key congressmen and political activists figured prominently in the Roosevelt presidency and in New Deal programs. Congressman Henry Steagall, the powerful chairman of the House Banking Committee, championed drastic reform to restore public confidence in the depression-scarred banking system.[30] His scheme was to protect small depositors by creating the Federal Deposit Insurance Corporation.

United States Senator John Bankhead, Jr., and his brother William Bankhead, the powerful Speaker of the House of Representatives until his death in 1940, were key supporters of the nation's farmers, putting together a coalition of southern Democrats and midwestern Republicans who found common ground on most agricultural issues. Edward O'Neal, president of the American Farm Bureau, was a Bankhead agricultural ally and an Alabamian. For the most part, this agricultural coalition represented the interests of the big farmers. H. L. Mitchell's Southern Tenant Farmers Union and Aubrey Williams's Farmers Union, on the other hand, represented the small farmers, but they were unsuccessful in welding Alabama's poor farmers into a competing political bloc.

Senator Lister Hill was generally acknowledged to be the state's leading supporter of President Roosevelt and the New Deal. At Hill's own request, he made the 1940 nominating speech for Roosevelt's unprecedented third bid for the presidency. A nervous Hill delivered a speech that moved—and, some said, sounded—like molasses.[31] Never again comfortable making radio speeches to national audiences, Hill nonetheless became a powerful figure in Congress. As Democratic whip, he steered the president's legislative agenda on labor, education, and health through the Senate. By 1944 he was one of Capitol Hill's leading advocates of a United Nations.

John Sparkman was another prominent Roosevelt torchbearer in Alabama's congressional delegation. The son of a tenant farmer in north Alabama, he was first elected to represent the Eighth District in 1936 and became the Democratic whip in the House of Representatives during World War II. After five terms in the House, Sparkman was elected the state's junior senator. Even though Hill and Sparkman were careful not to rock the boat on racial matters, they were leaders of the progressive wing of their party in Alabama, opposing efforts of such disgruntled Democrats as former governor Frank Dixon to form the breakaway Dixiecrat party in 1948.

Other New Dealers coalesced around Hugo Black, whom President Roosevelt nominated for a seat on the Supreme Court in 1937. Black's admission that he had briefly belonged to the Ku Klux Klan nearly sank his confirmation by the Senate. Black not only remained a confidant of the president during the war but he subsequently emerged as the most ardent defender on the bench of the Bill of Rights and individual liberties. Liberal New Dealers in Washington gravitated toward Justice Black's sister-in-law Virginia and her husband, Clifford Durr, who was the son of a prominent Montgomery businessman. As an administrator in the Reconstruction Finance Corporation and later the Federal Communications Commission, Clifford Durr was part of a small coterie of New Deal insiders from Alabama who were fiercely loyal to the Roosevelts and the national Democratic party.[32] For her part, Virginia Durr organized a nationwide effort to outlaw the poll tax.

Several Alabama congressmen opposed Roosevelt and the national Democratic party but for the duration of the war refrained from a frontal assault. Party loyalty bred some tolerance, but pork barrels were an even greater inducement, especially when the government in Washington could assign defense contracts and build new military encampments. Selma's Sam Hobbs was no Roosevelt partisan, but he cultivated contacts in Washington to get Craig Field built in his district.[33]

Frank Boykin from Mobile was a genial conservative and a person of great personal warmth and considerable imagination. He had never cut a big swath in Congress, but his nimbleness got the Army Air Corps to locate a major repair facility and supply depot at Brookley Field. As a ranking member of the House Merchant Marine and Fisheries Committee, Boykin leaned on the Maritime Commission to award contracts to Mobile's shipyards during the war.[34]

Congressman George W. Andrews, though he never achieved the national stature of his predecessor Henry Steagall, obtained several beneficial decisions for his district that profoundly affected the economic future of the Wiregrass. A lawyer from Union Springs, Andrews served as solicitor of the circuit court before volunteering for the Navy. In a political campaign managed by his brother, Andrews was elected to Congress while he was on active duty in the Pacific. Despite an initial setback, he lobbied successfully after the war to persuade the Army and Congress to transform Camp Rucker into a permanent military post.[35]

At home, state government functioned effectively during the war years. Economic prosperity amply funded state appropriations, although Alabama continued to lag far behind most of the nation in spending for education. Prodded by the Roosevelt administration to provide equality of opportunity for blacks and for women, state government politely equivocated. Privately, however, many leading state Democratic politicians were preparing to abandon the national party. On the federal scene, Alabama politicians played a key role in Congress and among opinion makers in Washington. Never before nor since has Alabama been more in the mainstream of American politics or provided more national leadership than during the World War II era.

Seven

The War and Society

The war years transformed Alabama's society in sweeping and sometimes traumatic ways. Some changes—tenant farming's slow but persistent demise, urbanization, and the continued outward migration of blacks—that began earlier in the century accelerated during the war. In 1910 more than 55 percent of Alabama's blacks were engaged in agriculture; by 1940 only about 35 percent farmed. In the 1940s Alabama's combined black and white farm population fell by 15 percent.[1] During that same period, 9 percent of Alabama's white population migrated to urban areas or out of state, while nearly 27 percent of the black population left rural Alabama. Blacks migrated to the North, West, or into Alabama's own industrial urban areas so steadily that in the plantation counties of western Alabama blacks constituted a smaller percentage of the population on the eve of World War II than in 1860.[2]

Depressed incomes and the inconveniences of rural life drove many Alabamians from the land. Agricultural income rose in the late 1930s and early 1940s but not as sharply as wages in construction, manufacturing, or mining occupations, where earnings were four to ten times greater than in farming. Cotton, which remained the leading cash crop and whose prices doubled from ten cents a pound in 1939 to twenty cents in 1942, paced the recovery in agricultural income. Still, cotton produced only about a third of predepression revenues, and on the eve of World War II, farmers were planting about half as much cotton as in 1929.[3]

Life in the countryside lacked the conveniences—as well as some of the banes—of modern living. Rural electrification cooperatives strung power lines in most counties and TVA generated cheap electricity in northern Alabama. Nonetheless, only 15 percent of the farms were electrified by December 1941. Telephones served fewer than 4 percent of Alabama's rural homes, and nearly 98 percent lacked indoor "facilities."[4]

Spangler cartoon in Montgomery Advertiser *showing the vast migration from countryside to manufacturing jobs in urban areas during the war. (Alabama Department of Archives and History)*

The population of Alabama's towns and cities, where the economic picture was brighter, grew by 57 percent during the 1940s. Between 1940 and 1943, 89,000 people—mostly poor whites and blacks—descended upon Mobile, whose population doubled during the war. Industrial jobs in Huntsville mushroomed from 3,500 in 1940 to 17,000 by 1944.[5] Twice as many Alabamians earned their livelihoods in nonfarming occupations in 1942 as in 1939.[6] Some entrepreneurs capitalized on the comparative prosperity of the towns and Alabamians' newfound mobility, such as Claude Flynt, whose family had struggled as tenant farmers for generations; Flynt now made a livelihood by using his old truck to move families and their possessions in and out of the Childersburg area.[7]

Cutbacks in defense outlays reduced manufacturing employment in the last two years of the war. Nonetheless, in 1946 there were 46 percent more industrial and commercial jobs in Alabama than at the beginning of the war. More remarkable, total wage payments in the state tripled, rising from $239 million in 1939 to $708 million in 1946. Inflation was negligible, and industrial wage earners could substantially improve their bank accounts because there was little to purchase and improvements in standards of living had to await the return of peace. In the meantime, Americans were encouraged to save for the future by purchasing war bonds.

The crush of humanity in Alabama's boom towns created severe strains on housing, education, public health, and moral standards. In Huntsville, if rooms could be found at all, they were likely to offer only worn linoleum and thin mattresses. Parked cars served as shelters, as did park benches on warm, clear nights. In Mobile, "hot beds" were rented by the hour. Unsightly trailer parks accommodated thousands. "Trailer wives" lived in mobile homes brought in by the federal government or installed by private enterprise. As the writer John Dos Passos observed during a journey to Mobile, "Housekeeping in a trailer with electric light and running water is a dazzling luxury to a woman who's lived all her life in a cabin with half-inch chinks between the splintered boards of the floor."[8] Federally financed projects ameliorated some housing and classroom shortages in areas where rapidly expanding military installations and defense industries placed great strains on local communities. The Federal Housing Authority came to the rescue in some war-impacted towns such as Mobile, where it built about 11,000 residential units in sixteen housing projects—all but two of which, however, were for whites.[9]

School classrooms bulged beyond capacity despite the fact that only 30 percent of Alabama's population attended school beyond the eighth grade.[10] Mobile's new Murphy High School, built to accommodate 2,200 students, had twice that number by 1944. Classes were taught in two shifts. Teachers in Childersburg, where the school population doubled in 1941, faced as many as 80 students in their classrooms. Overcrowded schools strained an already burdened educational system. Compared to the $3,592 spent per classroom in California, or even $1,526 in Iowa, Alabama allocated $748 per classroom in 1940—$840 for whites and $303 for blacks.[11]

Many fine teachers presided over Alabama classrooms during those years, but only 50 percent of the white teachers and 20 percent of the black teachers had completed four years at a senior university or teachers' college. More than a third of Alabama's black teachers had completed less than two years of college. That figure looked good compared to Mississippi where only 15 percent of the black teachers had at least two years of college. On the other hand, North Carolina's black schoolteachers were as likely to have graduated from four-year colleges as Alabama's white teachers.[12]

Pay scales for public school teachers varied widely. Those certified by "accredited" schools earned higher salaries than graduates of "approved" schools. Only white teachers' colleges, however, were accredited by the Southern Association of Colleges and Schools. Salaries, in any event, were not munificent. In the 1939–40 school year, white teachers averaged $874 per year; black teachers earned 40 percent less. Starting at $800 annually, teachers graduating from accredited schools could hope to reach a maximum salary of $1,300. In contrast, salaries of secretaries and assembly-line workers in Huntsville or Mobile began at $1,400. At the powder plant at Childersburg, skilled female laborers could earn as much as $3,600 annually.[13] It is not surprising that some teachers fled from overcrowded classrooms and low salaries.[14]

The quantity, if not the quality, of instruction in Alabama classrooms increased during the war years. Prior to the 1940s, schoolchildren attended 151 days of class annually, which fell below the national average. The shorter school year not only saved money but also accommodated farm families, whose children were needed in the fields. Prompted by Governor Frank Dixon, the Alabama legislature lengthened the school year to 166 days, a move that further burdened already underfunded school systems.[15]

World War II produced a watershed for higher education in the United States. In 1940 few Alabamians dreamed of a college education. Even relatively affluent families had found it difficult to send children to college during the 1930s. On the eve of World War II, less than 7 percent of the population had any education beyond high school.[16] Already reeling from the depression, Alabama's colleges had to be innovative to survive the world war. The condition of Alabama Polytechnic Institute, later renamed Auburn University, was typical. By the early 1940s, the school was more than $1 million in debt. Unable to pay wages in cash during the depression, API had issued scrip to the faculty and staff, who survived largely through the generosity of local merchants.[17]

The wartime draft left classrooms partly empty and depleted athletic teams so badly that some sports were canceled entirely or schedules were drastically curtailed. API's civilian student enrollment plunged from 3,600 in the fall term of 1942 to 1,700 a year later.[18] Military programs—such as the Army Specialized Training Program, a Navy radar training school, the Management War Training Program, and the Vocational Training for War Production Workers—took up some of the slack. With thousands of men and women attending API under these wartime programs, the campus acquired the appearance of a military encampment.[19]

Traditional liberal arts colleges survived by adapting to wartime demands. Birmingham-Southern College switched to the quarter system, emphasized physics and mathematics, and contracted with the Army Air Forces to provide basic education to 325 officer candidates each term.[20] Under president Harwell Davis's leadership, Howard College (now Samford University) became one of the nation's 131 colleges offering V-12 programs to educate future Navy officers. This program caused many changes on the tranquil campus. The V-12s were housed in two women's dormitories. The displaced coeds moved into a house purchased by the college and two former fraternity houses. The new women's dorms were known as "Ration," "Duration," and "Inflation." Undoubtedly the biggest wartime shock for this decorous Baptist college was the "smokers" and "dances" sponsored by the V-12 program on campus.[21]

War dramatically changed the composition of the student body at the University of Alabama. The number of civilian students decreased from 5,000 in 1941 to 1,500 three years later. The campus, however, bulged with servicemen. More than 13,000 students attended the university under one of the military- or defense-related programs. President Raymond Paty called it the "University at War." The Tuscaloosa campus was especially active in aviation training. In 1939 the Civilian Aeronautics Authority had selected the university for one of the first civilian pilot training schools. The Tuscaloosa campus had one of nine accredited aeronautical engineering programs in the country.[22]

The lean years experienced by higher education throughout the depression and in World War II ended with the passage of the GI Bill. Public Law 346 launched a more democratic era in which higher education became accessible to growing numbers of Americans. College enrollments exploded in the postwar period as veterans flooded college campuses. More than 10,000 World War II veterans enrolled at API between 1946 and 1950.[23] For the most part, students, especially the veterans, good-humoredly endured shortages of classrooms and housing. Among the most unusual living quarters at Alabama Polytechnic Institute were the deckhouses from never-completed Navy tugboats.

The war affected public health far less than officials had feared. Health authorities worried that large concentrations of soldiers at military encampments and widespread migration of job seekers into booming war towns would dramatically spread such communicable diseases as typhus and meningitis.[24] Luckily, other than an outbreak of polio and a higher than usual incidence of venereal diseases, Alabama was spared serious epidemics.

The "dread infantile paralysis" struck Alabama in 1941. The 871 cases of poliomyelitis were the state's worst epidemic of this crippling disease up to that time.[25] Local officials canceled county agricultural fairs and delayed the opening of school until late September.[26] The epidemic receded quickly but was a harbinger of the more widespread outbreak of polio in the 1950s.

Alarmed by the spread of venereal diseases, which reached epidemic proportions throughout the country during the war, the surgeon general of the United States launched a study of the spread and treatment of sexually transmitted diseases. As the only state in the South with public health offices in every county, Alabama agreed to establish voluntary statewide testing for venereal diseases. Moreover, as early as 1932, federal health officials in Alabama had already begun studying the spread of venereal diseases. Using the veterans' hospital in Tuskegee, the United States Public Health Service began gathering data about the pathology of syphilis among black males. Some of the methodology developed by the "Tuskegee experiment" was used in the broader study among volunteer participants who appeared before selective service boards in the state. Alabama's experiences served as a model and benchmark for subsequent nationwide testing.

Approximately 60 percent of the individuals appearing before draft boards in 1940 consented to testing for venereal diseases.[27] Although most of those who tested positive received medical treatment, some black victims in the Tuskegee study were only given placebos so that the course of the disease could be observed by federal health officials. Many medical practitioners and ethicists contend that the Tuskegee experiment callously ignored medical principles and state public health policy in order to conduct what these scientists regard as a flawed study. The "Tuskegee experiment" became especially tragic after World War II, when penicillin—which became readily available and which offered a cure for syphilis—was withheld from treatment.[28]

The war placed additional burdens on already strained private health care in Alabama. Prior to the attack on Pearl Harbor 2,075 physicians, including only 124 black practitioners, served the medical needs of 2.8 million Alabamians. Alabama had only half as many doctors per capita as most other states.[29] The critical shortage of physicians grew worse when 268 Alabama physicians, nearly 13 percent of the doctors in the state, donned military uniforms.[30] Only New Mexico surpassed Alabama in exceeding its quota for doctors in service.[31] Nationwide, more than 30 percent of the nurses volunteered for duty in military hospitals, further straining civilian health care.

Rural Alabamians, in particular, had little access to medical care. Only one physician served the 13,000 residents of Coosa County. To address the acute need for more doctors and nurses, Governor Chauncey Sparks promoted the creation of a four-year medical school. In 1944 the legislature appropriated funds for the Medical College of Alabama, which was located in Birmingham. Hillman Hospital, a charity institution, was used for teaching, and the new Jefferson Hospital, a county-owned facility for private patients, offered clinical opportunities for medical students.[32]

Alabama doctors first used penicillin, hailed as a miracle drug, to treat a case of blood poisoning in 1944. Administered in military hospitals to fight infections, penicillin was rarely used in civilian medicine until after the war. But in 1944 Senator Lister Hill interceded with doctors at Marine Hospital in Memphis to make the wonder drug available to Limestone County's Powers Hospital to treat Eugene Hillis, a young boy whose life was threatened by blood poisoning. Following a six-week battle, the "penicillin kid" recovered and was released from the hospital in March 1944.[33]

Only rudimentary sources of public welfare, including old-age assistance and aid to dependent children, the blind, and the unemployable, existed in Alabama. Some politicians, such as Jim Folsom, regarded Alabama's efforts as inadequate. Campaigning for governor in 1942, Big Jim stumped for old-age pensions for everyone sixty-five years of age or older.[34]

World War II had mixed effects on the state's social health. Crimes against property declined during the war. This phenomenon was generally explained by economic recovery from the depression and the rapid growth of employment and wages. One member of the State Board of Paroles and Pardons concluded that "high wages have tempted even the shiftless to some industrious effort."[35] State authorities, however, grew more concerned over vagrancy, prostitution, venereal diseases, drunkenness, and gambling. These problems appeared to be more acute near military installations or in towns that were attracting job seekers in defense industries. As early as 1940, state authorities were alert to charges that these problems existed in Phenix City. In the following summer, Governor Dixon ordered public safety officials to keep an eye on conditions in Childersburg.[36] Sheriffs and police chiefs in Alabama generally concluded that the most serious social problems were caused not by professional prostitutes but by young vagrants. The state confronted a not insignificant problem in locating runaway girls as young as thirteen or fourteen who had become military camp followers.[37]

Following the repeal of prohibition, the sale of alcoholic beverages had been made a local option. In "wet" counties, "state stores" dispensed alcoholic spirits. In "dry" counties, bootlegging flourished. When enterprising workers at the arsenals in dry Huntsville realized that thousands of gallons of 200-proof pure grain alcohol were used in the manufacturing process, it did not take them long to improvise ways to siphon off some of this potent coolant. Many of south Alabama's "Barnacle Bills"—fishermen, war workers, and dock hands—drove to Mississippi after work to drink in the roadhouses of an ostensibly dry state. There, right under the noses of local constables, suckers could gamble away their week's wages on the "one-armed Monte Carlos."[38]

Demon alcohol remained a powerful issue in the state, particularly for the Baptists. Ever vigilant against sin, the Alabama Baptist State Convention, meeting in Birmingham in November 1942, condemned the moral laxness of wartime Americans. Gambling, greed, sexual promiscuity, and especially alcohol fueled the "merry devil's dance."[39] The governing body contended that the catastrophe of Pearl Harbor would never have happened if Americans had been more sober-minded and morally resolute. Furthermore, it denounced liquor as the "patron saint of Washington," which "goes on debauching our soldiers and endangering our chances in the war."[40] Alabama Baptists wanted a national referendum as a means of reestablishing prohibition. The Methodists did not approve of alcohol, either, but did not seek an outright national ban on its sale. Worried about the corrupting influence of alcohol on young people, Alabama Methodists urged Congress to pass laws curtailing the sale of intoxicating drinks near military encampments.[41]

World War II posed other fundamental moral challenges to Alabama's religious denominations. Most Christian churches condemned war in principle but sanctioned the struggle against the Axis powers as a "just" war. Since the Middle Ages, Christianity had justified defensive wars as legitimate. In the Second World War, few Americans doubted the culpability of the Axis powers. A resolution adopted by the recently united Methodist Church typified the attitude of most Protestant denominations. Meeting in Montgomery in November 1942, the annual Methodist conference expressed its "abhorrence of war" but proclaimed this war to be a struggle pitting evil against good. Under these circumstances, the Methodists continued, Christians could not sit around "with piously folded hands" pretending "that war is not the business of the Church."[42] Alabama Baptists, too, expressed their loathing for war but justified this struggle as necessary to protect the freedoms enjoyed in a democracy, including religious freedom.

In a similar vein the southern Presbyterian Church—which after

World War I had said it would never again give its blessings to war—reversed itself after the attack on Pearl Harbor, proclaiming the struggle against the Axis powers to be a Christian duty.[13] The church saw the irony, however, of waging war abroad in defense of democracy when millions of Americans were deprived of the franchise in the United States. Pointing out that doctrines of racial supremacy threatened human liberty, the General Assembly of the southern Presbyterian Church decreed that it would be morally indefensible to wage war against racism abroad and leave intact those laws and customs at home that stood in the way of individual freedom. "Christians of America," this body proclaimed, "should practice justice and fairness to all races, including Negroes."[44]

As a universal church with large numbers of adherents in both the totalitarian states and the subjugated democracies of Europe, the Catholic Church was badly divided by the war. Although many Catholics regretted the papacy's silence on the racial doctrines of Adolf Hitler and national socialism, most were equally fearful of communism and Stalinist Russia. The dilemma was not as great for American Catholics, who tended to regard all totalitarianism as undesirable. To most Americans—Catholics, Protestants, or nonbelievers—the communist peril appeared remote, and Japan's threat loomed larger than Germany's. Francis Spellman, archbishop of New York after 1939 and leading Catholic spokesman in the United States, provided a workable compromise. He strongly supported President Roosevelt's foreign policy and the war against the Axis powers but at the same time continued to warn of the dangers of Soviet influence in the postwar world.[45] Still remembering the Ku Klux Klan's vicious Catholic baiting in the 1920s and 1930s, Alabama Catholics found foreign ideologies springing from racial and religious hatred to be distasteful. Archbishop Oscar Lipscomb of Mobile remembers from his boyhood in parochial school in the 1940s that prayers for Allied victory were offered daily.[46]

The religious denomination that experienced the greatest difficulty reconciling its faith with war was the rapidly expanding Pentecostal movement. Historically, the Church of God and other Pentecostal bodies had taken seriously God's admonition to Moses not to take human life. During World War I, the Church of God had been harassed and some of its members jailed because of their resistance to conscription. Throughout the 1930s the church continued to oppose military service for its members. But faced with the aggression and brutality of the Axis powers, the movement retreated from its traditional pacifism. After Congress enacted the draft law in 1940, the Church of God declared that it was the duty of males to register with selective service as long as adequate provision was made for conscientious objectors. Although some draft boards routinely sent conscientious objectors to induction centers that assigned them to combat units, most draft boards recognized the right of sincere religious opposition to war.[47]

Not all Pentecostals opposed the taking of human life in a justifiable war, and some volunteered for combat duty. On the home front many bought war bonds, worked in defense industries, or supported the war effort in other ways. Seeking to create a new image, the Church of God called upon its members to be patriotic. Summarizing the effect of World War II, a leading authority on southern Pentecostalism has written, "By 1944, the once strongly pacifist Church of God appeared to be moving into the mainstream of conservative evangelicalism and American society."[48]

Alabama's small Jewish community, of course, had the greatest stake in the outcome of the war. Until Germany's conquest of Poland in 1939, the implications of the racial policies espoused in Hitler's *Mein Kampf* had been only dimly perceived in the United States. Even during the war, the magnitude of the horrors perpetrated against European Jewry was unimagined. Nonetheless, war strengthened the bonds linking Alabama's small Jewish community to its persecuted coreligionists in Europe. From Birmingham's Jewish congregations alone, some 200 males served in the armed forces during the Second World War. Increasingly, Alabama's Jewish community gravitated toward Zionism. Birmingham's foremost Zionist, Abe Berkowitz, prodded the Alabama legislature into passing a resolution calling for the creation of a Jewish state in Palestine.[49]

Perhaps the most flamboyant personal gesture against Axis aggression came from Louis Pizitz, a leading member of Birmingham's Jewish community, businessman, and civic figure. A noted humanitarian, Pizitz had extended desperately needed credit at his store during the depression. On Thanksgiving, he fed the needy. Committed to higher education, he helped raise money for Tuskegee Institute. Quick to anger against aggression and totalitarianism, on 8 December 1941 Pizitz promised a check in the amount of $1,000 to the first American pilot who bombed Tokyo. Four months later, he made good his promise when Jimmy Doolittle's raiders flew from the carrier *Hornet* to deliver the first bombs on Japan. Although Colonel Doolittle refused the reward, Pizitz's check was sent to the unit fund, a gesture that Army Air Forces chief Henry "Hap" Arnold acknowledged in a warm letter of thanks.[50]

The depression and the Second World War not only challenged the spiritual lives of Alabamians but produced several important social changes as well. New demographic patterns emerged. Birthrates among both blacks and whites fell noticeably during the 1930s as families deferred children until times improved. This trend was not reversed until the postwar period's "baby boom." Also in the depression years, migration to urban areas had slowed as many Alabamians returned to the countryside. During the war, however, Alabamians—lured by defense jobs—flocked into the cities.[51]

Migration of African-Americans out of the state was another major trend. Between 1930 and 1950 the percentage of blacks in the total state population declined from nearly 36 percent to just under 32 percent. Southern blacks moved not only to cities in the East and Midwest but to the West Coast where jobs and a more open social climate attracted thousands. Contemporary black writers pointed out that "the outstanding fact concerning Negro migration during World War II . . . was the movement into cities in the West." Compared to Detroit's 47 percent increase in black population between 1930 and 1940, San Francisco's black population rose 227 percent; Los Angeles experienced a 78 percent rise, and the Portland-Vancouver area, a 90 percent jump.[52]

The westward trend continued during the war. Despite opposition from union leaders, southern blacks found jobs in industry, especially in shipbuilding—notably in flamboyant Henry Kaiser's shipyards in Oregon, at Moore Drydock in Alameda, California, and at Calship in Los Angeles. Although the aircraft industry experienced a fifteenfold increase in employment from 1940 to 1945, it hired few blacks except as menial laborers.[53] Although many southern black migrants discovered that segregationist attitudes were not a monopoly of the American

South, the increased prospects of greater personal freedom and prosperity proved to be a powerful magnet.

Even within Alabama the growth of urban jobs in industry, transportation, and the service sector, as well as in traditional domestic jobs, attracted rural blacks to the cities. From 29,000 in 1940, Mobile's black population grew to 46,000 by 1950. Many blacks came to Mobile looking for jobs on the waterfront, especially at the shipyards. Joe Williams, who hoboed from Birmingham to Mobile in 1940 to take a job at the docks, soon discovered money could be made in the restaurant business. Selling pork sandwiches for twenty-five cents and rib plates for forty cents, Williams's Electric Barbecue café grossed $70,000 in 1945.[54]

Steel and other industries drew rural blacks to Birmingham. Typical was Richard Arrington, Sr., who had struggled through the depression as a sharecropper and part-time blacksmith near Livingston in Sumter County. Desiring a better life for his family, Arrington got together enough money in the late 1930s to take the bus to Birmingham, where he found employment in a wire mill in Fairfield. Using a borrowed Model T, he moved the family to Birmingham in 1940. Although Richard Arrington, Jr., the future mayor of Birmingham, was only six years old at the time, he recalls that the move was "about the biggest thing that had ever happened to me."[55] The Arringtons, like nearly everyone else in Sumter County, were accustomed to kerosene lanterns and the stillness of evening. But from their new house in the Vinesville community, they could see the bright lights of the city and hear streetcars turning around in the distance. It was a memorable day when a toilet was installed on the back porch. Unlike many of their neighbors, the Arringtons would not have to make their way in rain or cold to the "dry toilet" in the backyard.

The catalyst of war brought to a head issues that promised to transform what was widely regarded as the natural order in relationships between men and women and between blacks and whites. Perhaps the most profound changes produced in the United States by the war related to the evolving role of women and to finding a resolution for the nagging inequalities suffered by blacks in society. War, especially the demand for labor but also the egalitarian principles for which the war was in part fought, eroded these traditions and the idealizations upon

An integrated crew at the ADDSCO shipyard in Mobile. (ADDSCO Collection, University of South Alabama Archives)

which the traditions were based. Half a century later, after many painful experiences, these transformations are still under way. Although impediments remain, both women and blacks have far greater opportunity to participate more fully in the life of the nation as a result of the changes stimulated by the war.

World War II prompted fundamental changes in the roles of women in society and in the nature of the home and the family. Whether wartime changes affected a lasting transformation of American society or proved only transitory remains a matter of debate.[56] In any event, as late as the 1940s the closely knit family and the creature comforts of home remained at the core of aspirations. As a result of the industrial revolution and the vast expansion of public education in the previous century, it was possible in the twentieth century for families—many of which were striving to pull themselves out of poverty and all of whose members knew only too well the grinding reality of back-breaking labor—to dream of being sufficiently well off to possess a comfortable home and the amenities of the modern world. It remained a matter of pride—nearly a caste distinction—if a single breadwinner, almost always expected to be the husband, could achieve this status. Deeply imbedded in this idealization was the role of woman as manager of home and hearth and the nurturer of children, tasks that American culture reinforced as worthy and satisfying.

Demand for labor in war industries led to the employment of millions of women across the nation to take the place of men who had been drafted into military service following the passage of the 1940 Selective Training and Service Act. The War Manpower Commission launched a recruitment drive to convince women that not only was war work patriotic but that they had the physical and mental skills to be successful. In Alabama thousands of women found jobs in industry, especially in the shipyards and at Brookley Field in Mobile, in the ordnance works in Huntsville, Childersburg, and Anniston, and in dozens of manufacturing plants.[57]

Not only did women work as mechanics in the aircraft modification plants, but a small band of adventuresome aviators also became Women's Airforce Service Pilots, or WASPs, ferrying planes from manufacturers to points of embarkation. Nancy Batson from Birmingham became one of the country's foremost service pilots.[58] After graduating from Ramsay High School, she enrolled at the University of Alabama where she led a very active academic, social, and political life. Nancy Batson joined Alpha Gamma Delta sorority, majored in history, and was elected president of the women's student government. Lured by the romance of flight, she convinced her parents in her junior year to indulge her in flying lessons at the recently established civilian pilot training school in Tuscaloosa. Soon she was soaring between clouds over the Black Warrior River. After graduation, Batson continued training at Southern Airways in Birmingham and earned licenses as an instructor and commercial pilot. Only 160 women had commercial pilot's licenses in the early 1940s.[59] When the United States went to war, Batson was teaching at the Embry-Riddle School of Aviation in Miami. Immediately, she packed her bags to join the Women's Auxiliary Ferrying Squadron at New Castle, Delaware. In September 1943, the WAFS and

Nancy Batson, an original WASP, flew warplanes from assembly lines to ports of embarkation. (U.S. Air Corps photograph)

other women service pilot organizations were unified into the Women's Airforce Service Pilots organization under Jacqueline Cochran's command.[60] Not only was Batson one of the original WASPs but her skills as a pilot were legendary. She commanded the Second Ferrying Group, whose flyers delivered P-47 Thunderbolts as well as B-24 and B-26 bombers to airfields, aircraft modification facilities, and ports of embarkation around the nation.

Still other women volunteered for duty as nurses at military hospitals in this country and abroad. The nursing school at Tuskegee trained many black nurses who served in World War II. In 1944 General Benjamin O. Davis, Sr., welcomed four young black lieutenants from Alabama when they arrived in England with a group of sixty-three nurses to minister to the needs of Allied soldiers during the invasion of the European continent.[61] At Fort McClellan nurses received special training for chemical warfare before being stationed overseas.[62]

The biggest employers of women in Alabama were the shipyards and Brookley Field in Mobile. Half of the 17,000 employees at the Mobile Air Service Command and the Southeast Army Air Depot at Brookley Field were women. Prodded by the Fair Employment Practices Committee, Brookley Field also hired black—mostly female— workers. At the Mobile Air Service Command, females worked as mechanics, welders, and inspectors—jobs normally held by men— modifying and repairing bombers. Women were preferred for some jobs, such as repairing delicate instruments, and for working in confined spaces. At the Southeast Army Air Depot, women performed clerical and shipping duties.[63]

Brookley Field pioneered in hiring employees with physical disabilities, which, in those days, included pregnancy. This pilot program was so successful that by 1943 nearly 1,400 individuals whose vision or hearing was impaired or who had other disabilities worked at Brookley Field cleaning spark plugs, typing reports, and repairing flight instruments.[64] The Bechtel-McCone-Parsons plant in Birmingham similarly hired women to work as welders and mechanics in bomber modification.

With 30,000 on its payroll, Alabama Drydock and Shipbuilding Company, or ADDSCO, became the largest employer in south Alabama. Nearby Gulf Shipbuilding in Chickasaw hired an additional 10,000. At the height of wartime production, women constituted approximately 10 percent of the shipyard workers.[65] Because of growing labor shortages, ADDSCO hired and trained women to weld and perform other tasks normally done by skilled men. Disparaged as "welderettes," these women soon earned high praise—and salaries— for the quality of their work and their reliability as employees.[66]

The ordnance plants in Huntsville, Childersburg, Talladega, and Anniston also employed many women. Females made up about 40 percent of the total work force at the Huntsville arsenals, and at times the Redstone Arsenal had more than 60 percent women.[67] These plants paid substantially higher wages than those earned by average workers. Between 1939 and 1946 average salaries in the ordnance plants rose from $900 to $1,800 annually. Depending upon skills, wages at the Childersburg plant, where 20 percent of the employees were women, ranged between $140 and $300 monthly. Because measuring and bagging gunpowder was regarded as unskilled labor, the top end of the pay scale for workers at the Brecon bagging facility at Talladega, where about 50 percent of the work force was female, was $115 per month.[68] Bowing to pressure from the Fair Employment Practices Committee, the Brecon plant hired black females during a period of critical labor shortage.

By 1943 perhaps as much as 25 percent of industry's labor force in Alabama was female.[69] Nationwide, the percentage of women holding industrial jobs rose from nearly 15 percent in May 1942 to slightly over 27 percent a year later.[70] In the following year, with the end of the war in sight, defense production dipped and women began receiving layoff notices. The War Manpower Commission, industries, and the military services had regarded the hiring of women as a pragmatic—and temporary—expedient necessitated by critical wartime labor shortages. When peace returned, it was expected that the "boys" on the front lines would return to claim the jobs then held by women. Although the measure of equality and independence that women achieved during the war proved transitory, many women, nonetheless, attained status and self-reliance heretofore virtually closed to them. They had proved their ability to compete in the essentially male domain of industry and business. It was a lesson with important implications for the future.

A very small contingent of female politicians and officeholders appeared on the public scene in the 1940s. In Huntsville, Myrtle Green became Madison County's first female probate judge.[71] Only one woman—Sybil Poole of Linden—sat among the 106 representatives and 35 senators in the Alabama legislature during the Second World War. She had served earlier as legislative clerk to a representative from Marengo County, and following the member's resignation in 1936, the Democratic Executive Committee appointed her to fill the vacancy. She was elected in her own right in 1938 and reelected in 1942. At first dismissed as a "comely young blonde," the press later described her as the "black widow of Alabama politics" on account of her political savvy and ability to defeat male challengers.[72] When she retired from her legislative seat in 1944, Poole was regarded by her colleagues as one of the ablest politicians in the legislature. From time to time her name was touted as a gubernatorial candidate, but instead she was elected to other constitutional statewide offices.[73]

The war also provided African-Americans with unparalleled but oftentimes impermanent opportunities in industry. Labor shortages forced industry, albeit sometimes reluctantly, to hire black workers. Additionally, President Roosevelt issued an executive order setting forth the principle that blacks and women should be treated fairly in the defense industry work place. Although southern politicians vehemently objected, Roosevelt created the Fair Employment Practices Committee as a wartime expedient to see that the guidelines were enforced. In essence, blacks and women were to have equality of opportunity with white men for jobs. Conditions of employment and wages for equal jobs were to be the same for all employees regardless of color or sex. Nationally, this policy had broad support. Platforms of both the Democratic and the Republican parties in 1940 and 1944 urged better political and economic treatment for blacks. In 1940 the Republicans pledged "that our American citizens of Negro descent shall be given a square deal in the economic and political life of the nation."[74] On the local level, black leaders and organizations urged equality of opportunity and improved conditions in local communities. John LeFlore, a leading member of the Mobile chapter of the NAACP, pushed vigorously for improved transportation and for the desegregation of lunch counters.[75]

By 1942 more blacks were being hired by construction, manufacturing, and service firms than ever before. Among the leading Alabama employers of blacks were the ordnance works, defense depots, and defense manufacturers. Under prodding from the Fair Employment Practices Committee, Alabama Drydock and Shipbuilding Company and the Union of Marine Shipbuilders agreed to train black welders and to integrate them into white crews. This policy led to much grumbling in the yard, culminating in a melee in May 1943 that left eight blacks and one white worker injured.[76] Tensions remained high at ADDSCO for weeks. In a letter to Governor Chauncey Sparks in early June, Mobile County Sheriff W. H. Holcombe labeled the ADDSCO shipyard as a

Pay day at the ADDSCO shipyard, Mobile. Note the separate lines for white and "colored" welders. (University of South Alabama, ADDSCO Collection)

"somewhat explosive situation."[77] Compared, however, with wartime rioting in Los Angeles, Detroit, Harlem, and Beaumont, Texas, turmoil in Mobile was mild.

Approximately 22 percent of the work force at the Huntsville Arsenal was black, equally divided between men and women. In a very unusual development, the president of Atlanta University, a black female college, negotiated the hiring at the Huntsville Arsenal of 100 members of his school's graduating class, undoubtedly much to the delight of the men at nearby Alabama Agricultural and Mechanical Institute.[78]

Cutbacks in defense industries during the last year of the war cost many blacks their jobs. The old adage about "the last hired, first fired" held true for both blacks and women. They were the first to be laid off to make way for the returning warriors, who expected to find normalcy in their own lives after months or years of sacrifice. Nonetheless, World War II had been a watershed, opening new possibilities for employment and improvement in material circumstances for women and blacks. These experiences gave rise to dreams of a better tomorrow for themselves and their children and to heightened expectations of a "square deal" in the years to come.

Eight

Prisoners of War

For many Alabamians, one of the most vivid memories of World War II is of the 17,000 Germans and Italians who were held in prisoner of war camps in the state between 1943 and 1946. Ted Spears of Sylacauga remembers the day his father packed him and his older brother into their black, four-door, 1936 Plymouth and drove down Highway 24 from Alexander City, where they lived at the time, to Opelika to see the German prisoners. He remembers his surprise at discovering that the POWs looked remarkably similar to Americans.[1] Indeed, many rural Alabamians were surprised that the Germans who helped them chop cotton, harvest peanuts, cut timber, or operate saws in lumberyards were much like themselves.

In the early days of the POW camps, however, the prisoners—especially the Germans—appeared sullen and defiant. The first contingent of POWs to arrive in the United States were tough desert soldiers of Rommel's North African campaign. Some of these troops were imbued with the doctrines of national socialism, regarded Hitler and the Reich as invincible, and remained convinced of Germany's ultimate triumph.

Not all POWs, however, were caricatures of Nazi ideology. As Alabamians learned, most POWs were decent human beings whose greatest concern—other than their own survival—was the welfare of loved ones at home. Especially later in the war, as the noose tightened around Germany, POWs were oftentimes middle-aged men or young boys hardly old enough to shave. Among the older men were many who, as democrats, socialists, communists, or traditional conservatives, had struggled vainly to prevent national socialism from coming to power in Germany. Friction between Nazis and anti-Nazis inside the camps occasionally led to harassment or even murder.[2]

The construction of POW camps in the United States accompanied the planning for Operation Torch in 1942. With British POW camps already bulging beyond capacity, it became necessary to ship additional war prisoners to the United States. Bowing to British wishes, combined Anglo-American forces commanded by General Dwight David Eisenhower landed in Morocco and Algeria in November 1942. In October, Bernard "Monty" Montgomery—with the aid of deciphered German signals—routed an Axis attack at El Alamein. In fierce desert fighting, the British and Commonwealth Eighth Army drove Field Marshal Erwin Rommel and his vaunted Afrika Korps back more than 1,400 miles across Libya into Tunisia. By May 1943 Axis forces were trapped. Ordered home by Hitler, Rommel had been replaced two months earlier by Jürgen von Arnim, whose army group of nearly a quarter million men surrendered in the Tunisian bridgehead anchored by Tunis and Bizerte.[3] For the first time in the war, Great Britain and the United States found it necessary to deal with large numbers of captured enemy troops.[4]

Having foreseen the likelihood of increased numbers of Axis war prisoners in Allied hands, the provost marshal general of the United States Army supervised the construction of POW facilities at existing military bases or at camps constructed for the purpose of holding prisoners until hostilities ceased and repatriation could commence. Construction of camps for an anticipated 70,000 war prisoners hastily began in late 1942. For security reasons these camps were located in sparsely inhabited areas and initially could not be located within 170 miles of seacoasts. Cheap land and mild winter temperatures led to the construction of camps in the southern and southwestern states, where approximately three-fourths of all POWs in American custody were eventually imprisoned. Before May 1943 only a few war prisoners were in the United States. By late August, however, more than 100,000 German and Italian POWs had arrived. At war's end, nearly 450,000 Axis POWs were held in camps in the United States.[5]

Construction of three base camps in Alabama had already begun by the time the Afrika Korps surrendered. A fourth camp was added in 1944. The first and largest POW camp in Alabama was just west of Aliceville, a town of not quite 5,000 residents, in Pickens County and not far from the Mississippi state line.[6] The site was located on land near the Frisco Railroad line so that POWs could be brought there by train. The 400 one-story dwellings and administrative buildings, constructed by the Algernon Blair firm of Montgomery, were designed to accommodate 6,000 prisoners and 900 guards and other camp personnel. Rarely did the population of the Aliceville camp exceed 3,500 during the three years of its existence.

The people of Aliceville, who had wondered why the government was constructing the gray buildings on the outskirts of town, learned the answer on 2 June 1943. Khaki-clad soldiers bristling with rifles, machine guns, pistols, bayonets, and shotguns and accompanied by Alabama Highway Patrolmen guarded the mile-long route from the Frisco Railroad track to the camp. Just before 5:00 P.M., a special train braked to a halt, disgorging the first load of 500 POWs only recently arrived from North Africa. The Germans expressed shock and surprise that America, contrary to what Propaganda Minister Joseph Goebbels had told them, had not been laid waste by German bombs.[7] By mid-June nearly 3,000 war prisoners had arrived.

The town's initial apprehension about the camp diminished as time passed, and Aliceville residents grew accustomed to the prisoners. The few escapes from the camp ended in failure. Two POWs were killed in August 1943 as they scrambled for the outer fence of the camp. Those who managed to get away were invariably apprehended in short order by the FBI or local authorities. Two escapees eluded captivity for sixty hours by hiding in the bottomlands of the Tombigbee River. Six POWs' dash to freedom in a stolen automobile ended in Memphis when they drove down the wrong side of a street.[8]

A second POW camp was built at Opelika. Curious local residents crowded the train station to get a glimpse of the several hundred prisoners who arrived in June 1943 from Boston. According to George Marlett, a guard at the Opelika camp, about 250 of the war prisoners had belonged to Schutzstaffel (SS) units. Fearing SS violence against POWs who wavered in their loyalty to national socialism, camp authorities segregated the SS prisoners from the rest of the camp. Unlike other POW camps, no politically inspired murders occurred at Opelika.[9] By 1945 there were more than 2,700 prisoners at Opelika. A third POW camp was activated at Fort McClellan in summer 1942. This camp, which housed more than 3,000 POWs at its height, was described by a reporter from the *Washington Post* as the most spacious and the best war prisoner facility he had seen. A somewhat smaller camp for approximately 1,700 Axis prisoners was located at Camp Rucker.[10]

Nearly all POW base camps were laid out in similar fashion. Most consisted of three or four compounds, each containing barracks for approximately 500 to 750 POWs. The barracks were cheaply constructed, consisting of wooden frames on concrete slabs and covered with tar paper. Each compound had a mess hall, recreation hall, workshop, canteen, infirmary, and administrative building. The camp had a hospital, chapel, warehouse, processing center, post office, showers, and athletic fields. Camps were surrounded by two chain-link fences ten feet high, with watchtowers and searchlights at intervals. Compounds within the camp were separated by a single fence.[11]

In addition to the four base camps, more than twenty side camps in Alabama were located in areas where POWs worked under contract for farmers, sawmills, loggers, and other private employers.[12] Many of these camps were temporary, sometimes consisting simply of tents.[13] Typically, POWs would be brought from a base camp in Alabama or from Camp Shelby, Mississippi, to a side camp where they would be given a minimum amount of training for the job for which they had been contracted.

War prisoners often remained skittish and fearful even after months of captivity. Montgomerian Mary Louise Caton Weed, who worked during summer 1945 in the Holding and Reconsignment Point near Maxwell Field, remembers seeing a group of POWs marching back to their quarters instinctively hit the dirt when a fighter plane playfully buzzed overhead.[14]

During work hours, POWs wore uniforms consisting of blue denim pants and shirts that had "PW" stenciled in white or yellow on the back. In the evenings or at other times when they were not working, they could wear their own military uniforms, which they had been permitted to keep. Daily routine varied little in POW camps. Roused by reveille at 5:30, prisoners trooped to the mess halls for breakfast, then shaved, and cleaned their barracks before reporting to work details at 7:00. Lunch was served at noon. POWs at work away from camp usually had sack picnic lunches that they could eat in the shade of a tree. The work details returned to camp at 4:30, and prisoners changed—if they wished—into their own service uniforms before dinner at 6:00. Evenings were free for recreation or educational pursuits.

The camps provided many diversions for the POWs. Movies, even those that had been chosen by camp authorities for their overt propaganda value, invariably attracted large crowds. Although lavish Hollywood spectaculars were most popular, POWs also turned out to see sleazy, grade-B productions.[15]

Most camps had activities organized and produced by the prisoners themselves. The POWs at Camp Aliceville organized an extensive array of cultural and intellectual activities. Initially using borrowed instruments, the prisoners formed an orchestra, which gave very competent and spirited performances of compositions by Beethoven, Verdi, and other European classical composers. With the help of the Red Cross and using canteen funds, the Aliceville POWs bought additional instruments. Subsequently, several choruses, a string quartet, a dance orchestra, and several bands that played popular music were formed. The POWs also delighted in building scenery and making costumes for numerous well-acted plays. A weekly newspaper, the *Zaungast*, was put out by the POWs. Forbidden from covering political matters, the paper mostly reported on camp activities and literary and other cultural matters.[16]

In their workshops, POWs could do such handicrafts as sculpting, wood carving, pottery, painting, and making inlay boxes and chess sets. Barracks competed for prizes awarded for the most beautifully landscaped grounds. Photographs from the Aliceville camp show trellises of stunning beauty and delightful topiaries that POWs had created in their compounds. War prisoners cultivated plants in hothouses for ornamental use.[17]

Camp libraries supported diverse reading habits and made possible the creation of a rather extensive educational program. Academic courses were sometimes taught by POWs who had been teachers or whose professions and educational backgrounds gave them useful skills or knowledge. American military personnel and professional educators also taught courses at the camps. Professors from Alabama Polytechnic Institute at Auburn instructed at Camp Opelika and Camp Rucker, while faculty from the University of Alabama in Tuscaloosa traveled to Camp Aliceville and Fort McClellan. English was, by far, the most popular course. At Camp Opelika, instruction in modern foreign languages as well as in Latin, mathematics, the sciences, shorthand, and law was offered. The level of instruction was so high that the Reich Ministry of Education awarded high school or college credit to POWs completing course requirements. "Transcripts" recording the level of performance in these courses and bearing the signatures of instructors and camp commanders were sent to Germany, where they became part of the permanent academic records of the prisoners, enabling them to complete high school or to get a head start toward a college degree upon their return. Most camps offered religious education, usually provided by a Protestant or Catholic chaplain from among the POWs.[18]

By far the most popular activities in the camps were sports, especially soccer and handball but also including basketball, horseshoes, weightlifting, volleyball, baseball, and even croquet. The camps organized intramural teams that developed spirited rivalries. Alfred Klein, who later became a lieutenant colonel in the Air Force of the Federal Republic of Germany, recalled that at Camp Opelika even the guards took an avid interest in the teams and "participated as cheerleaders from their towers and attended the games on weekends with their families shouting from the sidelines."[19] Sports equipment was at first scarce. POWs were dependent upon such outside organizations as the Red Cross, YMCA, and religious organizations for money and equipment. Eventually, war prisoners were permitted to use canteen funds for these kinds of activities.

The canteens, operated by the POWs themselves, were an interesting example of entrepreneurial ingenuity. Food, candy, cigarettes, beverages—including beer in wet counties—and toiletries were sold. POWs, in fact, obtained many items from their canteens that were scarce in Europe and could only be purchased on the black market. Cash did not change hands. Instead prisoners bought goods with chits, or coupons, which they earned by working outside the camps. Profits from canteen sales were used in whatever way the prisoners wished. In many cases, canteen funds bankrolled the purchase of sports equipment, musical instruments, books, or improvements to their quarters or recreation halls. Some canteens had tens of thousands of dollars in profits at the end of the war. When POWs were repatriated to Germany in 1946, it was not uncommon for some canteen funds to be donated to local charitable organizations. More often than not, however, POWs divided canteen funds among themselves, giving each war prisoner a small nest egg—usually fifty dollars, but sometimes several hundred dollars—with which to begin a new life.[20]

Guidelines for the treatment of prisoners of war were set forth in the

1929 Geneva convention, which required that they should be fed, clothed, and housed adequately and comparably to the captor nation's troops.[21] While some problems of interpretation arose, the War Department adhered as strictly as possible to the principles of the document. It was common knowledge that the Axis nations were not providing comparable amenities to POWs in their custody, but it was hoped that humane and generous treatment of POWs in this country would win improvements in the treatment of American war prisoners. The War Department also believed that controlling POWs in this country would be made easier if their treatment was good. In terms of psychological warfare, it was believed that fair and humane treatment of POWs— including well-stocked canteens—made it easier for Axis troops to surrender to Allied forces. There was also a belief that generous treatment of POWs would encourage their commitment to democratic values and human liberty in the postwar world.

The International Red Cross and the Swiss government, which represented Germany's diplomatic interests in Allied countries during the war, periodically inspected prisoner of war camps. Inspections of camps in the United States generally revealed compliance with the principles of the Geneva agreements. Also the War Prisoners Aid of the YMCA and the National Catholic Welfare Council involved themselves in camp conditions. In their concern for the religious and spiritual welfare of prisoners of war, both organizations provided chaplaincy services. War prisoners frequently wrote these organizations expressing gratitude for their efforts at making camp life more comfortable.

The camps required able-bodied POWs from the enlisted ranks, although not officers, to work. The government's policy was "no work, no eat." The Geneva convention recognized the right of host governments to require POWs to work, provided certain guidelines were followed. Jobs could not be hazardous, nor could they contribute directly to the war effort. Prisoners were to be compensated for their labor outside the camps, although not for routine work in the camps themselves.[22]

Within the camps, the POWs cooked, took care of laundry, and did routine maintenance work. Outside the camp, private employers contracted with camp officials for POW laborers. Because of labor scarcities created by the war, many employers welcomed this additional source of

German POWs at Aliceville. (Alabama Department of Archives and History)

workers. POWs were hired to chop cotton, cut timber, work in saw-mills, tap trees for resin, and harvest peanuts and other crops. One group of Aliceville POWs worked in the kitchen and laundry of the Northington General Hospital in Tuscaloosa. Labor was in such short supply in the Wiregrass that the 1944 peanut crop was nearly lost. With the support of the Alabama Extension Service and the state's congressional delegation, POW labor was mobilized. In October 1944 the *Birmingham News* reported that some 4,000 workers wearing shirts and pants stencilled with large PWs were helping harvest Alabama's $38 million peanut crop. Ironically, Nisei (Japanese-American) soldiers guarded these POWs.[23]

Organized labor, especially the Southern Tenant Farmers Union, opposed the use of POW workers in agriculture and industry. In order to ensure that prisoners were not undercutting the local labor market, the Army Service Command in Atlanta was required to obtain a ruling from the War Manpower Commission that local labor was, in fact, not readily available and that the proposed wage scale for POW labor was in line with prevailing wages. War prisoners were permitted to keep the equivalent of eighty cents a day, with the remainder of their wages going into the federal treasury to offset expenses for maintaining the POW camps.[24]

On balance, the POW contract labor program worked better than had been anticipated and provided an adequate substitute for scarce labor. By summer 1945, approximately 90 percent of the war prisoners in the United States were working in contract labor.[25] In that year one-third of the pulpwood cut in the southern states and in Appalachia was cut by POWs.[26] Because logging and sawmilling, along with mining, were among the most hazardous jobs in the work place, the use of war prisoners in the lumber industry came close to violating the Geneva convention guidelines. But the greatest single complaint from POWs was Alabama's climate, the humidity of which was even more debilitating than the heat. In later years, former POWs recalled their struggles with mosquitoes, red bugs, gnats, and horseflies that seemed irresistibly drawn to human perspiration.

Generally speaking, most POWs were content to bide their time in camps, grateful they had not become frozen corpses on the Russian steppes. But some were hostile and recalcitrant. Still others were ideological purists who sneered at the presumed decadence and weaknesses of the United States. The incorrigibles and those who were clearly prone to violence were isolated in special compounds or were sent to camps that provided tighter security. The Aliceville camp, originally designated as the confinement facility in the Southeast for German noncommissioned officers, had a segregation compound for trouble-makers.[27] The War Department authorized camp commanders to send "Nazi leaders, Gestapo agents, and extremists" to Camp Alva in Oklahoma.[28]

The treatment of German POWs deteriorated after May 1945. Liberation of Allied war prisoners in German camps and the discovery of the horrors in concentration camps in central Europe produced heightened resentment in the United States. By contrast, German POWs in the United States had been living in what were contemptuously called "Fritz Ritz" camps. After Germany's capitulation, some foods, such as meats, were served less frequently. On average, most German POWs lost ten pounds in this period, but few regarded this loss as a great calamity.[29]

Italian prisoners were the first to regain their freedom. Following Allied landings in Italy in 1943, the Mussolini government collapsed in July and Marshal Pietro Badoglio formed a new government. Badoglio dissolved the Fascist party, capitulated to the Allies, and declared war against Germany. The status of Italian war prisoners immediately improved. No longer treated as POWs, Italians could be used for war-related work. Hard-core fascists were segregated and turned over to the new Italian government, but rank-and-file Italians were free to volunteer for service units created by the Allies to assist in the war effort. Approximately 33,000 Italians volunteered for these service units and worked in ports of embarkation, ordnance plants, quartermaster depots, and service command posts.

Camp Rucker was designated as a training center for an engineer company of the Italian service units. These outfits received the same training as American military engineers with the exception of weapons training and tactics. For this work the Italians were paid $24 a month. They were also promised early repatriation as a reward for their efforts. By freeing American servicemen for other tasks, these Italians contributed to the Allies' war effort.[30]

The dreams of German POWs for an early return to their homeland were dashed. German war prisoners remained in Alabama until 1946 and in some cases 1947 before being repatriated. For one thing, war-devastated Germany would have been ill-prepared to deal with an influx of half a million POWs. Occupation authorities were already struggling with millions of ethnic German refugees from eastern Europe. Additionally, POW labor—especially in agriculture—was thought to be essential to the American economy. Gradually, the Alabama POW camps were phased out and the war prisoners shipped to other camps or to ports of embarkation. The Aliceville camp was deactivated in September 1945. Two months later the Opelika camp closed, followed by the deactivation of the McClellan and Rucker prisoner of war facilities in spring 1946.

Occasionally POWs formed lasting friendships in the United States, and fond memories lingered. Years after the war, some former prisoners returned to the site of their incarceration, hoping to find familiar faces or places. Alfred Klein, a future Bundeswehr officer, returned to Foley three times—1959, 1961, and 1972—and with his wife was invited to join the Elberta Social Club. Klein reveled in telling the story of how he and several other Germans had been given the keys to a farmer's automobile to return to his farm. Having the time of their lives cruising down a country road in Baldwin County and totally oblivious to the posted speed limit, they were stopped by two Alabama state troopers. "They started to write out speeding tickets," Klein reminisced from his Munich home in 1976, "when they realized we were POWs. They were absolutely speechless! I still laugh about it today."[31]

Another former POW, John Schroer, who became a successful insurance executive in Los Angeles, had warm memories of his days in Alabama. Schroer was based at Camp Rucker, but he also worked at a side camp in Montgomery loading boxes of foodstuffs onto trains. They mostly moved canned goods and flour, but occasionally a shipment of beer came through. The guards "encouraged us to break a case or two," Schroer gleefully remembered. Because it was such a pity the beer could not be shipped in that condition, the POWs and the guards "all sat down in the shade together and drank the beer."[32] Returning to Germany after the war, Schroer became an economist and a Marshall Aid administrator, working to rebuild Europe. Eventually fulfilling his dream to return to the United States, Schroer wound up as a senior vice-president in an American insurance company in California.

Few artifacts remain to remind us today of the Axis war prisoners who lived and worked briefly in Alabama. The camps themselves were turned over to local governments as inducements to lure private industry, while other facilities were dismantled and the materials sold under the terms of the Surplus Property Act of 1944. An ad in the *Birmingham Age-Herald* early in 1947, for example, announced the sale of the electrical distribution system, light poles, sewer pipes, and other supplies from the Aliceville POW camp. A few crafts—paintings, jewelry boxes, and carved wooden eagles—made by prisoners of war were given or sold to local residents. Today, few patrons who belly up to the handsome, ornately carved bar at the officers' club at Fort McClellan realize that it was made by German POWs. For several years after the war, American and Bundeswehr representatives conducted memorial services on the third Sunday of November at the small, inconspicuous cemetery on the base. Three Italian and twenty-six German POWs are interred there.[33] Otherwise, little remains to remind us of the more than 17,000 POWs who lived in Alabama during the Second World War.

Axis prisoner of war camps, especially those administered by the Japanese, generally contrasted starkly with facilities in the United

States. Although German captors sometimes inflicted great brutality upon American war prisoners, in general, conditions in POW camps in Europe conformed to the minimum requirements of the Geneva conventions regarding food and medical treatment. Chaotic and dangerous wartime conditions, however, hampered whatever goodwill the Germans intended to display. The Japanese, in contrast, displayed far less humanitarian concern for their prisoners. Whereas 1 percent of American POWs in German camps died from all causes, more than one-third of those in Japanese hands perished.[34] This contrast reinforced widely held racial stereotypes in the United States that were, in part, responsible for the internment of Japanese-Americans on the West Coast.

Several Alabama servicemen were held prisoners of war by the Germans. Three Jefferson County soldiers were imprisoned in Stalag Luft III, from which seventy-six Americans made a daring escape that was subsequently turned into a film, *The Great Escape,* starring Steve McQueen. One of these Jefferson County POWs, Alvin W. Vogtle, who had been captured when mechanical failure caused his plane to crash, escaped on his own to Switzerland after twenty-seven months of imprisonment.[35]

Wesley P. Newton of Montgomery fell into German hands when he was captured at Kesternich in the Ruhr Valley. Newton and his fellow war prisoners not only worried about their treatment at the hands of German captors but also about the accuracy of Allied bombing. He recalls that while he was in a German hospital atop a small mountain at Siegburg near the Rhine, American fighter planes dive-bombed the hospital, probably because it was being used as an artillery spotter post. The war prisoners escaped this bombing raid unscathed only to be threatened by the German SS security detail in Siegburg that vowed to execute Americans in retaliation. A courageous German doctor probably saved the lives of Newton and his fellow POWs by ordering the evacuation of the wounded to a camp farther east.[36]

In the Pacific theater war prisoners under Japanese control existed under even more terrifying conditions. Only general officers received treatment approximating standards imposed by the Geneva convention. For three and one-half years Lieutenant General Jonathan Wainwright, Brigadier General Carl Seals from Alabama, and others on MacArthur's staff (including Captain J. T. Traywick of Montgomery, who had been captured in the Philippines) were prisoners of the Japanese. In August 1942 they were moved from the Philippines to Formosa. Although subjected to considerable personal deprivation and inconvenience, the prisoners succeeded in maintaining a semblance of civility. When issued extra rations of rice, they invited one another over for dinner. Several officers, including Seals, had a bridge foursome that played as often as possible. In the course of their imprisonment, Seals formed a close friendship with Brigadier General William Edward Brougher, a Mississippian who maintained a diary of their experiences in prisoner of war camps.[37] In October 1944 Wainwright, Seals, and the other general officers were taken by ship and train to Manchuria, where they were confined first at Chengchiatun and then, in the following year, transferred to Hoten POW camp at Mukden. There they were liberated by Russian paratroopers in August 1945.

During this same period, General Seals's wife Margaret was interned at a camp for civilians that was located on the grounds of Santo Tomas University in Manila. Among the 5,000 prisoners at Santo Tomas were Jim Cullens of Ozark, a Red Cross worker, and Captain Ann Mealer of Birmingham, who since September 1941 had been the chief nurse at the fortress on Corregidor.[38] Mealer's determination to see her family in Birmingham helped sustain her during her captivity. She later said that her longing to walk through the lobby of the Tutwiler Hotel, to see the laurel bloom in the spring, and to enjoy the leaves on Red Mountain turning red and gold in the autumn made the months of incarceration bearable.

Troops of the First Cavalry Division liberated the Santo Tomas prisoner of war camp in early February 1945. Captain Mealer's dreams turned into reality: she was soon reunited with her brother and sister in Birmingham. Ironically and tragically, Margaret Seals, liberated at the same time, died five days after returning to the United States.

The American enlisted men taken prisoner after the fall of Bataan and the surrender of Corregidor faced more than three years of nearly unbearable hardship. The Bataan Death March was only the beginning for prisoners of war such as Bert Bank. A Tuscaloosa native and graduate of the University of Alabama, he was selling advertisements for the *Tuscaloosa News* on the eve of war. With a reserve commission,

Bank was called up for active duty in 1941 and wound up on Bataan, where he was taken prisoner in spring 1942. Joining a weary column that had already been on the move for five days, Bank trudged for five days without food or water. He was among those imprisoned in a camp at Cabanatuan about sixty miles north of Manila. Conditions there were desperate. Malnutrition, filth, and open latrines encouraged the spread of disease. Beriberi, dysentery, yellow jaundice, scurvy, dengue fever, and malaria plagued many of the prisoners. Because there were no medical supplies to offer cures or comfort in any event, diagnoses were irrelevant. In the first two months of imprisonment, 2,000 Americans died of hunger and disease. To supplement their meager allowances of rice and pig weed soup, the desperate prisoners ate dogs, cats, lizards, frogs, and virtually any other animal that had the misfortune of falling into their grasp.

Stuffed into boxcars, Bank and other prisoners were taken to Manila and then by boat to Davao on Mindanao. Red Cross packages arriving in January 1943 were plundered by their captors, who kept the cigarettes and chocolates. Gorging themselves on corned beef and Kraft cheese, which the Japanese snubbed, the prisoners were sick for two weeks afterward, but Bank recalled that it was "wonderful."[39] In summer 1944, as MacArthur's forces hopped islands toward the Philippines, Bank—by now blind from malnutrition—and his fellow prisoners at Davao were taken back to Cabanatuan, the scene of their earlier nightmarish imprisonment. Inexplicably, their Japanese captors disappeared at the beginning of 1945, abandoning the prison to the prisoners. Still behind Japanese lines, the prisoners remained at Cabanatuan, but conditions improved markedly when a massive search revealed vast stores of rice and live hogs upon which the prisoners feasted for three weeks. Finally, in late January, a detachment of U.S. Rangers and Filipino guerrillas made a daring raid twenty-eight miles behind enemy lines to rescue the 511 pitiful but grateful American, British, and Dutch POWs at Cabanatuan. Unlike their senior officers imprisoned on Formosa and in Manchuria, the survivors of the Death March had been nearly completely isolated from news of the outside world. At the Cabanatuan prison more than 25,000 letters from the United States remained undelivered because there was only one Japanese censor and he refused to approve more than 100 letters a day.[40] After his liberation in January 1945, Bert Bank heard the songs of Frank Sinatra for the first time and learned how new developments such as landing ships and bazookas had helped dislodge Japanese armies from the mountains and jungles of Pacific islands. But Bert Bank was one of the lucky ones. Death liberated nearly 300 Alabama war prisoners from their ordeals.

Nine

Liberating Europe

In the five years between autumn 1940 when the nation began inducting tens of thousands of civilians into military service and Japan's surrender in September 1945, nearly 15 million Americans donned military uniforms. More than 320,000 Alabamians enlisted or were called up for service. For many of the young recruits—some jaunty, others shy or reserved—military service meant leaving home for the first time. Although a hitch in the military generally produced good-humored jibes about regional differences and stereotypes, the war also forged a clearer sense of nationhood. Getting to know other servicemen and servicewomen from differing regional, ethnic, and racial backgrounds—coupled with the leveling influences of mass communications—encouraged the evolution of a more homogeneous society. Military assignments abroad or in other regions of the country often enriched Americans by broadening their global perspectives.

If there was one thing Americans in service learned to do well during the war, it was to wait. This was the universal gripe of servicemen. Initiation into service often began by waiting patiently on the platform of a train depot or in a dusty parking lot of a rural gas station that also served as a Trailway or Greyhound bus station. Most Alabama recruits or draftees reported to Fort McClellan, but those from the southern part of the state often went to Camp Blanding in Florida. In induction centers, waiting resumed and lines proliferated. Doctors and nurses performed routine, almost hurried, physical exams to ascertain that there was indeed a warm body at the end of the stethoscope. Intelligence and skills tests were administered, but all too often it seemed the results were rarely used to make assignments.[1] In the early months of the war, indoctrination and training proceeded at a leisurely stride. By 1944, however, as D-Day in Europe neared and with a direct assault on Japan's home islands looming in the future, the pace of training accelerated.

Increased demand for military personnel also led to recruitment of females. Numerous women from Alabama, both white and black, volunteered for a hitch in the military. By spring 1945 nearly 100,000 women from across the United States wore the uniforms of Wacs.[2] Laws prohibited women from combat duties, but as Wacs, Waves, Spars, WASPs, women Marines, or as members of the Nurse Corps they worked in clerical and administrative jobs, as drivers, as communications specialists, in supply rooms, as nurses or laboratory technicians, and as pilots. Women never warmed to the idea that they were merely holding down men's jobs, thus freeing the men to do more worthwhile tasks such as going to the battlefront. Women preferred challenging jobs that closely matched their educational level and skills. Morale among Wacs was highest when they were stationed in forward positions near combat.[3]

In Washington, considerable disagreement over priorities and objectives marked American policy in the first six months of 1942. Although Plan ABC-1, accepted a year earlier by Washington and London, prescribed a "Germany first" policy, Japan presented a more imminent danger to the United States in early 1942. In Europe, Britain's survival seemed assured at the moment. The British Isles had lived through a punishing Luftwaffe attack and, despite the perils of U-boats in the Atlantic, received massive amounts of American aid. American admirals therefore encouraged Roosevelt to make the first push in the Pacific against the Japanese Empire.

President Roosevelt decided to pursue both goals. Strategically, Europe would have top priority, but the United States would devote enough resources to reverse Japan's advance in the Pacific. At the Arcadia conference in Washington in early 1942, President Roosevelt committed the United States to Prime Minister Winston Churchill's view that the liberation of Europe should be the first priority of the Allies. Using Great Britain as a springboard for an invasion of the Continent, the United States promised to build up troops, supplies, and air power on British soil in anticipation of a cross-Channel attack sometime in 1943. Roosevelt, however, did not at that time share Churchill's view that North Africa should be swept clear of Axis troops before an assault on the European continent could begin. After the War Department and Roosevelt came to realize the enormity of preparations and meticulous planning required for a cross-Channel invasion, strategic thinking shifted toward opening a front in North Africa. In summer

1942, Chief of Staff George Marshall delegated the planning of Operation Torch, an invasion of North Africa, to Dwight David Eisenhower.[4] This operation had several goals. Most immediately, it would open up the Mediterranean by dislodging the Axis from North Africa, which would become the staging area for an invasion of Italy and eventually southern France. Furthermore, Operation Torch would extinguish the influence of Vichy France in North Africa and put pressure on French colonials elsewhere to abandon their allegiance to Marshal Henri Philippe Pétain and the collaborationists. Finally, a North African operation would assuage, in part, Joseph Stalin's urgent pleas to the Allies to open a new front, giving some relief to his beleaguered troops in the Caucasus.[5] In the meantime, the United States would continue amassing forces in the British Isles in anticipation of a landing on the French coast during 1943.

The opening of a new front, whether in North Africa or on the continent of Europe, required a vast amount of air power. U.S. carrier-based planes were committed to the war in the Pacific. In Europe and Africa, land-based bombers—protected by fighter craft—were needed to knock out strategic targets and, tactically, to prepare the way for the invasion of Europe. The Eighth Air Force—the Mighty Eighth as it was later known—carried out most of the daylight bombing missions against Germany and Nazi-occupied Europe until late 1944, when a second strategic air force, the Fifteenth, based in Italy, joined the campaign.

An Alabamian, Brigadier General Asa North Duncan, was a mainstay in helping Major General Carl Spaatz organize the Eighth Air Force.[6] Duncan was born in Leighton in Colbert County in 1892. After graduating from Alabama Polytechnic Institute, he enlisted in the National Guard, where he obtained a commission in the Air Service and became a flyer. In January 1942 Colonel Duncan arrived at the Savannah Army Air Base to begin the task of welding 24,000 men and more than 600 aircraft into the Eighth Air Force. Some of Duncan's planes were soon needed elsewhere. Lieutenant Colonel Jimmy Doolittle borrowed two dozen B-25s for his daring April raid on Japan. Nearer home, bombers from the fledgling outfit flew patrols in spring and summer 1942 against German U-boats terrorizing shipping off the East Coast of the United States in the Gulf of Mexico.[7]

In May General Carl "Tooey" Spaatz took over officially as commander of the Eighth Air Force, but Duncan stayed on as the chief of staff. In this capacity he coordinated the unit's transfer to England during the early summer. Brigadier General Ira Eaker exercised operational control until Spaatz arrived in Britain in June.[8] During July the vanguard of eventually thousands of B-17 Flying Fortresses touched down on British runways, often after harrowing flights via Labrador and Greenland. At the height of the European war, the Eighth Air Force occupied 112 of the 250 British airfields on which American planes were stationed.

The Eighth Air Force's first bombing raids were against strategic targets in France and the Netherlands. Attacks on targets in the German Reich itself began in January 1943. From the outset, American bombers flew during daylight and at high altitudes. Spaatz and Eaker had great confidence in the accuracy of the newly developed Norden bombsight, which, they believed, would enable American planes to drop bombs "inside a pickle barrel" at 20,000 feet. The British, especially Air Chief Marshal Arthur Harris, who headed the Royal Air Force's Bomber Command, scoffed at daylight bombing, which they regarded as too risky for planes and their crews. But from the American vantage point, Britain's area bombing at night was less accurate and produced unacceptably high civilian casualties.[9]

The first sortie flown by the Eighth Air Force against a continental target took off from Grafton Underwood shortly after 3:00 P.M. on 17 August 1942. The target was the marshaling yard at Rouen in western France. Colonel Frank Armstrong, riding in a B-17 named the *Butcher Shop* piloted by Paul Tibbets, who later flew the *Enola Gay* to Hiroshima, led the group. Armstrong's bombers included the *Birmingham Blitzkrieg* with an almost all-Alabama flight crew.[10]

Lieutenant Tom Borders, an Edgewood native who had played tackle on Alabama's 1938 Rose Bowl team, piloted this Flying Fortress whose bombs rained down on the marshaling yard from an altitude of 23,000 feet.[11] Upon his arrival in England, Borders had cockily declared: "I am ready to get a sock at Hitler." Borders's bombardier was Lieutenant W. C. Lewis from Birmingham, and the "belly gunner" was West Blocton's Sergeant Kent West. When a Messerschmitt 109 got within range, West fired a burst from his gun, apparently hitting the German craft. A jubilant homecoming at Grafton Underwood greeted the squadron and especially the flak-damaged *Birmingham Blitzkrieg,* which was credited with being the first plane in the Eighth Air Force to shoot down a German fighter. In one of his last letters home, Sergeant West enthused that he had just shot down a German plane over Rouen and was having a "swell time." Four months later, Borders and his crew died in a bombing raid on Bizerte in North Africa when flak hit the *Birmingham Blitzkrieg*'s bomb bay.[12]

In summer and autumn 1942, Spaatz and Duncan turned their attention to North Africa and the opening of Operation Torch. In October two vast flotillas transporting three task forces consisting of 125,000 troops set sail, one from New York and the other from Scotland. In the first flotilla, General George S. Patton, Jr., commanded the Western Task Force, which debarked at Casablanca. The second flotilla passed without incident through the Strait of Gibraltar, and its troops landed at Oran and Algiers. Only sporadic and light resistance greeted the Anglo-American forces in North Africa.

A newly formed Twelfth Air Force, some of whose bomber groups —including Tom Borders and the *Birmingham Blitzkrieg* until their loss in December—had recently been transferred from Britain, provided crucial air support for Allied troops in North Africa. As the senior air officer in Europe, Spaatz went to North Africa to assist Doolittle in the formation of the new air force, and Ira Eaker took command of the Eighth Air Force. Duncan, in Britain, coordinated the transfer of bomber groups to the Twelfth Air Force. Following the launching of Operation Torch in the second week of November, Duncan set out for Spaatz's headquarters in North Africa. Tragically, his plane disappeared—never to be found—somewhere off the northwest coast of France.[13]

The Twelfth Air Force pounded away at German and Italian positions until the surrender of the Afrika Korps in Tunisia in mid-May 1943. Among the Alabamians flying in North Africa was Lieutenant William Norred, who piloted the *Pine Apple Express,* named for his hometown in central Alabama. Another *Birmingham Blitzkrieg,* this one a Martin Marauder flown by Captain Bob Borders, took to the air in North Africa. Having graduated from Woodlawn High in Birmingham, he followed in his uncle Tom Borders's footsteps to Tuscaloosa and subsequently into the Army Air Corps. Bob Borders flew forty-seven combat missions, becoming one of the most celebrated pilots in the European and Mediterranean theaters. During the frantic last days of German resistance in North Africa, Borders and his *Birmingham Blitz-krieg* carried out bombing missions to prevent relief efforts from reaching Rommel and his trapped Axis forces in Tunisia. During one of these raids, Borders claimed to have unwittingly sunk an Axis warship, having mistaken—Borders jokingly boasted—his target for a troopship that could not fight back.[14] If Borders's claim is true, the warship would have been the *Trieste,* an Italian cruiser destroyed on 10 April 1943 as it lay anchored in antisubmarine nets off La Maddalena, Sardinia. Elsewhere in North Africa, Major William Lively, another Alabama pilot, claimed to have dropped the first paratroopers into Tunisia.[15]

Among the soldiers on the ground in North Africa who were grateful to have plenty of air support was Lieutenant Ralph "Shug" Jordan, who later became a legendary head football coach at Auburn University. When war broke out, the Selma native was teaching physical education and coaching freshman football and varsity basketball at Alabama Polytechnic Institute, his alma mater. Jordan had graduated with a degree in engineering and a Reserve Officers' Training Corps commission. A few months after the attack on Pearl Harbor, Jordan was assigned to the First Engineering Brigade and was en route to Scotland.[16] When the brigade received white overcoats and "long johns," nearly everyone figured their destination was Norway. Instead, Jordan's ship joined one of the convoys bound for North Africa, where his brigade constructed harbors and built roads. He wrote that there were about thirty API men in the area, enough to call a meeting of the North African Auburn Alumni chapter.[17] Master Sergeant John L. Mims from Dale County, who drove General Patton's jeep throughout the war, also welcomed close air support across North Africa and later in Europe.

The Mighty Eighth, now commanded by Ira Eaker, continued its strategic bombing of targets on the European continent. The transfer of about one hundred bombers—roughly a third of Eaker's planes—from Great Britain to the Mediterranean had diminished its striking power. Thomas K. McGhee of Greenville was lead pilot of eighteen Flying Fortresses that bombed the Renault motor vehicle factory near Paris in early April 1943. German resistance to the bomber offensive was fierce, but it was partially offset by a clever defensive tactic known as the combat box—which provided for mutual defensive coverage—developed by Colonel Curtis LeMay, the first commanding officer of the 305th "Can Do" Bombardment Group, to protect unescorted bombers.

American planes flew their first mission against a target inside Germany in January 1943.[18] The object was a submarine construction yard at Vegesack, but heavy cloud cover forced the mission to attack Wilhelmshaven instead. Operation Pointblank targeted Düsseldorf, the Ruhr, Hamburg, the ball-bearing plants at Schweinfurt, the Messerschmitt factory at Regensburg, and Berlin for destruction. In the months that followed, the Eighth Air Force bombed by day and the British by night.

Rod Calhoun, an Alabamian in the 303d "Hell's Angels" Bombardment Group, set out in January 1944 in his B-17 *The Eight Ball* for an attack on the Focke-Wulf plant at Oschersleben. Encountering fierce German fighter defense and with no fighter support because of the weather, the 303d group lost 34 of the 174 Flying Fortresses participating in the raid. The Hell's Angels received a Distinguished Unit Citation for this action and went on to complete more bombing missions than any other unit in the Eighth Air Force.[19]

By late 1944 the Luftwaffe's newly developed jet fighters took to the skies. Capable of achieving speeds greater than 500 miles per hour and ceilings over 37,000 feet, it was hoped that the Me-262s' outstanding performance would turn the tables. But this expectation proved illusive. In action over Aussig, Germany, Sergeant K. D. Adcock of Montgomery was among the Eighth Air Force's first gunners credited with downing one of these German interceptors.[20]

The fighter pilots of the Eighth Air Force scored many successes. Its first permanently assigned fighter group, the Fourth Fighter Group, was formed from personnel who had served in the RAF Eagle squadrons and was known to the Germans as the Debden Air Gangsters. The Fourth shot down more German planes than any other American unit in Europe. Grover C. Hall, Jr., whose father was the Pulitzer Prize–winning editor of the *Montgomery Advertiser*, was an officer and group historian of this outfit. Cecil Blackburn, a Birmingham-area physician, served as a squadron flight surgeon at Debden.[21] Lieutenant Arthur C. Cundy, a Birmingham native and University of Alabama alumnus, flew his P-51 Mustang, the *Alabama Rammer Jammer,* with the 353d Fighter Group. Cundy claimed six victories over German pilots.[22]

Even as combat raged in North Africa, Roosevelt and Churchill met at Casablanca to discuss engaging the enemy on the European continent in order to draw German troops away from the hard-pressed Russian front. In eastern Europe, German armies had violated the August 1939 Nazi-Soviet Non-Aggression Pact and invaded the Soviet Union in June 1941. Rolling the Soviet defenders back, Field Marshal Fedor von Bock's Army Group B drove deep into the Caucasus. By August 1942 General Friedrich Paulus and his Sixth Army had reached the outskirts of Stalingrad.

Eddy Gilmore, a journalist from Selma, reported from inside Russia throughout the war. Not knowing a word of Russian in 1941, Gilmore was uprooted from the relative comfort of wartime London, where he worked for the Associated Press, to cover the German advance into the Ukraine. By the time Gilmore returned to the United States twelve years later, few foreign journalists had become as intimately acquainted with Stalinist Russia as this Alabama native.[23]

The carnage at Stalingrad marked the turning of the tide on the eastern front, and German armies increasingly found themselves on the defensive. Nonetheless, conditions in Russia remained desperate. Beginning in summer 1941, Churchill and Roosevelt agreed to provide Russia with munitions, food, and other Lend-Lease aid. Most supplies reached Russia by convoy to Murmansk and Archangel. Some of these ships sailed from Mobile. The journey was a perilous one for the convoys, which contended with storm-tossed wintry seas, U-boats lying athwart their routes in the North Atlantic, and the German surface fleet in Arctic waters. Alabamians were among the officers and crewmen of the merchant fleet who were honored by the Russians for their part in the Murmansk run.

In the Mediterranean, the Americans wanted to wrap up the North African campaign as quickly as possible in order to concentrate on a cross-Channel operation in France. Because of their own strategic interests, the British favored opening a front in Italy and driving Axis influence out of the Mediterranean. Deferring again to Churchill's wishes, Roosevelt authorized an Anglo-American operation in Italy. On 10 July 1943, the British Eighth Army, commanded by the tenacious and arrogant Bernard Montgomery, and the Seventh Army of the flamboyant George Patton landed in Sicily.[24]

When troops from General Omar Bradley's Second Corps debarked from their landing craft near Licata, P-40 fighters of the Ninety-ninth Pursuit Squadron swept in to cover their landing. The pilots in the Air Corps's first black squadron had trained at the Tuskegee Army Air Field. Their commander, Benjamin O. Davis, Jr., graduated in the TAAF's first class. The Ninety-ninth's journey to the front began in early April 1943 at nearby Chehaw, Alabama, where the aviators boarded a New York–bound train. From there they sailed to Casablanca on the *Mariposa,* formerly a luxury passenger liner. From their base in Morocco, the pilots of the Ninety-ninth got their first taste of combat on 2 June 1943 when they strafed and dive-bombed Italian positions on the island of Pantelleria, which lies halfway between Sicily and North Africa.[25]

William Campbell, from Tuskegee and an original member of the Ninety-ninth Pursuit Squadron, was the first African-American to drop a bomb on an enemy.[26] On 11 June, after continued strafing and bombardment, the 11,000 Italians defending the island surrendered without firing a shot. Unique in the annals of warfare, an aerial offensive had compelled a garrison to lay down its arms. When Lieutenant Charles Hall shot down a Focke-Wulf 190 over southwestern Sicily in early July, he became the first African-American aviator in World War II to chalk up a victory against an Axis plane.[27] Soon afterward, in August, Colonel Davis returned to the United States to assume command of the newly activated 332d Fighter Group, which was training at Selfridge Field in Michigan.

The Ninety-ninth Pursuit Squadron moved first from North Africa to Sicily and later to southern Italy. Between October 1943 and April 1944, the Ninety-ninth operated with the Seventy-ninth Fighter Group—the first time the squadron participated in integrated operations with white units.[28] Lingering doubts about the abilities of black fighter pilots were dispelled by the skill and pugnacity with which they attacked German aircraft during the Anzio landing. The big break came on 27 January 1944 when the Ninety-ninth—outnumbered two to one—downed five Germans in the morning and three in the afternoon.[29]

In early July 1944 the Ninety-ninth joined Colonel Davis's 332d Fighter Group, which consisted of the all-black 100th, 301st, and 302d fighter squadrons. The 332d had arrived in Italy in early 1944. After a brief and disappointing assignment to coastal patrol, the 332d began flying combat missions in newly acquired P-47s. In July, when the Ninety-ninth joined the 332d at Ramitelli, the group switched to powerful P-51 Mustangs. Its mission was to escort bombers of the Fifteenth Air Force to targets deep inside enemy-held territory. By now the pilots of the 332d were painting the tails of their craft a brilliant red so that the bombers they escorted over Germany, Austria, and the Balkans—including missions to Berlin and to the refineries at Ploesti in Rumania—would know that they were being protected by the "Red Tails."[30] Known to the Germans as the "black birdmen," the pilots of the 332d earned the distinction of not losing a single bomber under their escort to enemy planes.[31]

Allied strategic bombing so far had failed to weaken the German infrastructure appreciably or to enfeeble Germany's will to fight. Moreover, Axis military might still threatened the success of an Allied landing in France. Therefore, in February and March 1944 the Eighth Air Force, from the United Kingdom, and the Fifteenth Air Force, from Italy, launched massive attacks on the German Reich itself, especially on aircraft and ball-bearing plants. Another major goal of these sorties was to draw the Luftwaffe into air battles of attrition that would so weaken German air power that it would no longer offer a significant threat.[32] Lieutenant William R. Lawley, Jr., a B-17 pilot from the Birmingham area, received the Congressional Medal of Honor for his role in one of these vital missions when he succeeded in skillfully flying his badly damaged plane back to the British Isles.[33] The success of these attacks produced a crucial turning point in the war in Europe, clearing the way for Allied landings on the Continent.

British and American staff officers busied themselves during spring and summer 1943 with planning a cross-Channel invasion. Roosevelt and Churchill, meeting in Quebec in August, approved the outlines of Operation Overlord, which called for landing three Allied divisions on the Normandy coast in May 1944. Montgomery and his chief, Eisenhower, who had recently arrived in London from North Africa, insisted that the invading force should be strengthened to include at least five infantry and armored divisions joined by three airborne divisions. As a result, southern England became a vast armed bivouac for three million troops.

Reconnaissance flights over the landing zones were crucial to the success of Operation Overlord. Hoyt Warren, an Alabamian and graduate of API who completed advanced flight training at Craig Field in early 1943, flew a P-51 in a reconnaissance squadron that photographed in detail the Normandy beaches.[34] In March 1944 Warren flew his first mission to France. Clearing the white cliffs of Dover, reconnaissance pilots skimmed low across the English Channel to avoid detection by the Germans. When he reached the French coastline near Le Havre, Warren looked for marshaling yards, antiaircraft batteries, and V-1 "buzz bomb" launch sites. His squadron flew eighty-three missions to France in preparation for D-Day.

In the meantime, strategic air strikes launched from British airfields targeted French and German transportation systems to make it difficult for the Germans to reinforce their positions in Normandy. Delaying the invasion to round up additional landing craft, Eisenhower set 5 June for the landing on the Normandy beaches if the weather cooperated.

Allied feints and deceptions confused the Germans about invasion plans. Rommel, who had been evacuated from Tunisia before the surrender of the Afrika Korps, now commanded the defense of the French coast. His problem was to decide which areas along the 3,000 miles of European coastline controlled by German armies to reinforce against an Allied invasion. A mythical British army in Scotland appeared to be preparing for a landing in Norway. Deceptive information passed to German intelligence through "turned" agents indicated that the main cross-Channel invasion would occur at Pas de Calais. This supposition grew more plausible when the Germans were allowed to learn that General George Patton commanded Allied forces in southeastern England. What the Germans did not know was that Patton's army was a decoy, complete with fake tents and tanks. The Allies successfully misled the Germans into believing the impending attack on the Normandy coast was merely a feint. Rommel reinforced German positions as best he could, but Allied intentions remained baffling.

At the last moment and with troops already loaded on their landing craft, Eisenhower postponed Operation Overlord for twenty-four hours. The weather had taken a turn for the worse. Finally, on the evening of 5 June 1944, the great Allied armada set sail. Lieutenant Isham "Ike" Dorsey of Opelika, a pilot with the Ninth Air Force, marveled at the invasion force that stretched below him from horizon to horizon. It was "great to have a ringside seat at the largest operation

Lieutenant Isham "Ike" Dorsey flew his Thunderbolt over the Allied invasion fleet during the Normandy invasion. (Isham "Ike" Dorsey Collection, Auburn University Archives)

yet," he confided to a diary that he kept in a small English laundry book.[35] D-Day went smoothly except at Omaha Beach, where the First Infantry Division ran into trouble when its amphibious tanks were swamped, and near Caen, where the landings faced organized, large-scale resistance. Many Alabamians, including combat veteran Shug Jordan, took part in the Normandy landings.

Among those decorated for organizing supply activities on the Normandy beachhead were two black Alabama corporals, Henry P. Harvest of Montgomery and Julius C. Adams of Verbena. They were members of the 262d Quartermaster Battalion, which set up headquarters three days after D-Day in an apple orchard near the Normandy coast using ration boxes for desks.[36]

Two months after the Normandy landings, the American Seventh Army under General Alexander M. Patch and French troops commanded by General Jean de Lattre de Tassigny landed in southern France. A major goal of Operation Anvil was to gain seaports through which supplies destined for Allied armies driving into northern France could flow. Although this campaign siphoned resources from the fighting in Italy, Eisenhower had no regrets. In any case, he regarded events in Italy as a sideshow. The war in Europe would be won by destroying German forces in France and in the Reich. American and French forces moved north swiftly after securing ports in southern France. By mid-September they had linked up with the Third Army, which was now commanded by General Patton. Sergeant Rhey Palmer of Greenville landed in Marseilles with the Forty-second Rainbow Division late in 1944. By spring 1945 his machine-gun squad had crossed the Rhine and was in the thick of the fighting at Würzburg, Schweinfurt, and Nuremberg before joining the race to Munich.[37]

In the breakout from Normandy, Patton drove in a broad front to the Loire in the south and eastward to Argentan, trapping large numbers of regular and SS Panzer troops in a pocket bounded to the north by Canadian troops at Falaise. Aerial reconnaissance pilots—such as Lieutenant William O. Davenport from Valley Head in north Alabama—spotted enemy tanks and convoys for Patton's advancing forces while flying their P-51s over France and Germany.[38] In fierce tank battles, Captain William B. Patterson of Birmingham commanded a unit that destroyed eighty tanks of General Paul Hausser's Seventh Army. Patterson's unit belonged to the 773d Tank Destroyer Battalion, which wiped out more German tanks than any other outfit in Patton's Third Army as it drove through central France, pushing Field Marshal Günther von Kluge back toward Paris and beyond. Subsequently, the 773d participated in a crossing of the flooded Mosel River that Patton praised as "one of the epic river crossings of history."[39] Captain J. R. Willingham, whose parents lived in Tuscaloosa, commanded a Thunderbolt squadron that captured 300 Germans in France by circling overhead like a sheepdog, herding the German soldiers toward an armored column.[40] In mid-August Patton urged a vigorous prosecution of the offensive against reeling German forces to end the war quickly. He believed his Third Army could be inside Germany within ten days.[41] Eisenhower, however, preferred a more deliberate campaign across a broad front.

German forces in France retreated doggedly. Hitler's obsession that von Kluge had participated in a failed 20 July coup and planned to surrender his troops in the Falaise-Argentan area led to the field marshal's dismissal and suicide. Walter Model, who had worked miracles on the eastern front, replaced von Kluge and became commander in chief west. But Model had no better success in stemming the Allied advance.

The Allied breakout from Normandy received vital assistance from the French underground and from the largely cooperative French public. Responsibility for organizing these relationships primarily fell to the Office of Strategic Services, better known as the OSS, and to the Counter Intelligence Corps, or CIC, which had been created by the War Department to foil the intelligence operations of Axis nations. One of the CIC's operatives was Lieutenant Miles Copeland, a graduate of Ramsay High School in Birmingham and a future senior figure in the postwar Central Intelligence Agency. Before the war, Copeland played poker and blackjack to supplement his earnings as a jazz musician. Hoping to play his trumpet in Glenn Miller's service band, Copeland had volunteered for the Rainbow Cavalry of the Alabama National Guard.

Prospects of weeks of training in the dusty surroundings of unfinished Camp Blanding in Florida's panhandle or slogging through swamps in Louisiana maneuvers prompted the eager Copeland to take tests for an assignment in military intelligence. Alabama congressman John Sparkman's intercession helped Copeland get a posting to the CIC. From London, where he worked on intelligence aspects of Operation Overlord, Copeland crossed to France when the Allied drive to Paris began. Denying the persistent CIA legend that he was the first operative to reach Paris, Copeland admits to being the first American to enter Paris for no particularly good reason. Copeland claims that another Alabamian, an African-American named Moses Decter, who had a flair for foreign languages, was instrumental in getting the Paris public works into working order after the German withdrawal.[42]

After landing at Omaha Beach at Normandy, the First Army, commanded by Lieutenant General Courtney Hicks Hodges, raced through France and Belgium, overran Aachen, fought a bitter battle in the Huertgen Forest, and, after helping repulse the Germans in the Battle of the Bulge, captured Remagen, where a bridge over the Rhine was secured. Subsequently, Hodges and the First Army participated in the encirclement of the Ruhr. Although not as famous as Patton, Hodges was an outstanding commander. Among his subordinates was William F. Nichols, an artillery officer in the Eighth Division and later a longtime congressman from Alabama's Third District.[43] Nichols lost a leg when he stepped on a land mine in the Huertgen Forest. His exemplary leadership won the praise of those under his command, including Edward Williamson, a feisty Pennsylvanian who later settled in Auburn to teach history.

In a last desperate attempt to reverse the fortunes of war on the western front, Hitler launched a massive winter counteroffensive in the Ardennes. The goal of Operation Watch on the Rhine was to seize Antwerp by driving a wedge in the Allied forces. Some Allied units were decimated by the fierce fighting. After zigzagging for sixteen miserable days across the Atlantic in the crowded hold of an "ancient" freighter, James E. "Ed" Thompson of Jasper joined the Seventh Armored Division in Belgium. The "Lucky Seventh" had almost been wiped out at Saint Vith and desperately needed replacements. The first combat casualties Thompson saw were tank crews. They had been raw recruits, replacements like himself, who had been thrown into battle with insufficient training before their baptism of fire. "I had the uneasy feeling," Thompson wrote, "we were being led to slaughter."[44]

Shortly after Thompson's arrival at the Belgian front, the Allied advance resumed. William H. Simpson's Ninth Army reached the Rhine River opposite Düsseldorf in early March. Farther south, on 7 March 1945 the Allies had a bit of good luck when the Third Corps of Hodges's First Army discovered that the Ludendorff bridge spanning the Rhine River at Remagen was still intact. Although two demolition devices exploded, little damage occurred and the Ninth Armored Division pushed across the bridge and established a perimeter east of the Rhine.[45]

By the end of March, Allied armies had made further Rhine crossings over hastily constructed bridges, driving toward Berlin and Munich on a broad front stretching from the North Sea to Switzerland. In a letter to his family in Jasper, Ed Thompson described the chaos in northern Germany as German civilians fled from advancing Russian armies near the Elbe River. "The roads were jammed with refugees," he wrote, "walking and traveling in every imaginable means of transportation."[46] On 12 April 1945 President Roosevelt died at his Warm Springs, Georgia, retreat. Hitler was jubilant, thinking this event would destroy the Allied coalition. But within hours Vice-President Harry Truman from Missouri had taken the oath of office to become the thirty-third president of the United States. By mid-April Russian armies raced westward in a headlong effort to reach Berlin before the Americans or the British. With Berlin encircled, Hitler dictated his last will and testament and appointed Grand Admiral Karl Doenitz as his successor. On the following day, 30 April, Hitler and his mistress, Eva Braun, whom he married in the last moments in the Berlin bunker, committed suicide. Germany's fate was sealed.

The buzz bombs, the jet fighters, and other miracle weapons on which Hitler vainly pinned his hopes failed to reverse the tide of battle. In the darkness of the morning of 7 May 1945 General Alfred Jodl signed the German surrender at an unpretentious schoolhouse in Rheims. On the next day, the ceremony was repeated in Berlin for the benefit of the Russians. Throughout Allied countries cheering throngs welcomed the victory over nazism. Clear-sighted leaders foresaw that permanent peace had not yet descended upon Europe. In the meantime, however, attentions turned to the Pacific, where the flags of the Empire of the Rising Sun still fluttered.

Ten

Alabama and the War at Sea

War at sea played a larger, different role in the struggle against the Axis powers than in previous American conflicts. This was a two-ocean war in which American sea power engaged the enemy and protected merchant shipping in the Pacific as well as in the Atlantic. Although traditional surface craft and submarines continued to be of utmost importance, carrier-borne aircraft radically altered the conduct of war, as the shocking attack at Pearl Harbor proved. Alabama played a notable part in the battle at sea. Warships closely identified with the state were in the thick of fighting. Alabamians played conspicuous roles in naval actions and in convoying supplies to allied nations. Alabama's shipyards, using steel manufactured in the state, launched scores of vital freighters and tankers.

Three cruisers named for Alabama cities—*Birmingham, Tuscaloosa,* and *Mobile*—as well as the battleship *Alabama* took part in the war at sea. Although few Alabamians saw duty aboard these vessels, emotional bonds developed between those ships and the state and cities for which they were named. Alabamians read with interest about the exploits and fate of these warships and their crews. Two decades after the war's end, officials and civic groups mounted a campaign to have the battleship *Alabama* towed to Mobile and turned into a permanent memorial honoring the men and women of Alabama who served in World War II.

The heavy cruiser *Tuscaloosa* was the oldest of these warships and the first to see action.[1] After being commissioned in 1934, the *Tuscaloosa* steamed to the Pacific for maneuvers and routine cruises. With war looming in Europe, the ship joined Cruiser Division Seven in the Atlantic. President Roosevelt had a fondness for this vessel, which was involved in several significant political and diplomatic episodes. In August 1939 FDR enjoyed the late summer sea breezes as he cruised aboard *Tuscaloosa* along the New England coast to his Campobello retreat. The ship's first significant war-related sea duty was the rescue of passengers and crew of the German vessel *Columbus*. After having broken out of the Gulf of Mexico into the open Atlantic, *Columbus*—one of Germany's largest merchant vessels—was challenged by a British cruiser off the American East Coast. Not wanting his valuable ship to become a British prize, the German master ordered his vessel to be scuttled. Nearly 600 passengers and crewmen took to the sea in lifeboats. *Tuscaloosa,* which had been shadowing both the German vessel and the pursuing British warship, rescued these survivors, who were taken to New York.[2]

Shortly after the *Columbus* episode, Roosevelt boarded *Tuscaloosa* for a cruise to the Caribbean and passage through the Panama Canal to the west coast of Central America. In late 1940, in the wake of his successful bid for a third presidential term, FDR again sailed on *Tuscaloosa* to the Caribbean to inspect several of the British bases exchanged for fifty aged U.S. destroyers. While at sea, Roosevelt received desperate appeals from British Prime Minister Churchill for war supplies. Roosevelt and his top political adviser, Harry Hopkins, decided to abandon the "Short of War Policy" in favor of a Lend-Lease program to aid Great Britain. Six days later, on 22 December 1940, *Tuscaloosa* steamed across the Atlantic with Admiral William Leahy, the president's close confidant and newly appointed ambassador to Vichy France. In August 1941 *Tuscaloosa* accompanied the cruiser *Augusta,* which was taking Roosevelt to a rendezvous with Prime Minister Churchill at Argentia, Newfoundland. There, in Canadian waters, the two leaders forged the Atlantic Charter. In late 1942 *Tuscaloosa* again hosted the president on another voyage to the Caribbean.

In the meantime, between Caribbean missions, the heavy cruiser did convoy duty in the Atlantic and participated in Operation Torch on the North African coast. On the heels of the disastrous PQ-17 convoy (in which twenty-four of thirty-five merchant ships carrying war cargo to the Soviet Union were sunk by the Germans), *Tuscaloosa* transported a valuable load of torpedoes and other munitions to Russia in late summer 1942.[3] Two months later, in October, the cruiser sailed with an armada of 500 warships and 350 troop and transport vessels that rendezvoused on the coast of North Africa. Opening fire with its eight-inch guns against the French fleet at Casablanca, *Tuscaloosa* helped repulse a Vichy counterattack.[4] Abandoning their forced subservience to the

Germans, French leaders in North Africa rallied to the Free French cause of General Henri Giraud and his rival, General Charles de Gaulle.

In October 1943, during the first American carrier strikes against Nazi-occupied Europe, *Tuscaloosa* provided cover for the carrier *Ranger.* Eight months later, gunfire from the heavy cruiser supported the landings of Operation Overlord on the beaches of Normandy. After subsequently battling German gun emplacements at Cherbourg and German positions on the Italian coasts, the *Tuscaloosa* was transferred to the Third Fleet in the Pacific and participated in action at Iwo Jima and Okinawa.[5] Having earned seven battle stars for meritorious service, *Tuscaloosa*'s last mission was to transport weary but happy veterans to San Francisco before steaming to Philadelphia where the ship was decommissioned in 1946.

The newer, faster, and more expensive light cruisers *Birmingham* and *Mobile* were also highly decorated ships. *Birmingham* was badly damaged in combat on no less than three occasions.[6] Having been christened by Hattie Taylor Green, the wife of Birmingham's mayor, Cooper Green, the vessel was commissioned in early 1943. After shelling Sicily during the Allied invasion in the summer, the cruiser shifted to the Pacific and provided cover for aircraft carriers in action off Tarawa and Wake Island. Damages from a torpedo and two bombs forced the ship out of action for several months. After repairs, the cruiser participated in the invasions of Saipan, Guam, the Philippines, and Okinawa.

In October 1944 *Birmingham,* along with the cruiser *Mobile* and the battleship *Alabama,* formed part of Admiral Halsey's Third Fleet in the Philippine Sea. As a prelude to the invasion of Leyte, these vessels participated in carrier strikes against Formosa.[7] A few days later, during the Battle of Leyte Gulf, *Birmingham* came to the aid of the burning and abandoned light carrier *Princeton*. While the crew of the *Birmingham* attempted to douse the fires aboard the carrier, the main magazine of the *Princeton* exploded, hurling chunks of steel fragments on the nearby cruiser. The blast killed 237 sailors and wounded 426. It was the worst disaster suffered by any of the Alabama-named vessels in the war. After repairs in San Francisco, the ship returned to action off Iwo Jima. During the invasion of Okinawa, *Birmingham*—whose assistant executive officer was Lieutenant Commander William Jelks Cabannis of Birmingham—repelled wave after wave of Japanese planes. In early May 1945 at Okinawa, a kamikaze struck the ship, killing more than 30 seamen.[8] Again repaired, this cruiser, which earned nine battle stars and a Navy Unit Commendation, returned to duty in the Pacific, ending its wartime career in Australia.

The cruiser *Mobile* participated in most major operations in the Pacific from late summer 1943 until the surrender of Japan.[9] In those operations the ship earned eleven battle stars. Besides shelling Japanese positions in the Gilberts, Marshalls, Carolines, Marianas, Philippines, and Ryukyus, *Mobile* provided protection for carriers against kamikazes and attacked Japanese shipping with its six-inch guns. In Ulithi lagoon, the cruiser's lookouts spotted a periscope. Sharpshooting by the cruiser, succeeded by depth charge patterns laid down by destroyers, obliterated an enemy midget submarine. Following Japan's surrender, *Mobile* twice steamed into harbor at Nagasaki—which had been leveled by an atomic blast less than a month earlier—to embark liberated prisoners of war.

The state's namesake, the battleship USS *Alabama,* was the fourth ship in American naval history to bear that name. Until World War II the best-known *Alabama* was the Confederate raider commanded by Admiral Raphael Semmes. The modern 35,000-ton battleship *Alabama* was the first capital ship to be built at the Norfolk Navy Yard in almost fifty years. Construction began early in 1940, and the ship was christened on 15 February 1942, slid into the Elizabeth River, and was commissioned six months later. A delegation of Alabamians, headed by Governor Frank Dixon, took part in the christening. Among the prominent citizens attending the festivities were Secretary of the Navy Frank Knox; Supreme Court Justice and Alabama native Hugo Black; Senator and Mrs. Lister Hill; Governor Colgate W. Darden of Virginia; Governor and Mrs. Joseph Broughton of North Carolina; and the Alabama legislative delegation. Lieutenant Raphael Semmes, a descendant of the famous Confederate admiral, presented a silver service to the ship.[10]

Problems plagued the recently launched *Alabama* and its first captain. According to one crew member, the new battleship ran aground twice during trial cruises.[11] The first episode, in Chesapeake Bay, caused concern among the sailors, but after the ship again ran aground, this time in Maine's Casco Bay, the ratings practically mutinied. To restore the morale of the crew, the Navy Department relieved the skipper who, despite his apparent shortcomings in navigation, was promoted to admiral during the war. Under the able seamanship of his replacement, Captain Fred D. Kirtland, *Alabama* set out in spring 1943 for European waters, where it served with the British Home Fleet.[12] The battleship cruised in Norwegian waters, participating in the relief of British troops at Spitsbergen, and later vainly sought to tease the German battleship *Tirpitz* into a showdown on the high seas.

After returning to Norfolk, *Alabama* set sail for the Pacific in August 1943. Except for one brief period in early 1945 when the ship put into a West Coast port for repairs, *Alabama* remained in the western Pacific, providing cover for aircraft carriers and pounding Japanese-held islands with its sixteen-inch guns. The battleship's first action in the Pacific came in the Gilbert Islands in autumn 1943 when its big guns thudded against Japanese positions on Makin Island. A few weeks later, in November, *Alabama*'s antiaircraft crews had their first opportunity to defend American carriers against Japanese aircraft.

After bombarding Japanese positions on phosphate-rich Nauru Island, followed by a brief respite at Pearl Harbor, *Alabama* joined the invasion task force steaming for Kwajalein atoll in the Marshall Islands and then sailed due west for Truk. As a part of Task Force Fifty-Eight, the *Alabama* made hit-and-run attacks on Saipan, Guam, and Tinian in the Marianas, followed by bombardment of Palau to the southwest. During this period the battleship came under the most intense Japanese air assault it had yet experienced. A thirteen-hour battle during the night in late February 1944 left five crewmen dead and eleven wounded.

The attacks on Japanese-held islands in the Pacific formed a prelude to retaking the Philippines, which began with MacArthur's invasion of New Guinea. *Alabama*'s guns fired in support of MacArthur's landings at Hollandia, Aitape, and Humboldt Bay on New Guinea's northern coast in the spring. In June the battleship was part of a task force that bombarded the Marianas and provided support for the invasion of Saipan. At the beginning of the Battle of the Philippine Sea later in the month, the battleship provided the rest of the fleet with valuable intelligence about an approaching large Japanese air fleet. This timely warning enabled American forces to prepare for the biggest carrier

USS Alabama *(BB-60) in December 1942. (U.S. Navy photograph, courtesy of USS* Alabama *Battleship Memorial Park)*

battle of the war—the Great Marianas Turkey Shoot—which broke the back of Japanese air power. Sending four waves of planes against Allied vessels in the Philippine Sea on 19 June 1944, Vice Admiral Jisaburo Ozawa lost more than 300 airplanes and three carriers, while the Americans lost 38 aircraft.[13]

In the aftermath of this Japanese debacle, reconnaissance and probing missions revealed that Japanese defenses were deteriorating. After participating in operations that secured new bases at Palau and the Ulithi atoll, *Alabama* conducted sorties against Okinawa, Formosa, and Japanese airfields in the Philippines. Relatively feeble resistance convinced MacArthur to advance the invasion of the Philippines by several weeks. By the time operations commenced in Leyte Gulf, the Japanese were virtually incapable of mounting stiff air opposition. *Alabama* had participated in twelve consecutive campaigns in the Pacific. Not only had the battleship escaped relatively unscathed, but it had also carried out its mission with great success: no carrier protected by

Alabama had been touched by a bomb, a kamikaze, or a torpedo. Captain Vincent R. Murphy replaced Captain Kirtland, who had ably commanded the vessel from the first mission in northern Europe.

In the rare moments when the ship was in port, the crew of the *Alabama* fielded an exceptionally fine baseball team. Behind the outstanding pitching arm of Chief Petty Officer Bob Feller, who in civilian life hurled fastballs for the Cleveland Indians, the *Alabama* team won the "World Series" of the Third Fleet. News that the *Alabama* was to sail to the States for overhaul was greeted enthusiastically by the crew on Christmas Eve 1944.

After a brief respite at Bremerton, Washington, the ship—now under the command of Captain William Goggins—returned to the western Pacific where its guns supported ground troops on Okinawa. At the beginning of July 1945, *Alabama* sailed for the Japanese home islands to blast industrial sites and protect carriers whose planes were bombing Japan from Nagasaki northward to Hokkaido with little opposition.

Rather than risk a costly invasion of the Japanese home islands, President Truman decided to use atomic bombs, which led to a speedy Japanese surrender. At the head of the American fleet, the battleship *Alabama* steamed into Tokyo Bay, where surrender ceremonies were held aboard USS *Missouri* in September. After two weeks in Japan, *Alabama* hoisted anchor for Okinawa to take on some 700 passengers, including a large number of jubilant Seabees, who were taken to San Francisco for a grand victory celebration. Of the original crew of approximately 2,300, only 10 officers and 395 enlisted men still served on *Alabama* at the end of the war. After decommissioning, the battleship remained in mothballs in Puget Sound for nearly two decades. Following a successful campaign to create a memorial park honoring *Alabama,* the battleship was towed in 1964 to Mobile, where it serves as a vivid reminder of its contributions in the Second World War.

Numerous individual Alabamians served with great distinction in the Navy. Rear Admiral Charles H. "Socrates" McMorris from Wetumpka, war plans chief for Admiral Husband Kimmel at Pearl Harbor, emerged unscathed from the catastrophe and was given command of USS *San Francisco.* By autumn 1942, his heavy cruiser served as the flagship for Task Force Sixty-Four operating in the Solomon Islands. During the night of 11–12 October 1942, the task force encountered Japanese Cruiser Division Six steaming down the "Slot," a fifty-mile wide channel between the eastern and western Solomons. The Japanese hoped to dislodge the Americans from Henderson Field on Guadalcanal, which had been taken by the Marines in the summer. In the ensuing battle off Cape Esperance, a Japanese cruiser and destroyer were sunk. The flagship of Japanese Rear Admiral Aritomo Goto, mortally wounded by an exploding shell, was reduced to a "floating junk heap."[14] This was the Navy's first victory in a night battle with Japanese surface vessels, and for his part in this victory McMorris was awarded the Navy Cross.

McMorris's life was probably saved when he was transferred to the North Pacific just three days before another major naval engagement at Guadalcanal in November. In the Battle of Ironbottom Sound, the *San Francisco* took several direct hits, destroying the bridge and killing both the fleet admiral and McMorris's replacement as commander of the cruiser. Not as fortunate as McMorris was Seaman Second Class Frank Slater from Fyffe in northeastern Alabama. A gunner on the *San Francisco,* Slater was killed when a Japanese plane crashed into his battle station as he was blazing away at incoming planes. For his intrepid conduct, Seaman Slater was posthumously awarded the Navy Cross.

In the northern Pacific, off Russia's Komandorski Islands, a task force under McMorris's command—and consisting of the heavy cruiser *Salt Lake City,* the light cruiser *Richmond,* and four destroyers—lay in wait in March 1943 for escorted Japanese merchant ships en route to the Aleutians. Among the destroyers was the USS *Bailey,* commanded by a cigar-chomping Alabamian, Lieutenant Commander John C. Atkeson of Columbia, who earned a Navy Cross in this battle. Although outnumbered two to one, McMorris's task force inflicted heavy damage on the Japanese convoy, preventing it from resupplying Japanese troops in the Aleutians.[15] This was the kind of "long-range daylight gunnery duel" that naval officers dreamed of fighting.[16]

From May 1943 until war's end, McMorris—whose reputation had been boosted by the Battle of Komandorski Islands—served as innermost confidant and chief of staff to Admiral Chester Nimitz, the commander in chief Pacific Fleet. McMorris became an architect of American strategy in the Pacific. The Alabamian, dressed in shorts, accompanied Nimitz on his daily walks to his hilltop quonset headquarters on Guam after that island had been taken from the Japanese in 1944.[17]

Alabama also produced one of the Navy's most authentic heroes and two of the most successful submarine commanders of the war. The skipper of *Growler,* Howard Gilmore from Selma, was the first submarine commander in World War II to be awarded the Congressional Medal of Honor. Pell City's Lieutenant Joseph H. Willingham had tours of duty on two submarines, one of which was *Tautog,* which sank more enemy vessels than any other submarine in the United States Navy. William B. Parham from Birmingham commanded the fifth war cruise of *Gabilan,* one of three submarines in a wolfpack that terrorized Japanese shipping in the Java Sea in spring 1945 and sank the cruiser *Isuzu.*

Under Willingham, who took command at its commissioning on 3 July 1940, *Tautog* was assigned to Pearl Harbor, where it was one of Rear Admiral Thomas Withers's twenty-two submarines.[18] The *Tautog* escaped the Pearl Harbor attack unscathed. On the day after Christmas Willingham and *Tautog* slipped out of Pearl Harbor to head for the Marshall Islands on the sub's first war cruise. The observations made by *Tautog* and *Dolphin* provided important intelligence to Admiral William "Bull" Halsey, whose carrier task force in February 1942 carried out the first American retaliatory strike against the Japanese. Willingham made three more war cruises as skipper of *Tautog.* On the last of these cruises, in autumn 1942, his submarine laid mines off French Indochina. With a Navy Cross for his four missions on *Tautog,* Willingham was transferred to *Bowfin,* which he commanded on its first war cruise in the South China Sea. During this mission, Willingham not only sank three enemy vessels but also delivered supplies to anti-Japanese forces near Mindanao in the Philippines. Admiral Ralph Waldo Christie, commander of the Southwest Pacific fleet at Brisbane, got this very successful and popular submarine officer transferred to his staff. *Tautog* went on to sink 72,000 tons of Japanese shipping and is credited with destroying more enemy ships than any other American submarine.

The Crommelins from Wetumpka were perhaps Alabama's most decorated and distinguished naval family in World War II. Each of the five sons of John Gereart and Katherine Gunter Crommelin graduated from the United States Naval Academy at Annapolis. Two of the brothers—both serving in Halsey's Third Fleet in the western Pacific—lost their lives in the last months of the war.[19] Commander Charles Crommelin, one of the first combat pilots to fly a Hellcat, served as air group commander on the new *Yorktown* and led strikes against the Gilbert Islands in autumn 1943. He was lost in combat over Okinawa in March 1945. His brother Richard, a fighter squadron leader who had already been shot down in his Wildcat in the Coral Sea and who had earned a Navy Cross at Midway, failed to return from a mission over Hokkaido in the last weeks of the war.[20] The youngest brother, Quentin, who graduated from the naval academy in 1941, saw service at Guadalcanal and the eastern Solomons before taking flight training and becoming a naval flight instructor. Henry, the only nonflier among the Crommelin boys, skippered a destroyer in the Pacific.

The eldest Crommelin son, John, pulled a tour aboard the carrier *Enterprise*. As flight officer, it was his responsibility to provide pilots with tactical information to ensure the success of their missions. In late October 1942, planes from *Enterprise* and the *Hornet* engaged an enemy carrier task force steaming for Guadalcanal. Encountering the Japanese force near Santa Cruz Island, *Hornet* was sunk and *Enterprise* damaged.[21] Japanese losses, however, were heavy. The downing of 100 Japanese planes, many of them to Commander Crommelin's pilots, took some of the pressure off the U.S. positions on Guadalcanal. As a skilled pilot and leader, Crommelin earned near-legendary respect of the airmen and sailors of the *Enterprise*. As they flew to their rapidly approaching targets, pilots could hear ringing in their ears John Crommelin's Alabama-accented remonstrance: "There is no room for waste, no excuse for misses. If you're going to go out there and miss, you should have stayed home and let a *good* pilot have your bunk and your crack at the Japs."[22]

Promoted to captain, Crommelin subsequently became chief of staff to Rear Admiral H. M. Mullinnix on the escort carrier *Liscome Bay*. During the invasion of the Gilbert Islands, the ship was torpedoed and sunk off Makin Island on 24 November 1943 with great loss of life, including Mullinnix, 52 other officers, and nearly 600 men. With the vessel listing severely, John Crommelin, himself badly burned, jumped overboard. Floating for an hour in a sea with flaming fuel all about, Crommelin was rescued.

By 1944 Crommelin was serving as chief of staff of a carrier task force. Stationed aboard *Gambier Bay,* he was responsible for aviation briefings and helped direct the attack on the Marshall Islands and the preinvasion strike on the Palau Islands. Returning to Montgomery in late September 1944—honored by a Legion of Merit award—John Crommelin was fortuitously not aboard *Gambier Bay* when it was sunk in October in a battle off Samar in Leyte Gulf.[23]

Merchant vessels and merchant seaman, many from Alabama, also served the Allied cause. Sailing singly or in convoys, merchant ships courageously carried troops, military matériel, and vital industrial goods despite the lurking danger of enemy submarines, warships, and mined harbors. Departing from Mobile and other Gulf of Mexico ports, ships bound for Murmansk or Liverpool joined convoys at Key West to sail under the protective watch of American and British destroyers along the sub-infested East Coast and across the Atlantic.

One Alabamian who made five voyages in convoy across the Atlantic was John Beecher. The son of a steel company executive who moved his family to Birmingham in the aftermath of the panic of 1907, Beecher in 1942 signed on as a crew member of the recently commissioned Liberty ship, *Booker T. Washington.*[24] With a West Indian master and a crew, including other Alabamians, that was evenly split between blacks and whites, *Booker T. Washington* was one of four vessels operated by the War Shipping Administration with black captains and integrated crews. In the Pacific theater, Commander James S. Freeman from Jasper was awarded the Navy Cross for sailing his cargo vessel through enemy waters, surviving attacks by torpedo planes and bombs, to deliver supplies to General MacArthur's troops in the Solomon Islands.[25]

Desperately needing more Navy and Marine Corps officers than could be produced by the naval academy and the twenty-seven existing Naval Reserve Officer Training Corps programs, several procurement and training programs were established at colleges and universities across the nation. The largest of these was the V-12 program, which was established on 131 campuses.

In Alabama there were two V-12 programs. One, an undergraduate curriculum, was established at Howard College (now Samford University) in Birmingham. President Harwell Davis believed the Navy program would be the answer to the prayers of his institution, which, like so many other schools, suffered declining enrollments during the war years. Howard College tailored its traditional curriculum to offer more technical courses required by the Navy. At the height of the program in 1943 and 1944, approximately 225 Navy cadets enrolled each term.[26] A smaller V-12 program for medical training was operated by the University of Alabama School of Medicine. Across the state, Alabama Polytechnic Institute operated a War Training Service School—a "Little Pensacola"—that taught principles of flight to Navy cadets.[27]

Carrying on a strong seafaring tradition, tens of thousands of Alabamians served in the Navy, stood watches as coastal pickets, sailed as merchant seamen, or worked in the shipbuilding industry to do their part for victory over the Axis nations. Of these, more than 1,100 Alabamians lost their lives in the service of the Navy and Marines in World War II, and an additional 1,400 were wounded or became prisoners of war.

Eleven

Capturing the Pacific

Following the attack on Pearl Harbor, Japan's offensive in the Pacific and in Asia rapidly overpowered the feeble resistance of the Western powers. By spring 1942 Japan had nearly realized its plan for a Greater East Asia Co-Prosperity Sphere and seemed bent on further conquests. The situation in the Philippines appeared hopeless. President Roosevelt ordered General Douglas MacArthur to leave Luzon, where American and Filipino troops, now under General Jonathan Wainwright's command, were bottled up at Corregidor. Explosive discontent over British colonialism on the Indian subcontinent invited Japanese meddling in South Asia. Using recently captured Rabaul as a staging area, the Japanese were within striking distance of New Guinea and Australia.

The most immediate priority in the Pacific was the defense of Australia. Barring help from the Americans, its fall seemed imminent. Only one Australian division was available for home defense. One division had surrendered at Singapore, and three others were fighting in Greece and the Middle East.[1] Japan's attacks on Pearl Harbor and the Philippines diverted, in mid-Pacific, a Manila-bound convoy that made for Australia instead. The first contingent of Yanks arrived "down under" on 22 December 1941. In the weeks that followed, thousands of American troops under General Alexander M. Patch, who had served as chief infantry instructor of the Alabama National Guard in 1939–40, poured into the Southwest Pacific in preparation for invading Guadalcanal.

Antiaircraft batteries from Alabama's 104th Coast Artillery Battalion were among the earliest American units establishing defensive perimeters in northern Australia. After a forty-day journey aboard the *Queen Mary,* the battalion arrived in Australia, where it was issued modern Bofors guns to help defend Queensland. Corporal Robert Bain from Phenix City remembers how unprepared the Australians were for Japanese aggression: "They only had a few transports. They would push bombs out the doors. When they didn't have bombs, they would put razor blades on beer bottles and throw them from the planes."[2] By the early summer, MacArthur had 25,000 troops and 260 aircraft in Australia to begin his campaign to drive the Japanese from their Pacific empire.

Thomas H. Moorer, an Alabama native and the first naval officer to head the Joint Chiefs of Staff, was an early hero of the war in the Southwest Pacific. Having survived Pearl Harbor, where he was flying a Navy patrol plane over Ford Island at the time of the Japanese attack, Lieutenant Moorer was sent to Australia. There, his PBY-5 patrol bomber made reconnaissance flights from Port Darwin. On one of these flights in late February 1942, nine Zeros—en route to bomb northern Australia—came out of the sun to attack the Annapolis graduate's plane. With his Catalina in flames, an engine out, and his fuel tanks and fuselage ripped by gunfire, the wounded Moorer managed to set his seaplane down. Rescued by a Philippine merchant ship, Moorer's misfortune, however, did not end. A bomb from a Japanese plane scored a direct hit on the small ship, sinking it within minutes. Moorer and most of the PBY crew managed to reach a nearby island, from which they were later rescued by an Australian subchaser.[3] Despite the bombing of northern Australia, the anticipated Japanese invasion of the continent never materialized.

Even with pitifully thin military forces in the Pacific, the Allies succeeded in landing several counterblows. As a first step, the Allies reorganized the Pacific command. From his headquarters at Pearl Harbor, Commander in Chief Pacific Fleet Chester Nimitz had direct responsibility for the northern and central Pacific. General MacArthur, ordered to quit Corregidor for Australia, assumed the Southwest Pacific Theater command, which planned and conducted operations in New Guinea, the Dutch East Indies, and the Philippines.[4]

Events in the Coral Sea in May 1942 demonstrated the significance of carrier-borne air power and foreshadowed shifting fortunes of war in the Pacific. Unknown to the Japanese, the Allies had acquired the ability to intercept and decipher coded enemy naval messages.[5] Code breakers learned that Japan planned to dispatch a task force to seize Port Moresby as a prelude to invading Australia. Armed with this intelligence, Nimitz ordered the carriers *Lexington* and *Yorktown* to the Coral Sea in late April 1942 to await the arrival of the Japanese.[6]

Among the flyers on the *Lexington* was Birmingham native Lieutenant Noel Gayler, who won three Navy Crosses for action in this theater.
His combat initiation came in late February near Bougainville Island
when his squadron of F4F Wildcats flew off the *Lexington* to take on
seventeen Japanese bombers and their fighter escorts. Gayler downed
one of the bombers before a bullet smashed into his front windscreen,
forcing him out of action.[7] Three weeks later, with his carrier operating
in the Gulf of Papua, Gayler's squadron escorted dive-bombers and
torpedo planes over New Guinea's rugged Owen Stanley Mountains to
deliver a damaging attack on ships and harbor facilities at Lae and
Salamaua. To date, this was the most stunning American operation in
the Pacific.[8]

The Battle of the Coral Sea, in which Gayler's squadron again
distinguished itself in fierce aerial combat, was the first naval engagement fought entirely by carrier-based aircraft without surface vessels
ever seeing one another. Because the opposing carriers were often 200
miles apart, aerial reconnaissance was crucial. Lieutenant Hoyt Mann
from Roanoke, Alabama, flew scouting missions and was commended
for locating Japanese naval targets.[9]

The two-day battle opened on 7 May 1942 with a Japanese attack on
the American oiler *Neosho,* which had nearly been sunk five months
earlier at Pearl Harbor. Among the sailors killed on the *Neosho* in the
Coral Sea was Henry W. Tucker, a pharmacist's mate from York,
Alabama, to whom the Navy Cross was posthumously awarded for his
heroic efforts to save the lives of injured shipmates. The whereabouts of
the main body of Admiral Frank Jack Fletcher's Task Force Seventeen
remained unknown to the Japanese. Lieutenant Richard Crommelin
from Wetumpka, flying a Wildcat from the *Yorktown,* destroyed a
Japanese reconnaissance plane before it discovered the American carriers. American flyers, however, located the Japanese fleet, and on 7 May
they sank the *Shoho,* the first Japanese flattop destroyed by American
planes in the war. On the following day, American bombs badly damaged the carrier *Shokaku,* which, along with *Zuikaku,* withdrew to a
home port for repairs and to replace planes and sailors lost in the Coral
Sea. The absence of these carriers dealt a severe blow to Japan's attack on
Midway Island in the following month.[10]

American and Australian losses in the Coral Sea were also heavy, particularly on the second day of the battle. Aviators contended not only with Japanese adversaries but also with antiaircraft fire from "friendly" surface vessels. Of the four planes in Noel Gayler's group escorting torpedo planes and dive-bombers against the Japanese task force, only Gayler, who took cover in the clouds, returned to the *Lexington*. Elsewhere, Richard Crommelin, whose F4F Wildcat began losing oil pressure, hobbled back to the carriers. A nearby destroyer plucked him from the sea when he ditched his plane near the *Lexington*.[11]

On the second day of the battle, Japanese aircraft finally found Admiral Fletcher's task force. Chief Quartermaster Frank "Pork Chops" McKenzie, an Alabamian, was at the helm of the *Lexington* when Japanese torpedo bombers arrived late in the morning.[12] As many as five torpedoes struck the *Lexington,* and although the carrier listed slightly, it was believed the fires could be brought under control.[13] Two hours later, however, the first of several internal explosions wracked the carrier, and by late afternoon 2,400 crewmen and officers abandoned ship. Japanese torpedoes also scored minor damage on the *Yorktown,* forcing it to Pearl Harbor for repairs.

Although Fletcher withdrew from the Coral Sea, giving the impression of Japanese victory, the battle proved to be a strategic victory for the United States. The damage inflicted on the Japanese forced Admiral Shigeyoshi Inouye to postpone the attack on Port Moresby, causing great anguish among senior officers in Tokyo who had been receiving overly optimistic reports from the scene. For the first time in the war, American forces had frustrated a Japanese operation.

Barely a month later, Japan embarked on a bold strategy in the northern and central Pacific to push the Americans back to the West Coast. An attack by a small carrier task force on Dutch Harbor on Unalaska Island in the Aleutians in early June 1942 left Glen Howard Tate, a native of Madison County, dead and three other Alabamians injured.[14] Attu and Kiska soon fell. It was 1943 before the United States undertook to drive the Japanese from American soil in Alaska.[15]

To the south, however, Japan suffered a telling defeat in an epic sea battle at Midway Island. Admiral Isoroku Yamamoto, architect of the victory at Pearl Harbor, planned this attack as well. As he had promised in 1941, the stunning setback to the United States at Pearl Harbor enabled Japanese forces to run wild in the Pacific for six months. The attack on Pearl Harbor, however, had not eliminated the United States as a naval power in the Pacific. The attack on Midway Island had two objectives. Known as the sentinel of Pearl Harbor, the island could be used as a base from which the Japanese could operate at will against American bases in Hawaii. Yamamoto also hoped to lure Nimitz into a pitched sea battle, which the Japanese strategist confidently expected to win. His task force, consisting of 8 carriers and 11 battleships among its nearly 200 warships, was the largest Japan had ever assembled.[16]

Once again the ability of American cryptographers to read Japanese naval messages gave Admiral Nimitz a decisive edge.[17] Learning of Japan's intentions to strike at Midway, Nimitz quickly gathered a task force under Admiral Raymond A. Spruance and another under Fletcher to await the Japanese fleet plowing toward this relatively obscure island lying 1,200 miles northwest of Hawaii. Although the United States lost the carrier *Yorktown* in the ensuing Battle of Midway in early June, American air power reigned supreme, inflicting heavy damage on Yamamoto's forces. The Japanese lost four carriers, a heavy cruiser, over 300 aircraft, and 5,000 sailors and troops. Six months after the attack on Pearl Harbor, the tide of battle in the Pacific began to shift. After the "miracle at Midway," the Japanese never again directly threatened Hawaii or the U.S. West Coast. "At Midway," Gordon W. Prange wrote, "the United States set aside the shield and picked up the sword, and through all the engagements to follow, never again yielded the strategic offensive."[18]

American hopes rose further following the landing of General Alexander Vandegrift's First Marine Division on Guadalcanal in the Solomon Islands in August 1942. This was the first American land offensive in the war against the Axis. Meeting little resistance, the Marines quickly established a beachhead. The capture of an airfield, which the Japanese were building and which the Americans named Henderson Field, proved decisive. Harold H. "Swede" Larsen of Birmingham, a Navy pilot, flew in the first squadron of six TBF torpedo planes to Henderson Field.[19] As his squadron prepared to attack Japanese cruisers and destroyers during the Solomons campaign, Larsen's advice to his men was: "Go after the nearest big one."[20] The *Long Island,* with Alabama naval reservists as crew members, and other small escort carriers delivered Wildcat fighters and Dauntless dive-bombers to

Guadalcanal.[21] John Howard McEniry from Bessemer and other Marine dive-bomber pilots pounded Japanese positions in the Solomons by day and by night.[22] Months of bloody fighting followed on Guadalcanal and in adjacent waters. Japan's loss of 24,000 troops in the Guadalcanal campaign—especially the 600 aviators—took its toll and in early February 1943 forced the evacuation of the last Japanese soldiers from the island.[23] This action in the Solomon Islands marked the beginning of the arduous campaign to liberate the Pacific from Japanese domination.

During 1943 and into the early part of 1944, the Allies drove the Japanese from their strongholds in the Solomon Islands, Bismarck Archipelago, and New Guinea. Only heavily fortified Rabaul on New Britain Island remained in Japanese hands. MacArthur decided to bypass Rabaul, isolating the stronghold and subjecting it to nearly constant bombing. The task of reducing Rabaul fell to the Thirteenth Air Force, which contained a squadron of former Alabama National Guard flyers who had earlier gained combat experience conducting antisubmarine missions off the East Coast of the United States before being shipped to the Pacific.[24]

American strategy in the Pacific envisioned dislodging the Japanese from their island strongholds and using the liberated islands as stepping-stones to launch an eventual attack on the Japanese home islands. Military planners concluded that only a full-scale invasion of the main islands would force Japan to its knees. Vast resources of naval power, air power, and ground troops would be necessary, and the success of this strategy required unparalleled cooperation among all branches of the military and the utmost care in planning amphibious operations. It can be argued that amphibious operations were the most important tactical innovation in World War II and that the defeat of the Axis powers hinged upon them. All of the great Allied victories—North Africa, southern Italy, Normandy, and the Pacific campaigns from Guadalcanal to Okinawa—were achieved by landing great numbers of troops by sea, protected by massive firepower from offshore warships and a commanding control of the skies.

The architect of American amphibious tactics was General Holland McTyeire Smith, an Alabama native. Having begun work on amphibious tactics in the early 1920s, Smith devoted more thought to that subject than any previous American officer. In World War II he planned and led some of the most famous amphibious landings in the Pacific, including Tarawa and Makin islands in the Gilbert chain, Kwajalein and Eniwetok in the Marshall group, Saipan and Tinian in the Marianas, Guam, and Iwo Jima. As commander of the Fifth Amphibious Corps and later as commanding general of Fleet Marine Force Pacific, Smith had more troops under his authority than any previous Marine officer in history.[25]

Smith grew up in Russell County in eastern Alabama around the turn of the century. In 1898 at the age of sixteen he entered nearby Alabama Polytechnic Institute at Auburn. Other than reading widely into the lives of Napoleon Bonaparte and Andrew Jackson, Smith exhibited little intellectual curiosity or accomplishment in those youthful years. Obedient to his father's wishes, he studied law in Tuscaloosa and returned to Seale. Unhappy with the prospects of spending the rest of his life as a courthouse lawyer in east Alabama, he obtained a commission in the Marines and saw combat duty in France during World War I.

In the twenties Smith boldly advanced his ideas on amphibious warfare. Exercises in the Caribbean and in the Hawaiian Islands taught many lessons, one of the most important being that the Marine Corps needed a shallow-draft landing craft with a retractable ramp in the bow so that combatants could debark close to shore. In the midthirties Smith began writing the manual for amphibious landings, and in 1937 the recently promoted Colonel Smith arrived in Washington to build an amphibious force shaped by his doctrines.

The search for a suitable landing craft led to collaboration with famous New Orleans boat builder Andrew Jackson Higgins, who had developed shallow-draft vessels for the Louisiana bayous.[26] In 1940 a Higgins prototype landing craft was used in fleet exercises, and in the following year a retractable bow ramp was added. By 1941 Marines were carrying out exercises that rivaled in scale many of the nearly one hundred future landings on Pacific islands during the war.

In the aftermath of the Japanese attack on Pearl Harbor, Smith was bypassed for combat command. His reputation was that of a trainer. Only in 1943 did Chief of Naval Operations Ernest King, the grand strategist of the war in the Pacific, and Admiral Nimitz, the operational commander in the Pacific, select Smith as commander of the Marine's

Marine General Holland Smith developed the tactics of modern amphibious warfare. (Holland Smith Collection, Auburn University Archives)

Fifth Amphibious Corps, whose mission was to take Japanese-held islands across the central Pacific.

The Marine Corps applauded Smith's selection. Numerous battles over turf with the Army and Navy were anticipated, and General Smith was known as someone "who can sit at the table and pound it harder than any naval officer."[27] After all, it was not a retiring personality that had earned him the nickname "Howlin' Mad" more than three decades earlier, when he regularly force-marched subordinates over nearly impossible terrain in the debilitating tropical climate of the Philippines. Although admitting to a penchant for speaking his mind when the occasion demanded, Smith denied being unreasonable and thought the "Howlin' Mad" moniker unjustified.

On several celebrated occasions Smith crossed swords with the Navy and the Army. He acrimoniously complained that the Navy failed to bombard islands with sufficient thoroughness before his Marines hit the beaches. In particular, the landing on Tarawa, which he later characterized as unnecessary and wasteful, had been marred by what he regarded as the Navy's ineptness. In this and other operations, he roundly condemned inadequate and poorly coordinated air support.

During operations on Saipan in June 1944 Smith took the unusual—and highly publicized—step of relieving a popular Army general from command. He accused the general and his division of slackness in combat, but many observers regarded the episode as interservice rivalry or attributed the incident to a personal vendetta. Much of the press back in the States, many Army officers, and most infantrymen believed that the Pacific islands could have been taken with far fewer casualties, and they blamed Smith for needless loss of life.[28]

Despite the spat with the Army over Saipan, continued successful landings coupled with growing air and naval superiority vindicated Smith's basic doctrines. Japan's setbacks in June 1944—the defeat at Saipan, the annihilation of Japanese air power in the Battle of the Philippine Sea, and the beginning of B-29 raids on the home islands followed by the landing of Marines at Tinian in July—dealt a staggering blow to the Japanese, leading to the resignation of Premier Hideki Tojo's cabinet.

A unit with deep Alabama ties that participated in the island hopping across the Southwest Pacific was the Thirty-first, or Dixie, Division. This was originally a National Guard outfit composed of units from Alabama, Mississippi, Louisiana, and Florida. In World War II, the Thirty-first Division gained distinction as one of the Army's most outstanding training divisions before being sent in 1944 to the Pacific, where it fought in New Guinea, on Morotai, and in the Philippines.[29]

Some of the division's units traced their origins to the nineteenth

century. The Thirty-first Signal Company had originated as the Mobile
Cadets, a group that was formed in 1845 and saw service in the Civil
War, the Spanish-American War, World War I, and the Mexican
Expedition. The Thirty-first Headquarters Company, commanded
during World War II by Colonel Joseph A. Langan, had formerly been
known as the Mobile Rifles.[30]

Major General John C. Persons, the commander of the Thirty-first
Division from October 1940 to late September 1944, had the distinction
of being one of only two National Guard generals to lead their divisions
into combat in World War II. Born in Atlanta on 9 May 1888, Persons
moved to Birmingham in 1904. After brief employment with the Alabama Consolidated Coal and Iron Company, he studied law at the
University of Alabama and became a partner in a Tuscaloosa law firm.
Persons volunteered for military duty in World War I and served as an
officer in France. He received the Distinguished Service Cross for his
participation in the Second Battle of the Marne.[31]

Following the armistice, Persons returned to law practice in
Tuscaloosa but remained active in the Alabama National Guard. In
1927 a banking job lured him back to Birmingham. Three years later
the First National Bank of Birmingham made him president. In August of that same year, the Alabama National Guard promoted Persons
to brigadier general and gave him command of the Sixty-second Infantry Brigade. Called "Old Stone Face" by his troops, General Persons was
regarded as a tough but fair commander.

National Guard training grew more determined and purposeful,
taking on a warlike tone, as the international situation worsened in
1938. Serious and physically demanding military maneuvers replaced
the "Boy Scout" atmosphere that prevailed in earlier encampments. In
one of these maneuvers, a hard-hitting and straightforward attack by
George Patton's tanks literally ran out of gas after Persons's Sixty-
second Brigade infiltrated Patton's rear guard and stole his reserve
gasoline.[32]

In October 1940 Persons succeeded General Albert H. Blanding
from Florida as commander of the Thirty-first Division. This promotion coincided with the federalization of National Guard units throughout the country. In December 1940 the division reported to a newly
established, and still not completed, encampment at Camp Blanding,

Florida. The division's first job was to build shelters and to lend a helping hand to the civilian contractors. Persons believed strongly in physical conditioning, and throughout 1941 the division combined rigorous exercising with field training in Ocala Forest and maneuvers in Louisiana and the Carolinas.[33]

Toward the end of 1941, after more than twelve months on active duty, the troops of the Dixie Division eagerly anticipated their return to civilian life in time for the Christmas holidays. The attack on Pearl Harbor shattered those hopes. Fearing an imminent German invasion on the heels of Pearl Harbor, elements of the division were hastily sent to the Atlantic seaboard. Maneuvers in Louisiana demonstrated the fitness of the Dixie Division for combat duty, but there followed a disappointing series of assignments to Camp Bowie, Texas; Fort Sill, Oklahoma; Camp Shelby, Mississippi; and, finally, Camp Pickett, Virginia. Many of the original members of the division had been sent as replacements to combat divisions. By 1943 General Persons complained that his division was far better prepared for combat than many less-experienced divisions that were already overseas.

Woolen uniforms and overcoats were eventually issued, and it finally looked as though the Thirty-first Division was heading for the European theater. However, when the eleven tightly packed transports shipped out from Hampton Roads in early 1944, they sailed south to the Caribbean and through the Panama Canal for the Southwest Pacific. General Persons, in the meantime, flew separately to Brisbane in Australia to confer with General Douglas MacArthur about the role of the Thirty-first Division in the liberation of the Philippines.[34]

Arriving in New Guinea in mid-April 1944, the Dixie Division assembled at Oro Bay where it became part of the Sixth Army, which had already acquired battle experience in the tough Cape Gloucester and Hollandia operations. Lieutenant General Walter Krueger, the Sixth Army commander, had great respect for the Thirty-first Division and its officers. Having headed the Southern Defense Command earlier in the war, Krueger was well acquainted with Persons from the days of the Louisiana maneuvers. The Sixth Army commander welcomed Persons's disciplined and well-led division.[35]

During the next six weeks the Thirty-first Division acclimated itself as best it could to the heat and humidity of the tropics. Early in July 1944 the division had its first taste of jungle combat when Krueger assigned a combat team from the 124th Regiment to help defend a beachhead in the Aitape area of New Guinea against an anticipated counteroffensive by the Japanese Eighteenth Army. The three battalions, under Colonel Edward M. Starr, slogged their way through difficult terrain and warded off fierce Japanese bayonet attacks.[36] One of the units of Colonel Starr's 124th Regiment made a phenomenal night march that was cited as a "feat unparalleled in the history of jungle warfare."[37] By 10 August 1944, organized Japanese resistance had ceased in the Aitape area.

In the meantime, General Persons and the rest of the division arrived at Toem on New Guinea's Maffin Bay to relieve the Sixth Division, which along with the Forty-first Division had seized Wakde Island, which served as a staging area for a landing near the village of Sarmi on the mainland. General Persons, who now commanded the Wakde Task Force, mounted an offensive against Japanese troops on his perimeter to enlarge his sector. The 155th and 167th regiments received their baptism of fire on probing missions in this operation. The 155th Regiment was commanded by Colonel Walter J. Hanna, nicknamed "Crack" Hanna because of his reputation as the best marksman in the Alabama National Guard.[38] In addition to protecting the airfield at Maffin Bay, the Dixie Division labored through the unending rains and the ever-present mud to improve the port for Liberty ships and to unload supplies.[39] The capture of Sansapor by Krueger's Sixth Army completed the New Guinea campaign except for mopping up isolated Japanese resistance.

MacArthur's next goal was the liberation of the Philippines, for which he needed an airfield so that bombers could soften Japanese resistance as a prelude to an amphibious operation. Mountainous and jungle-covered Morotai Island appeared to be a good choice. Northernmost of the Spice Islands and straddling the equator, it lay halfway between New Guinea and the Philippines. Although the Japanese had begun construction of an airfield, the island was thought to be lightly defended.[40] Planning for an amphibious landing began in July while the Aitape and Maffin Bay operations were under way. Krueger entrusted this operation to General Persons, whose Thirty-first Division would spearhead the amphibious landing.[41]

A combined American and Australian naval task force, consisting of

New Guinea 31st "Dixie" Division. (John Persons Collection, Alabama Department of Archives and History)

General Douglas MacArthur (center) during a visit to Morotai Island to congratulate General John Persons (left) and the 31st "Dixie" Division for their successful invasion in September 1944. Persons was one of only two National Guard generals to command their divisions in combat in World War II. (John Persons Collection, Alabama Department of Archives and History)

cruisers, destroyers, escort carriers, forty-five LSTs (landing ship tanks), and assorted other landing craft, set sail on 11 September for the 700-mile trip to Morotai. Counting a regimental combat team from the Thirty-second Division in reserve, General Persons had 28,000 men under his command for Operation Tradewind. Following a heavy naval and air bombardment on the morning of 15 September 1944, landing craft began ferrying soldiers to two beaches. Surprisingly treacherous conditions on the fringing reefs and in the surf marred the landing, nearly turning it into a disaster. The official Army history of the Morotai invasion concludes that "offshore conditions at Red Beach were undoubtedly the worst encountered in the Southwest Pacific Area throughout the entire war."[42] In his memoir, General Krueger described the beach conditions in the landing area as "the worst we had ever seen in our operations, and that was saying a lot."[43]

Coral heads in shallow water extended 150 yards off Morotai at the White Beach, forcing the tank landing craft to locate a more suitable landing spot. Infantrymen waded ashore over treacherously difficult coral and muddy terrain, often in water up to their armpits. At the Red Beach some 2,000 yards to the north, bulldozers towed ashore vehicles that had tumbled into deep holes and fissures in the reef. Both beaches were, in Krueger's words, "wholly unsuitable for unloading LSTs."

Fortunately, little Japanese resistance greeted the Dixie Division at the beaches, and the three battalions moved inland within three hours after landing. By early afternoon General Persons established his headquarters on the island, and before sunset the Thirty-first Division secured the airfield. The Dixie Division extended its beachhead into the interior, despite isolated Japanese counteroffensives and sporadic air attacks over the next few days. By 4 October the island had been cleared of its last remaining Japanese defenders.

The partially completed airfield on Morotai, however, proved unsuitable for heavy bombers because of the marshy terrain upon which it was built. The Dixie Division converted the field into a landing strip for fighters and constructed a new airstrip near the beach for bombers. Planes were soon taking off from Morotai to attack Japanese positions on Mindanao and to escort bombing raids against oil fields in Borneo. The capture of Morotai completed the preliminaries for the campaign to regain the Philippines. General MacArthur, who was a step closer to

Supply dump, Morotai invasion, 1944, 31st Division. (John Persons Collection, Alabama Department of Archives and History)

fulfilling his vow to return, visited General Persons and the Thirty-first Division to extend his personal congratulations for the successful operation.

Ten days after the landing on Morotai, in a highly unusual move, fifty-six-year-old General Persons requested permission to return to Alabama. Attempting to explain this surprising development, Persons maintained that his five-year absence with the Dixie Division threatened his position at his Birmingham bank.[44] If this were indeed the reason for General Persons's step, it was wholly uncharacteristic. Personal advantages had always been sacrificed to duty to country and the Dixie Division. Perhaps more plausible was his realization that the citizen-soldier would have to give way to hard-bitten Army and Marine commanders in the weeks ahead. He only had to remind himself of the recent dismissal by Marine General Holland Smith of the only other National Guard commander, General Ralph Smith of the Twenty-seventh Division, during the invasion of Saipan three months earlier.

Many of John Persons's subordinates in the Dixie Division believed his return to civilian life was prompted in part by disappointment over the Army's failure to promote him to a corps command. Writing from New Guinea to a Birmingham friend in summer 1944, Colonel Hanna described John Persons as "without question the most brilliant leader in the Army."[45] Others hinted in letters to Persons that they could read between the lines of his resignation, indicating they believed the story about the necessity of his returning to the bank to be a smoke screen. Joseph Langan, a retired Mobile attorney and in 1944 in charge of division headquarters, remains convinced that the Army's failure to promote Persons had a decisive influence on his decision to leave his command.[46]

Technically, General MacArthur approved a thirty-day leave of absence for the Dixie Division commander. A month later, in October 1944, the Army approved a three-month leave of absence, which was to be followed by Persons's transfer to inactive officer status.[47] His unexpected arrival in San Francisco in early October greatly surprised his family and friends. After a warm reunion in Alabama, Persons went to Washington, where General George C. Marshall bestowed the Distinguished Service Medal upon him, closing a chapter in an exemplary military career that spanned a quarter century, from the Second Battle of the Marne to the campaign for the Philippines.

On the same day that General Persons and the Dixie Division landed on Morotai with only scattered Japanese resistance, another Alabamian was in the thick of one of the bloodiest battles fought in the Pacific. Private Eugene B. Sledge, a young enlistee from Mobile, waded ashore with his First Marine Division at Peleliu. General MacArthur considered it absolutely essential to take this small island at the western end of the Carolines before pushing on to the Philippines. Ironically, many strategists later regarded the Peleliu operation—like the taking of Tarawa—as unnecessary. "Sledgehammer," as his buddies called him, had little opportunity to consider the strategic implications of this adventure. His more immediate concern was sheer survival. Many of Sledge's companions on his landing craft were veterans of Guadalcanal and the tough Gloucester campaign and knew what to expect as the sun peaked over the horizon on this mid-September morning. But their advice and war stories hardly prepared him for the realities of what he was about to encounter.

Private Eugene Sledge of Mobile in the Pacific. Sledge's memoir With the Old Breed at Peleliu and Okinawa *has been hailed as the finest description of combat to come out of World War II. (Courtesy of Eugene Sledge)*

Eugene Sledge, soft-spoken and today retired from a long career of teaching biology at Montevallo University in central Alabama, has written what many regard as a classic memoir of a soldier at war.[48] The significance of his *With the Old Breed at Peleliu and Okinawa* is often compared to Erich Maria Remarque's *All Quiet on the Western Front* or Henri Barbusse's *Under Fire*. Paul Fussell, himself a platoon leader in France in World War II and an authority on the literature of war, writes that Sledge's book is "one of the finest memoirs to emerge from any war."[49]

Sledge's story is that of a front-line soldier, a grunt, who endures firsthand the terrors of war and who slogs through the muck and mire of battle. Aided by a forbidden diary, Sledge remembers his first morning of battle: "We waited a seeming eternity for the signal to start toward the beach. . . . Waiting is a major part of war, but I never experienced any more supremely agonizing suspense than the excruciating torture of those moments." Of course, the fear of the moment produced physical reactions:

> I broke out in a cold sweat as the tension mounted with the intensity of bombardment. My stomach was tied in knots. I had a lump in my throat and swallowed only with great difficulty. My knees nearly buckled, so I clung weakly to the side of the tractor. I felt nauseated and feared that my bladder would surely empty itself and reveal me to be the coward I was.[50]

Sledge experienced the universal emotions and thoughts of frontline soldiers of all nationalities and all ages. What kept him going on the battlefield when he was weary or terrified was not idealism or patriotism but the fear of letting his buddies down. Camaraderie was a powerful motivator. "Friendship," he wrote, "was the only comfort a man had." Although proud to be a Marine, Sledge regretted the inhumanity of war. At Peleliu and later at Okinawa, his belief in the goodness of human nature slipped away. "Something in me died at Peleliu," he wrote. "Perhaps it was a childish innocence that accepted as faith the claim that man is basically good."[51]

Peleliu also marked the beginning of a new—and in some ways more terrifying—form of warfare on the Pacific islands.[52] The Japanese still attacked at night, making what seemed to be fanatical banzai charges into the foxholes. But no longer did they make all-out efforts to stop amphibious landings on the beaches. Rather, the Japanese built fortifications in the interior, in the coral, in hillside caves, and in bunkers. Only rarely did individual Japanese soldiers surrender, even to a clearly superior enemy force. To defeat them it became necessary to advance toward a heavily defended position, often facing thundering mortar barrages or, if close enough, withering machine-gun fire, grenades, or intense rifle fire. A Marine corporal from Carbon Hill, Clarence Nicholas, defied the odds when he single-handedly destroyed a Japanese pillbox that he stumbled upon behind the lines on Peleliu.[53] Few combatants were so fortunate. Of the 235 members of Sledgehammer's unit—Company K, Third Battalion, Fifth Regiment,

First Division—that landed at Peleliu, only 85 came through un-scathed. His unit suffered over 60 percent casualties.

Replacements arriving on the front lines were bewildered not only by the incessant gunfire but also by the squalid conditions they found. Many times, Sledge and the few remaining veterans never even learned their names: "They came up confused, frightened and hopeful, got wounded or killed, and went right back to the rear on the route by which they had come, shocked, bleeding or stiff. They were forlorn figures coming up to the meat grinder . . . and going right back out of it like unread books on a shelf."[54] At Okinawa, where Sledge's unit went through fifty days of "hell," casualties—including original members and replacements—exceeded 100 percent. Only 26 of the original 235 members and only 24 of the 254 replacements survived. As one of the few members of his company not to receive a Purple Heart, Sledge claims that he escaped as a "fugitive from the law of averages."[55]

While the battles in the Philippines and for the Pacific islands gripped the public's attention, a "forgotten war" in the China-Burma-India theater—involving a quarter-million American troops—straggled along. Japan's conquest of Burma threatened India with nationalist insurrection and left China isolated. For years an American, General Joseph Stilwell, had served as military attaché in China and since 1942 as chief of staff to Chiang Kai-shek's army. In India, the arrival of General William Slim to command a British imperial army that operated jointly with Stilwell's forces partially restored morale.[56] Irregular troops, such as Merrill's Marauders and Orde Wingate's Chindits, developed guerrilla tactics for jungle warfare to keep the Japanese off balance.

American planners regarded China as vital to the struggle against Japan. Not only did the forces of Chiang Kai-shek's Kuomintang and Mao Tse-tung's communist movement tie down large numbers of Japanese troops but eventually, it was thought, China would become a base from which the Allies would operate against Japan. In 1942 supplies reached China by air from India, but the 100 planes flying across the "Hump" could deliver only 5,000 tons of Lend-Lease supplies to China monthly.

Vital, therefore, was the need for a road from India's eastern prov-ince, Assam, across northern Burma into southern China. Already existing was an old Burma road, but it was in a sorry state of repair over its course of some 600 miles from Mong Yu in northern Burma to Kunming in China's Yunnan province. From Kunming the road led north to Chungking, Chiang Kai-shek's headquarters. Earlier surveys indicated the most feasible route out of India would be from Ledo in Assam, across the Patkai Mountains and across the Irrawady River to Mong Yu, where it would intersect with the old Burma road. The 500-mile route crossed some of the most difficult terrain and climate on earth. If the road were ever completed—and there were many skeptics—it would be one of history's greatest engineering feats.

Construction on the Ledo Road began in late 1942, but because it progressed only slowly, a new supervising engineer—General Lewis A. Pick—was put in charge of the project.[57] Pick, an adopted Alabamian, was a native of Virginia who had commanded an engineering company in the hard-fought Meuse-Argonne offensive in 1918. After World War I his military career took him to the ROTC program at API where he married Alice Cary, whose father had founded the college's School of Veterinary Medicine. Prior to building the Ledo Road, Pick's most ambitious undertaking was the development of a billion-dollar flood-control plan for the Missouri Valley.

Burdened by lack of supplies, torrential monsoon rains, mud slides, malaria, dysentery, leeches, and occasionally Japanese soldiers, the 28,000 "engineers" and 35,000 local laborers pushed a mile a day through jungle, across swollen rivers, and over tropical mountains. Supplies were dropped by plane or arrived by pack animals. By early 1945 "Pick's Pike" neared completion. Leaving Ledo in January, it took nearly a month for the first convoy, with General Pick at its head, to reach China, where a tumultuous crowd greeted the Americans on 4 February 1945 as they drove through the pavilioned gateway at Kunming.

In the following months more than 5,000 vehicles traveled over the Ledo-Burma road to deliver tens of thousands of tons of supplies to America's Chinese allies. Defying Winston Churchill's prediction that the road would not be completed before the war ended, General Pick and his "road gang" built what incontestably can be called "the greatest military highway undertaken."[58] Perhaps as important as the highway itself was the four-inch pipeline for petroleum laid alongside the road from Ledo to Myitkyina, which became the principal terminus for air transports flying into China.

Much disagreement was generated over the question of whether the amount of supplies delivered over the road justified the costs and the enormous efforts. Fortunately, American success in driving the Japanese out of the Philippines and taking islands such as Iwo Jima and Okinawa much nearer to the Japanese home islands ended the war sooner than had been predicted in late 1942 when the Ledo Road was begun. Had it been necessary, as earlier war plans envisioned, to use China as the main base from which to operate against the Japanese homeland, the Ledo Road and the Burma campaign would have been crucial to Japan's defeat.

In the campaign for the Philippines, the Dixie Division—now under the command of Major General Clarence E. Martin—remained in the thick of events. In November 1944, while most of the division was securing Morotai, one battalion from the 167th Regiment engaged in vicious combat against well-entrenched Japanese troops on the small island of Mapia off western New Guinea. At the same time elements of the 124th Regiment took the unfortified Asia Island group.[59] Krueger's Sixth Army in the meantime opened fronts on Leyte, Mindoro, and Luzon islands and began advancing toward Manila.

In April 1945 the Dixie Division landed at Parang on the Philippine island of Mindanao. Some units, such as the 167th Regiment patrolling the Taloma Trail outside Davao, suffered some of the heaviest casualties of the war during this period. Corporal Harry R. Harr, a native of Pennsylvania serving with the 124th Regiment, became Dixie Division's only Congressional Medal of Honor recipient. When his machine-gun squad's position came under heavy enemy fire near Maglamin, Mindanao, in early June 1945, he threw himself on a grenade to save the lives of four fellow soldiers.[60] Following Japan's surrender in mid-August 1945, large numbers of Japanese troops surrendered to the Thirty-first Division on Mindanao. The Dixie Division had made a major contribution to the victories of Krueger's Sixth Army and to MacArthur's triumphs in New Guinea and in the Philippines.

As the drive across the central Pacific reached closer to Japan in early 1944, Admiral Nimitz reorganized the Marine command, making Holland Smith commander of the Fleet Marine Force Pacific. This promotion, however, removed him from operational command. At Iwo Jima in February 1945, Smith shared command with Admirals Raymond A. Spruance and R. Kelly Turner. Major General Harry

Schmidt, who had succeeded Smith as Fifth Amphibious Corps commander, led the troops onto the beaches. Smith, along with Secretary of the Navy James V. Forrestal, observed the Iwo Jima operation from aboard Turner's flagship, *Eldorado,* where "Howlin' Mad" once again fretted over the limited bombardment preceding the landing.

Iwo Jima, a volcanic rock, was useless except as an air base from which fighters could rendezvous with B-29 bombers coming from their bases in the Marianas to drop their loads on Japanese cities and industries. Nearly 30,000 Americans hit the beaches of Iwo Jima with little opposition on 19 February 1945, but taking out the pillboxes, bunkers, and fortified caves proved costly. The capture of the island produced more American casualties—7,000 dead and twice that many wounded—than any other battle in the Pacific up to that point in time. Assisting the medical corpsmen was Rex, a German shepherd from Birmingham who was wounded while delivering blood plasma to units at the front.[61] Japan suffered even more staggering casualties. Of the nearly 22,000 Japanese troops garrisoned at Iwo Jima, only 1,100 survived.

After Iwo Jima was secured and its airfields made operational, increased fighter protection could be given General Curtis LeMay's long-range bombers. High-altitude conventional bombing rocked Japan by day. At night, low-altitude incendiary bombs scorched the cities. The most destructive raid prior to the atomic bombs came in March 1945 when 334 Superfortresses from Guam, Saipan, and Tinian—and protected by fighters from Iwo Jima—dropped newly developed and highly destructive incendiary bombs on Japan, setting off fire storms in Tokyo that killed an estimated 90,000 civilians and caused the water in the canals to boil.[62] Some of the small but highly lethal bombs filled with a jellylike material called napalm were manufactured at the Huntsville Arsenal.[63]

Hundreds of American aviators flying B-29s made emergency landings at Iwo Jima when, returning from bombing missions over Japan, they were unable to reach their bases in the Marianas. As Ben Johnson, a physician from Bessemer and flight surgeon on Iwo Jima, has pointed out, many of the accidents and emergencies were caused by the stress and fatigue of flight crews and their planes.[64] Fighter escort pilots in cramped cockpits flew one and sometimes two round-trip missions of

1,500 miles from Iwo Jima to Japan on a daily basis. When exhausted bomber crews passed over Iwo Jima after their bombing runs over the Japanese home islands, they still had another 300 miles to fly before reaching their bases in the Marianas.

The island of Okinawa, lying less than 400 miles from Kyushu, was the last objective before a direct assault could be undertaken against the main Japanese islands. When American troops stormed ashore on Easter Day, 1 April 1945, Army General Simon Buckner was in command of the operation. It took nearly two months to subdue the Japanese in some of the most bitter fighting of the war.

For Eugene Sledge, already hardened by the bitter fighting at Peleliu, Okinawa proved more unnerving and physically enervating. Sledge encountered civilians, caught in a confused, lethal crossfire, whose condition was pitiful. Adding to the misery were the torrential rains that began falling in the third week of May, just as Company K began an assault on Half Moon Hill. Sledge thought he "had been flung into hell's own cesspool." Bodies half covered with mud and whose hands clutched rusting rifles lay where they had been felled by bullets or shrapnel. "For several feet around each corpse," Sledge remembers, "maggots crawled about in the muck and then were washed away by the runoff of the rain." Everywhere, the "smell of death saturated my nostrils. It was there with every breath I took."[65] Although some Japanese—about 7,000—surrendered, another 110,000 were killed or committed suicide. For the Americans, the battle for Okinawa took the lives of 12,500—including General Buckner, who was killed by flying shrapnel—and an additional 40,000 were wounded.[66]

In April 1945, as the Okinawa assault was getting under way, the Allies began planning for an invasion of the Japanese home islands. Victory was in sight. The "Great Marianas Turkey Shoot" in the Philippine Sea, in which over 300 Japanese aircraft from Guam and from Admiral Ozawa's carrier force were destroyed almost a year earlier, broke the back of Japanese air power, and gave the Allies air supremacy in the Pacific. General Douglas MacArthur had waded ashore in the Philippines in early January, and Manila was cleared in March. Japanese armies had been defeated in Burma, and supplies were reaching China over the Ledo Road. American bombers were pounding Japan's cities, harbors, industries, and communications network.

Germany was collapsing, and Adolf Hitler committed suicide in his Berlin bunker.

Franklin Roosevelt's death in April 1945 elevated Vice President Harry Truman from Missouri to the presidency and made him commander in chief of American military forces. For the first time Truman learned about the Manhattan Project, which had developed a feasible way to build bombs from uranium and plutonium. In mid-July an atomic bomb was successfully detonated in the New Mexico desert near Alamogordo. For Truman, the decision to use atomic bombs against Japan was a military, not a moral, decision. With little hesitation, Truman approved the use of atomic bombs to end the war with Japan as quickly as possible and with as little loss of life as practicable.

On 6 August 1945 a B-29—the *Enola Gay*—took off from Tinian carrying an atomic bomb. The pilot was Colonel Paul Tibbets, who along with Edgewood's Tom Borders three years earlier had flown the first American bombing mission against German targets on the European continent. The U-235 bomb, nicknamed "Little Boy," snuffed out 80,000 lives at Hiroshima. Three days later, another atomic bomb—"Fat Boy"—fell on Nagasaki, killing immediately another 35,000 Japanese. Simultaneously, the Soviet Union declared war against Japan and Soviet troops poured into the puppet state of Manchukuo.

On the following day, Emperor Hirohito indicated Japan's willingness to consider peace proposals. On 15 August 1945, the emperor—in the first public broadcast by a Japanese emperor—announced his nation's surrender. Occupation forces began arriving in Japan two weeks later. American warships, including the USS *Alabama,* sailed into Tokyo Bay, and on 2 September General Douglas MacArthur presided over Japan's formal surrender aboard the USS *Missouri.*[67] It was now time for the peacemakers to begin their work to create a new order in the Pacific and in Asia that guaranteed peace with justice. A new era in warfare had dawned, posing new challenges to the very survival of humanity.

Twelve

The End of the War

y mid-1944 Allied triumph seemed certain. Most Alabamians, in service or on the home front, probably shared the sentiments of Lieutenant Charlie Beavers of Birmingham. Writing from Italy to his uncle Jack, Charlie Beavers confidently—but without arrogance or malice—predicted that the United States was going to win this war:

> We'll win this war, Jack, people like myself will win it, for winning the war means returning to home, and home and what it stands for is what we are fighting for. Americans are not good soldiers, but they are the best fighters in the world. They are not good soldiers because they don't know how to hate, but they are the best fighters, because they have the best thing in the world to fight for.
>
> Let's hope it won't be too long before we can go down to the river again. I might want to look up one of those girls you were talking about, and take her along too.[1]

Allied strength on the battlefields, in the factories, and on farmlands at home prevailed, vindicating Charlie Beavers's optimism. Having done his part for victory, Charlie Beavers returned to Alabama to go to college.

Alabamians greeted Germany's surrender in May 1945 with much cheering and horn honking. Mayors spoke from atop fire trucks, and factory whistles shrilly proclaimed victory in Europe. Sober reflection, however, led to the realization that the rejoicing was premature. Months of savage island fighting in the Pacific lay in the future. An editorial in the *Birmingham World* anticipated that the war against Japan "may easily prove long and costly."[2] Thus, President Truman's decision to drop atomic bombs, which hastened the end of the war, found little condemnation at the time. Although Alabamians recognized the destructive power of the dawning atomic age and dimly comprehended the chilling dangers it held for the future, they welcomed Japan's defeat in August with unrestrained enthusiasm.

Within minutes of President Truman's announcement on 14 August 1945 that Emperor Hirohito had agreed to surrender, crowds poured into the streets of Alabama's towns. Businesses closed so employees could join the revelry. In Montgomery, automobiles and pedestrians surged up and down Dexter Avenue between the capitol and the Exchange Hotel. In a scene reminiscent of Mount Suribachi on Iwo Jima, a boy climbed to the top of the fountain on Court Square where he planted a small American flag. In Birmingham a "tin can band" formed spontaneously to lead a parade down Fourth Avenue, while pedestrians jitterbugged on sidewalks. Jalopies filled with flag-waving teenagers careened through town. Servicemen waded through confetti-filled streets, kissing as many girls as possible. Liquor sales in wet counties were halted. Montgomery's commissioner of public safety hoped, none too optimistically, that the merrymaking would soon end so that people would be in a sufficiently sober mood for thanksgiving services in area churches on the following day.[3]

Alabamians rejoiced not only over the impending return of the troops from overseas but also for the end of rationing, blackouts, housing shortages, and other home-front inconveniences. Restrictions on gasoline purchases were immediately rescinded. After an absence of more than three years, "fill 'er up" was once again heard at the gasoline pump. At first, drivers went on a binge and for several weeks most service stations ran out of gasoline by the end of every day. Rationing of tires, sugar, and meats, however, continued for several more months.

At great cost in lives and treasure, the Allies had repulsed the aggression and militarism of the Axis nations. It is estimated that 50 million persons perished as a result of the conflict, and millions more were left homeless or scarred physically or psychologically for life.[4] Of all the combatants, Russia suffered the most casualties, having lost as many as 7 million battle deaths and another 7 million civilian deaths. Proportionately, Poland suffered the greatest casualties—approximately 6 million (nearly half of whom were Jews), which amounted to about 20 percent of its prewar population.

Among the Axis nations, Germany had more than 4 million battle deaths and nearly 600,000 civilians killed (60 percent of whom were women), many of them in air raids on Hamburg, Dresden, Berlin, and other military targets. Including civilian deaths, more than 300,000

V-E Day, 20 May 1945, at the ADDSCO shipyard. (ADDSCO Collection, University of South Alabama Archives)

Italians lost their lives. Over 20 percent of the 5 million Japanese inducted into military service were killed. The atomic bombs dropped on Hiroshima and Nagasaki quickly came to symbolize the destructiveness of war on civilian populations, but conventional and fire bombing of Japanese cities left nearly 90,000 dead in Tokyo and another 260,000 civilians entombed in the smoldering ruins of Osaka, Kobe, Yokohama, and other industrial cities, which were 60 percent destroyed at war's end.

Virtually every Alabamian had a loved one, relative, or friend serving abroad. One-third of Alabama's male population—321,000 of 938,000 adult males—had volunteered or were drafted for military service. Thousands of Alabama women also served as Wacs, Waves, Spars, WASPs, or as nurses. Of the more than 15 million Americans who served in the armed forces, nearly 300,000—or 2 percent—lost their lives and 800,000 were wounded. More than 4,500 Alabamians lost their lives in combat or perished in prisoner of war camps. Approximately 75 percent of Alabama's war deaths, or 3,400, occurred in the Army and Army Air Corps. Another 1,100 Alabamians in the Navy, Marine Corps, and Coast Guard gave their lives.[5] Nearly 20 percent of Alabama's naval casualties came from Birmingham alone.[6]

Without doubt, the Second World War—following on the heels of the Great Depression—had a greater impact on Alabama than any event since the Civil War. Wartime labor shortages and higher manufacturing wages produced unparalleled economic opportunities for Alabamians on the home front. A vast migration from countryside to cities in Alabama and the industrial North and West Coast, involving nearly 10 percent of Alabama's rural whites and more than 25 percent of rural blacks, occurred during the 1940s. Women, too, acquired greater mobility. At the height of World War II, women made up nearly a quarter of Alabama's work force. Similarly, the war broadened opportunities for black Alabamians to gain better-paying jobs at shipyards, aircraft modification plants, steel mills, and ordnance works. Although the impending defeat of the Axis led to defense cutbacks, layoffs, and plant closings, especially of the ordnance works, Alabama's industrial base remained larger in the immediate postwar period than ever before. Industrial wages in 1946 were three times greater than they had been in the prewar era. Measured by public investments in defense plants and purchases of military goods at the peak of wartime production, Alabama profited more from World War II than any other state in the South.[7]

Both economically and politically, Alabama joined the mainstream of American life. Neither before nor since has Alabama enjoyed as much political influence in Washington as during the late 1930s and the war years. At the same time, the war touched a raw nerve. While on the one hand the war had an integrating effect and seemed to heal fissures left over from the Civil War and Reconstruction, the vast expanse of federal power during the depression and in the war years aggravated a dispute over states' rights. This quarrel, especially as it related to race relations, would culminate in later years in a bitter division among Alabama's Democrats and the emergence of the Dixiecrat movement.

The war also had a globalizing and educating effect on Alabamians. Uprooted by the tens of thousands from their farms and towns, they came to know other regions of the United States as well as other parts of the world. Because two-thirds of the nation's military bases were located below the Mason-Dixon line, millions of servicemen and servicewomen from diverse areas of the nation came south for their training.[8] The end of the war and the GI Bill launched a democratic era in education. In 1941 less than 7 percent of Alabama's adult population had obtained any schooling beyond high school. Indeed, only 22 percent of the population had gone beyond the eighth grade. By 1950 the number of Alabamians with some college education had increased by 43 percent, and the percentage of Alabamians with at least some high school education had risen to almost 30 percent. Increased opportunities in higher education had the most dramatic impact on black Alabamians. By 1950 there had been a 90 percent increase in the number of African-Americans in the state with at least one year of college education.[9]

For the second time in a generation, Americans had been called upon to go to war in defense of liberty and freedom. Once again, most Alabamians selflessly bore their sacrifices with dignity. As best they could, Alabamians—in a world that promised never to be quite the same—set about restoring normalcy to their lives. Some Alabamians feared the social, economic, political, and moral forces that wartime had unleashed in the nation, while for others the future held great promise. World War II presented the state and its people with a unique opportunity to transform society. Whether the war became a genuine watershed in the history of Alabama and the South remained a question for the future.

Alabama's War Heroes

World War II revealed some of the worst evils of which human nature is capable. It also summoned forth honorable, indeed noble, behavior. Numerous Alabamians served beyond the call of duty or performed acts of gallantry and heroism. Oftentimes those deeds were recorded only in the memories of those who performed them or their comrades. Occasionally, acts of personal bravery or uncommon performance were rewarded by public recognition.

Action in the Pacific provided the first test of strength and character in combat. Eager to have an authentic hero, newspapers hailed Auburn's Hoyt "Hap" Jolly, an Army Air Corps captain, as Alabama's first war hero. Jolly, who received his wings in 1940, was seriously wounded when leading his squadron of four Flying Fortresses against a Japanese airdrome and harbor facilities in the South Pacific.[1] Private First Class Verbon C. Sanders of Montgomery, who received the Silver Star for gallantry in action on Guadalcanal, was another early war hero. Marine Lieutenant Howell Heflin of Leighton, a future chief justice of the Alabama Supreme Court and United States senator, led his platoon against a heavily defended Japanese position in the jungles of Bougainville in 1943. A fierce three-hour firefight under "a deluge of grenades and gunfire" merited a Silver Star for young Heflin, who was invited to make numerous appearances during a visit to Alabama later in the war.[2]

From its inception in 1862, the Medal of Honor has been recognized as the nation's most distinguished award for gallantry and sacrifice in combat. Of the 469 Medals of Honor conferred upon servicemen during World War II, 12 went to men with Alabama connections. Seven of the recipients entered service from Alabama and were credited to the state. Five others had been born or lived in Alabama but entered service in another state. Jefferson and Madison counties each produced two recipients of the Medal of Honor.

The first Alabamian to be honored by a Medal of Honor during the Second World War was Charles W. Davis, a native of Gordo in Pickens County, who was commended for gallantry in the Battle of Galloping Horse Hill on Guadalcanal.[3] When the medal was awarded several months later, it marked the first time in U.S. military history that the Medal of Honor had been bestowed in the field. "Gordo" Davis attended high school in Montgomery and pitched baseball for the University of Alabama. As an Army captain in the Twenty-fifth Infantry Division fighting in the jungles of the Solomon Islands in January 1943, he volunteered to take orders to the forward companies in his battalion, which were pinned down by gunfire near the crest of Galloping Horse Hill. Remaining on the front lines, he led an assault against Japanese machine guns. When his rifle jammed, Davis unholstered his pistol, which he waved in the air while charging the enemy line. This act of bravery inspired others to join the attack against enemy positions. Davis came home to a hero's welcome and to see his first child, who was born during his absence.

Madison County celebrated the return of its two Medal of Honor recipients with a festive parade in Huntsville that drew a crowd of 10,000 jubilant people. Lieutenant Cecil "Bushy" Bolton was a professional boxer who was born in Florida but had moved to Madison County, where he entered service. He became one of Alabama's most decorated soldiers. As a member of the 104th Timberwolf Infantry Division, which first engaged the enemy in combat in October 1944, he participated in an Allied thrust across the Mark River in Holland in early November. Despite receiving wounds in both legs, Lieutenant Bolton led a bazooka team across an icy canal in chest-deep water, knocked out a machine-gun nest, and, in the dimly moonlit night, silenced an 88-mm gun firing on American positions. Wounded again, Bolton ordered his men to return to their unit without him, while he crawled back to his unit and collapsed.[4] The actions of Bolton's squad enabled the battalion to push the German line beyond the Maas River estuary.

Staff Sergeant Paul Bolden was cut from a somewhat different swatch. He was a quiet-spoken farm boy who was born in Iowa but grew up in Madison County. He entered combat on 15 June 1944, which also happened to be his twenty-second birthday. "I didn't think I would last two minutes," he later recounted.[5] On Christmas Eve 1944, his Company I of the Thirtieth Infantry Division was pinned down by withering fire emanating from a house in the town of Petit-Coo in Belgium. Inching their way forward, Bolden and a comrade reached the German position. After tossing two grenades into the house, Bolden rushed through the door, only to find thirty-five SS troops inside. Catching the Germans by surprise, Bolden killed twenty of them with grenades or bursts from his submachine gun. The survivors returned fire, wounding Bolden in the shoulder, chest, and stomach and killing his comrade across the street. Mustering his strength, Bolden dashed back into the house, firing away and killing the remaining fifteen SS troops. This brazen and impetuous attack against impossible odds cleared the way for his company's advance through Petit-Coo.[6]

Two Marine recipients of the Medal of Honor from Alabama, Private

First Class John Henry New of Mobile and Sergeant Ross Franklin Gray of Marvel Valley in Bibb County, were killed in some of the fiercest fighting in the Pacific. As a member of the First Marine Division, New fought in what Eugene Sledge, himself a survivor of the Peleliu campaign in September 1944, called the "assault into Hell."[7] The island of Peleliu was a rabbit warren of caves and other redoubts. It was from such a cave that a Japanese soldier tossed a grenade at a Marine mortar team. In utter disregard for his own safety, Private New hurled himself on the grenade to save the life of his fellow Marines.

Sergeant Ross Gray, also awarded the Medal of Honor posthumously, fought at Iwo Jima. Known to his fellow soldiers in the Fourth Marine Division as "the Deacon" or the "Fightin' Preacher," Gray had been a minister before the war. As a platoon sergeant on the third day of the assault on the volcanic island in February 1945, Gray single-handedly cleared a mine field and destroyed six Japanese positions, saving his platoon from certain destruction.[8]

Two Jefferson County natives in the Army Air Forces received the nation's highest award for valor. One was Lieutenant William R. Lawley, Jr., a Leeds native and the son of a Baptist minister. Shortly after the Japanese attack on Pearl Harbor, twenty-four-year-old Lawley enlisted in the Army Air Corps. By early 1944 Lawley commanded a Flying Fortress named *Cabin in the Sky* with the Eighth Air Force in England. On his tenth bombing mission over the Continent, about twenty German fighters attacked his bomber, severely damaging his controls. With the plane in a steep dive and an engine in flames, Lawley ordered the crew to bail out. But two crew members were so badly injured that parachuting from the plane was out of the question. Though wounded himself by a cannon shell that shattered the windshield and killed his copilot, Lieutenant Lawley pulled the plane from its steep dive, through skillful flying put out the fires, and managed to make a belly landing on a British airfield with only one engine still functioning.[9] This incredible feat of grit and skill earned him one of the fourteen Medals of Honor awarded to members of the Eighth Air Force.

Jefferson County's other Medal of Honor winner, Staff Sergeant Henry "Red" Erwin, hailed from Adamsville. At the age of twelve, following the death of his coal-miner father, Erwin began working in a grocery store. At the height of the depression he quit school to take a job with the Civilian Conservation Corps. From his salary of thirty dollars a month he managed to send twenty-two dollars to his mother. Because he was smart and willing to take the initiative, Erwin rose quickly in the CCC and, by taking an equivalency exam, earned a high school diploma. In the early 1940s he found a better-paying job at Fairfield Steel. Because he was working in a vital defense industry, Erwin could have obtained a deferment, but when the draft board said either he or a younger brother would be inducted, Erwin volunteered for the Army Air Forces.

Staff Sergeant Erwin became a radio operator on *City of Los Angeles,* a B-29 Superfortress, and by spring 1945 he was in the Pacific. On his second mission over Tokyo, a phosphorous bomb used as a visual marker for the group's bombing run accidentally detonated inside the plane. Sergeant Erwin picked up the burning explosive and, although seriously injured and nearly blinded by the blast, managed to toss the device from the plane. As the smoke cleared in the cockpit, the pilot regained control of the plunging aircraft and at an altitude of 300 feet pulled the plane out of its steep dive. Commending Erwin for his selfless actions, President Truman authorized an immediate conferral of the Medal of Honor. Having to break into a display case on Pearl Harbor to get a medal, Army personnel rushed the award to the sergeant's hospital bed. Upon his return to Alabama, citizens of Bessemer poured into the streets to welcome Erwin as a hero. The road to recovery was difficult. Over the next two years Red Erwin had no less than thirty-three operations, mostly skin grafts, but his buoyant spirit endeared him to everyone.[10]

Five other recipients of the Medal of Honor were born in Alabama but credited to other states. David McCampbell, born in Bessemer in 1910, became the Navy's leading World War II ace. After entering service in Florida, McCampbell obtained an appointment to the United States Naval Academy. In the early months of the war, he flew Hellcats and was aboard the carrier *Wasp* when Japanese submarines sank it on 15 September 1942 off the Solomon Islands. Surviving that incident, Commander McCampbell became an inspiring leader of Air Group Fifteen—the Fabled Fifteen—which flew off the carrier *Enterprise* in the Philippine Sea in 1944. In June, when the task force came under attack by 80 Japanese aircraft, his squadron routed the enemy. McCampbell shot down 7 planes, establishing the Navy record for most enemy aircraft shot down by one pilot in a single day. Four months later— with the odds stacked against them—he and another Hellcat pilot fended off 60 Japanese planes bearing down on the *Enterprise* and the fleet. Single-handedly, McCampbell shot down 9 Japanese planes, thus breaking his old record and setting a new one that remains the American combat record for enemy aircraft destroyed in a single day.[11] Altogether, Commander McCampbell was credited with knocking 34 enemy planes from the skies of the South Pacific, making him the most successful Navy pilot in the Second World War. In addition, he destroyed 20 Japanese planes on the ground. His Air Group Fifteen destroyed more enemy aircraft—315 in dogfights and 348

Lieutenant Howell Heflin received a Silver Star for leading an attack on a heavily defended Japanese position at Bougainville in the Pacific. (Courtesy of Howell Heflin)

Red Erwin was the first B-29 crew member to receive the Congressional Medal of Honor. (U.S. Army photograph, courtesy of American Legion)

on the ground—and more shipping tonnage than any other group in the Pacific. For his "extraordinary heroism" and "outstanding leadership," McCampbell was awarded the Navy Cross and the Medal of Honor. Promoted to captain, McCampbell held a number of command and staff positions after World War II.

Two Medal of Honor recipients were born in Tuscumbia but entered service in other states. Private Wilson Douglas Watson, whose family moved to Arkansas, was honored for his bravery and inspiring leadership in two pitched battles against seemingly impregnable Japanese positions on Iwo Jima in late February 1945. In the European theater, Lieutenant Jack Treadwell, who joined the Army in Oklahoma, single-handedly rushed and captured six German pillboxes on the Siegfried line. His bravery and success inspired his company to follow him into fierce enemy gunfire, driving a wedge in the German position and effectively breaking up enemy resistance.

Jake Lindsey, born in the Isney community of Choctaw County, had moved to Mississippi before entering service. As a technical sergeant in the Sixteenth Infantry Regiment, First Infantry Division, he saw action in western Germany. During a fierce German counterattack in November 1944 east of Aachen, Lindsey's sharpshooting knocked out two machine-gun nests, forced two tanks to withdraw, and halted enemy flanking movements. Although wounded, the sergeant took on eight Germans in close-range combat, killing three and capturing three. Lindsey's courageous action enabled his platoon to escape serious harm.[12]

The nation's first submarine commander in World War II to receive the Medal of Honor was Howard Walter Gilmore, who was born in Selma in 1902.[13] After enlisting in the Navy, he entered the naval academy through examination. He flourished at Annapolis, where he was in the top 10 percent of his class. Following graduation in 1926, Gilmore began a very successful career in the submarine arm, eventually commanding the USS *Growler*.

After operating in the Aleutians, Gilmore's submarine was transferred to the South Pacific. On New Year's Day 1943 he left Brisbane on his fourth war mission, searching for Japanese shipping between Rabaul and the Solomons. In mid-January the *Growler* sank two troop transports and at the end of the month again made frequent contacts with the enemy. In early February Gilmore encountered a Japanese convoy that aggressively fought back. By now the Japanese were arming their merchant vessels with deck guns manned by trained gun crews. Unknown to the U.S. Navy, the Japanese were better able to detect and locate American radar.

During the night of 7 February, as the *Growler* waited patiently on the surface for Japanese shipping, the watch suddenly spotted a vessel less than two miles away. In the darkness, Gilmore maneuvered to attack. The Japanese craft, a heavily armed auxiliary, abruptly reversed course and steamed straight for the *Growler*. Too late to fire torpedoes, Gilmore decided to ram the Japanese vessel. Suddenly, his submarine came under intense machine-gun fire, wounding Gilmore and killing two crewmen. With the Japanese vessel closing quickly, the only hope to save the submarine and its crew was to take it down as quickly as possible. Badly wounded and unable to move, Gilmore gave the order "Clear the bridge!" The remaining members of the watch scurried through the conning tower hatch. In the control room at the bottom of the ladder, the executive officer waited for the skipper. With time running out and with the Japanese still raking the deck with their .50-caliber machine guns, Gilmore issued his final order, "Take her down!" As the submarine plunged to safety, the sea swept the bodies of the *Growler*'s skipper and the two sailors overboard. Gilmore's selfless concern for the welfare of his vessel and its crew became legendary in the submarine service.

Alabamians took note of the heroes on the home front as well. The *Birmingham Post* launched a contest in August 1942 to honor the "Alabama War Mother" and "Alabama War Grandmother." Prizes of fifty-dollar war bonds were to be awarded to the mothers and grandmothers with the most "boys" in service. Taking an early lead was Mrs. William B. McDonald of Huntsville, who had six sons in service—four in the Army and one each in the Navy and Marines. In addition, her husband worked in one of the arsenals.[14] The paper noted that the Crommelin family of Wetumpka had five sons in the Navy, four of them aviators and the fifth the commander of a destroyer. There were six Taylor brothers from Opp in service. Mrs. James Jones of Frisco City had four sons in World War I and ten grandsons in World War II. Emma Grady—billed as the mother who "backs the attack"—sent seven sons from their farm near Montevallo into service and bought war bonds to help end the war sooner. The *Birmingham Post* declared Charity Deason of Lomax, near Clanton, as the Alabama War Mother. She had eight sons in service, five of whom were on active duty and another who died during the sinking of the aircraft carrier *Wasp*.

In a similar competition, black Alabamians selected their own Alabama War Mother. The winner, Hattie B. Fletcher, was announced during a Mother's Day rally at Birmingham's Legion Field kicking off the seventh war loan campaign. Nearly nine thousand African-Americans gathered on this Sunday in mid-May 1945 after Germany's defeat for a musical program by the Tuskegee Army Air Base band and to hear Birmingham businessman A. G. Gaston pay homage to the sacrifices of the mothers of Alabama's black servicemen.[15]

Notes

1. The Eve of War

1. Leah Rawls Atkins, *The Valley and the Hills: An Illustrated History of Birmingham and Jefferson County* (Woodland Hills, Calif.: Windsor Publications, 1981), 148.

2. *Montgomery Advertiser*, 31 December 1941. Also see Chauncey Sparks, "The Impact of War on Alabama," in Hallie Farmer, ed., *War Comes to Alabama* (University: Bureau of Public Administration, University of Alabama, 1943), 1–9.

3. *Montgomery Advertiser*, 27 January 1942.

4. "No American city underwent such drastic, sweeping change as a result of the Second World War as did Mobile," according to Melton McLaurin and Michael Thomason, *Mobile: The Life and Times of a Great Southern City* (Woodland Hills, Calif.: Windsor Publications, 1981), 123. After visiting American cities that had been transformed in the early war years, John Dos Passos described Mobile as "a city that's been taken by storm." See John Dos Passos, *State of the Nation* (Boston: Houghton Mifflin, 1944), 92.

5. McLaurin and Thomason, *Mobile*, 124.

6. Edward Boykin, *Everything's Made for Love in this Man's World: Vignettes from the Life of Frank W. Boykin* (Mobile: Privately printed, 1973), 102–3; Mary Martha Thomas, *Riveting and Rationing in Dixie: Alabama Women and the Second World War* (Tuscaloosa: University of Alabama Press, 1987), 36. Congressman Boykin was a great booster of the port city. He loved telling people that "If you can't get into Heaven, at least visit Mobile." Boykin, *Everything's Made for Love,* 59.

7. John H. Napier III, "The Military, Montgomery, and Maxwell," *Aerospace Historian* 24 (Winter 1977): 191.

8. Office of Information, Air University, Maxwell Air Force Base, *Fifty Years of Aviation at Maxwell Air Force Base, 1910–1960* (Montgomery: Air University, Maxwell Air Force Base, 1960), 41; for a general history of Maxwell Field, also see *Montgomery Salutes Maxwell and Gunter* (El Cajon, Calif.: National Military Publications, 1985).

9. Mary C. Lane, ed., "The History of Fort McClellan" (manuscript, Fisher Library, U.S. Army Chemical School, Fort McClellan, Ala., 1955; revised 1958).

10. See the very informative book by Val L. McGee, *The Origins of Fort Rucker* (Ozark, Ala.: Dale County Historical Society, 1987); on Steagall's early career, see Jack Brien Key, "Henry B. Steagall: The Conservative as a Reformer," *Alabama Review* 17 (July 1964): 198–209.

11. On the establishment of the Tuskegee Army Air Field and flight school, see Robert J. Jakeman, *The Divided Skies: Establishing Segregated Flight Training at Tuskegee, Alabama, 1934–1942* (Tuscaloosa: University of Alabama Press, 1992), especially 183–239; idem, "Jim Crow Earns His Wings: The Establishment of Segregated Flight Training at Tuskegee, Alabama, 1934–1942" (Ph.D. diss., Auburn University, 1988); Benjamin O. Davis, Jr., *Benjamin O. Davis, Jr., American: An Autobiography* (Washington, D.C.: Smithsonian Institution Press, 1991), 68–89; James R. McGovern, *Black Eagle: General Daniel 'Chappie' James, Jr.* (University: University of Alabama Press, 1985), 25–40; Robert A. Rose, *Lonely Eagles: The Story of America's Black Air Force in World War II* (Los Angeles: Tuskegee Airmen, 1976), 9–54; Von Hardesty and Dominick Pisano, *Black Wings: The*

American Black in Aviation (Washington, D.C.: Smithsonian Institution Press, 1983), 19–33; "The Negro in the Army Air Forces," in Jessie Parkhurst Guzman, ed., *Negro Year Book: A Review of Events Affecting Negro Life, 1941–1946* (Tuskegee Institute: Department of Records and Research, 1947), 354–58.

12. Jakeman, *Divided Skies*, 142–44.

13. Rose, *Lonely Eagles*, 13–14; Jakeman, *Divided Skies*, 248–49.

14. Jakeman, *Divided Skies*, 224–37.

15. Ibid., 267.

16. The issue of where to locate the black flight school generated much controversy. The east end of Tuskegee was predominantly inhabited by whites whose leaders expressed opposition to locating the base near them. A site near Chehaw, about six miles outside of town, was selected, thus allaying some misgivings in the white community. A black construction firm from Nashville, Tennessee, McKissack and McKissack, built the TAAF at a cost of nearly $2.5 million (ibid., 271–92). This was the largest construction contract awarded to a black firm during World War II (Guzman, *Negro Year Book*, 188).

17. Jakeman, *Divided Skies*, 303–4.

18. Survey of Commercialized Prostitution Conditions, February–March 1940, Alabama Governor (1939–1943: Frank Murray Dixon), Administrative Files (henceforth cited as Dixon files): Law Enforcement—Phenix City, Alabama Department of Archives and History, Montgomery.

19. Director of Public Safety, J. F. Brawner, to Governor Frank Dixon, 17 July 1941, in ibid.: Childersburg Operations.

20. Elise Hopkins Stephens, *Historic Huntsville: A City of New Beginnings* (Woodland Hills, Calif.: Windsor Publications, 1984), 106; James Record, *A Dream Come True: The Story of Madison County and Incidentally of Alabama and the United States*, 2 vols. (Huntsville: N.p., 1970–78), vol. 2; Cleo Cason and Winona Stroup, "The Early Years of Redstone Arsenal," *Huntsville Historical Review* 1 (July 1971): 29–43.

21. Maurice Matloff, ed., *American Military History*, rev. ed., Army Historical Series (Washington, D.C.: Office of the Chief of Military History, Department of the Army, 1973), 419.

22. Franklin D. Roosevelt to Governor Frank M. Dixon, 21 September 1940, Dixon files: Selective Service System Plan, September 1940–October 1941.

23. Clinton William Whitten, "Alabama Editorial Opinion on American Entry into World War II, 1939–1942" (Master's thesis, Auburn University, 1961), 118.

24. *Birmingham Age-Herald*, 30 September 1940.

25. Alabama State Military Department, Office of the Adjutant General, *Quadrennial Report of the Adjutant General for Four Year Period Ending September 30, 1942* (N.p., n.d.), 151.

26. C. A. Dykstra (National Director of Selective Service) to Governor Frank Dixon, 1 November 1940, Dixon files: Selective Service System Plan, 1940–1941.

27. Approximately $303 was spent for each class of black students in Alabama. Guzman, *Negro Year Book*, 103; also Report of Rejections, 13 November 1940, Dixon files: Selective Service System Plan, 1940–1941.

28. Alabama Military Department, *Quadrennial Report*, 46.

2. The United States Goes to War

1. Samuel Eliot Morison, *The Battle of the Atlantic, September 1939–May 1943* (Boston: Little, Brown, 1948), 27–55.

2. Ibid., 79–81.

3. *Birmingham News*, 20 October 1941. On the *Kearney* episode, see Morison, *Battle of the Atlantic*, 92–93.

4. United States War Department, Bureau of Public Relations, *World War II Honor List of Dead and Missing: State of Alabama* (Washington, D.C.: N.p., 1946).

5. Dan van der Vat, *The Atlantic Campaign: World War II's Great Struggle at Sea* (New York: Harper and Row, 1988), 210; Morison, *Battle of the Atlantic*, 94–98.

6. *Selma Times-Journal*, 8 December 1941.

7. *Montgomery Advertiser*, 7 December 1941.

8. *Birmingham Age-Herald*, 6 December 1941.

9. *Montgomery Advertiser*, 7 December 1941; *Mobile Press Register*, 7 December 1941.

10. *Selma Times-Journal*, 7 December 1941.

11. J. L. Chestnut, Jr., and Julia Cass, *Black in Selma: The Uncommon Life of J. L. Chestnut, Jr.* (New York: Farrar, Straus and Giroux, 1990), 21.

12. Roger Lax and Frederick Smith, *The Great Song Thesaurus*, 2d ed. (New York: Oxford University Press, 1989), 73–75.

13. Local newspapers regularly printed schedules of radio programs. For the programs being broadcast on the day Pearl Harbor was attacked, see, for instance, *Mobile Press Register*, 7 December 1941.

14. Hoyt M. Warren has described his reaction to events at Pearl Harbor in his World War II memoirs entitled *The Making of a Spy in the Sky: A Story of a World War II Pilot* (Abbeville, Ala.: Henry County Historical Society, 1982), 3.

15. Joan Nist, "Memories of World War II" (a talk at "World War II: A Time Remembered," conference sponsored by the Alabama Humanities Foundation and Auburn University Center for the Arts and Humanities, Auburn, 4 October 1991). Also see Tom Gordon, Scottie Vickery, and Ginny MacDonald, "The Day of Infamy Relived," *Birmingham News/Birmingham Post-Herald*, 7 December 1991, and Allen Cronenberg, "Pearl Harbor's Legacy," *Birmingham News*, 8 December 1991.

16. "The Day of Infamy Relived," *Birmingham News/Birmingham Post-Herald*, 7 December 1991.

17. *Montgomery Advertiser*, 8 December 1941.

18. *Birmingham World*, 19 December 1941. Crispus Attucks, a black merchant seaman, was one of five patriots killed by British troops in the Boston Massacre in 1770.

19. *Montgomery Advertiser*, 14 December 1941.

20. Gordon W. Prange, *At Dawn We Slept: The Untold Story of Pearl Harbor* (New York: Penguin Books, 1982), 362, 401.

21. On McMorris's command of the *San Francisco*, see Russell Harris, "Battle of Cape Esperance," *Sea Classics* 23 (April 1990): 14–21. Also see *Montgomery Advertiser*, 23 October 1944; *Birmingham News*, 29 January 1945; and George E. Jones, "Brain Center of the Pacific War," *New York Times Magazine*, 8 April 1945, sec. 6, 10–11, 38–39.

22. On the *Tautog* during the attack on Pearl Harbor and in the aftermath, see Theodore Roscoe, *United States Submarine Operations in World War II* (Annapolis: United States Naval Institute, 1949), 8–10; Clay Blair, Jr., *Silent Victory: The U.S. Submarine War against Japan* (Philadelphia: J. B. Lippincott, 1975), 83, 99; Robert Thew, "America's Most Successful Submarines," *Sea Classics* 23 (April 1990): 28–31.

23. Matloff, *American Military History*, 423–24.

24. Drafted into service, Howard and Robinson would both be killed in action during the Allied surge to the Rhine River in March 1945. Wesley P. Newton, "The Deaths of Two Alabama Soldiers" (presentation to "World War II: A Time Remembered" seminar at ADAH, 26 January 1992).

25. Photo, Auburn University Archives. This photo appeared in the 1942 *Glomerata*, Alabama Polytechnic Institute's student yearbook.

26. *Birmingham News*, 8 December 1941.

27. Ibid.; Edmund G. Love, *The 27th Infantry Division in World War II* (Washington, D.C.: Infantry Journal Press, 1949), 14–17. The Twenty-seventh "Empire" Division had the longest overseas wartime service of any division in the U.S. Army. For an account of the personnel and activities of the Twenty-seventh Division during training at Fort McClellan, see *Pictorial History: Twenty-Seventh Division, United States Army, 1940–1941* (Atlanta: Army-Navy Publishers, 1941).

28. Basil Collier, *The War in the Far East, 1941–1945: A Military History* (London: Heinemann, 1969), 202–19.

29. Ronald H. Spector, *Eagle against the Sun: The American War with Japan* (New York: Free Press, 1985), 106–9.

30. *Birmingham News*, 25 January 1942, 11 February 1945; *Birmingham Age-Herald*, 29 August 1945.

31. See a feature article in the *Birmingham News*, 25 November 1945, which describes Barker's life in considerable detail. Copy in Birmingham Public Library, Tutwiler Collection of Southern History, "World War II Scrapbooks, 1939–1945," vol. 6.

32. Louis Taruc, *Born of the People* (Westport, Conn.: Greenwood Press, 1973), 70–73; Benedict John Kerkvliet, *The Huk Rebellion: A Study of Peasant Revolt in the Philippines* (Berkeley and Los Angeles: University of California Press, 1977), 114–15.

33. *Birmingham News*, 25 November 1945; see program for "Memorial Service—Captain Joseph Rhett Barker, II—26th Cavalry, Philippine Scouts, U.S.A." in "World War II Scrapbooks," vol. 6.

3. Alabama Goes to War

1. Lee Kennett, *For the Duration: The United States Goes to War, Pearl Harbor—1942* (New York: Charles Scribner's Sons, 1985), 15, quoting from *December 7: The First Thirty Hours* by correspondents of *Time*, *Life*, and *Fortune* (New York: Alfred A. Knopf, 1942), 20.

2. *Montgomery Advertiser*, 10 December 1941.

3. Cited in Maxine D. Jones and Joe M. Richardson, *Talladega College: The First Century* (Tuscaloosa: University of Alabama Press, 1990), 140.

4. German Foreign Minister Joachim Ribbentrop handed his government's declaration of war to the American chargé d'affaires in Berlin at noon, German time, on 11 December 1941. Less than two hours later, Benito Mussolini declared war on the United States during a four-minute speech to 150,000 people assembled on Rome's Piazza Venezia. In Washington, both houses of Congress voted unanimously—with Jeanette Rankin abstaining—for war against the European Axis powers. Mary H. Williams, ed., *U.S. Army in World War II: Chronology, 1941–1945* (Washington, D.C.: Office of the Chief of Military History, Department of the Army, 1960), 4; *New York Times*, 12 December 1941.

5. Faye A. Axford, *Limestone County during World War II* (Athens, Ala.: Limestone County Historical Society, 1983), 14.

6. *Mobile Press Register*, 17 May 1942.

7. *Alabama* 7 (24 April 1942): 5; Public Information Subject Files—General, SG6952, Folder 568: "Defense Program WWII," ADAH.

8. Axford, *Limestone County*, 14.

9. Dixon files: Governor's Speeches, 14 March 1942.

10. A useful contemporary account of the CAP's origins and activities is William B. Mellor, Jr., *Sank Same* (New York: Howell, Soskin, 1944).

11. Hank Jones, "50 Years of Civilian Air Patrol," *Retired Officer Magazine* (January 1992): 38–42. Logs of U-boats that operated in American waters frequently make note of crash dives on account of aircraft sightings, especially "flying boats" but also smaller craft. See, for example, War Diary of U-67, 31 March 1942–8 August 1942, PG 30664, National Archives Microfilm Publication T-1022, roll 3030. The U-boat's commander, Gunter Müller-Stöckheim, described frequent dives because of aircraft. At the time of his mission in the Gulf of Mexico in June and July 1942, the Navy had only a handful of bombers conducting antisubmarine flights. When aircraft were sighted in the distance, U-boat captains could not run the risk of remaining on the surface. On 16 June 1942, for example, U-67 had just passed through the Florida Straits and entered the Gulf of Mexico. Müller-Stöckheim sighted a stream of smoke on the horizon and decided to give chase to what appeared to be a freighter. An hour into the chase, the lookout spotted an airplane at a great altitude and some two to three miles away. Sounding the alarm, U-67 rapidly submerged. Fifty minutes later, when the U-boat searched the horizon with its periscope, nothing was to be seen. "Anyhow," Müller-Stöckheim wrote in his log, "I could not catch up with my freighter." War Diary of U-67, 16 June 1942.

12. Karl Doenitz, *Memoirs: Ten Years and Twenty Days* (Annapolis: Naval Institute Press, 1990), 223; also see Michael Gannon, *Operation Drumbeat: The Dramatic True Story of Germany's First U-Boat Attacks along the American Coast in World War II* (New York: Harper and Row, 1990), 388–89.

13. Gannon, *Operation Drumbeat*, 347.

14. War Diary of U-506, 26 March 1942–15 June 1942, PG30566/2, National Archives Microfilm Publication T1022, roll 3066.

15. Gannon, *Operation Drumbeat*, 344–45.

16. *Mobile Press Register*, 16 May 1942.

17. Remembering her childhood, Leah Rawls Atkins of Auburn recollects that in summer 1942 her family rented a beach cottage on the Gulf coast, probably in Panama City, Florida. Having no air conditioning in those days, the children slept on the porch overlooking the Gulf. She recalls that heavy wool blankets were tacked to the windows across the "sleeping porch." During the day the blankets were pulled to the side with rope or string. At night and with the lights extinguished, the children pulled back the blankets in order to hear the lapping of the surf and perhaps to see a U-boat offshore.

18. These auxiliary, civilian vessels that stood watch for U-boats and rescued surviving merchant sailors were also called the "Cockleshell Fleet." Mellor, *Sank Same*, 144–57.

19. See correspondence between Frank Boykin and Joe Danciger in the Frank Boykin Collection, Folder 3, ADAH; also Dixon files: Jack Danciger.

20. Boykin, *Everything's Made for Love*, 111.

21. Jefferson County Chapter, American Red Cross, *World War II History of Jefferson County Chapter American Red Cross: A Report to the Membership . . . , September 1, 1939–December 31, 1945* (Birmingham: [Jefferson County Chapter, American Red Cross], 1946), 29.

22. Ibid., 26

23. Edward John Pluth, "The Administration and Operation of German Prisoner of War Camps in the United States during World War II" (Ph.D. diss., Ball State University, 1970), 211–13.

24. Thomas, *Riveting and Rationing*, 99.

25. McGee, *Origins of Fort Rucker*, 132.

26. Axford, *Limestone County*, 55.

27. Dixon files: USO.

28. Vera Ruth "Millie" (Gomillion) Prentiss Collection, ADAH. This collection includes hundreds of postcards and letters from servicemen whom "Willy-Nilly" had befriended at the Montgomery USO club.

29. The Original Salvation Army World War I Doughnut recipe (from Dixon files: USO):

7 1/2 cups sugar	3 cans water
3/4 cup lard	18 cups flour
9 eggs	18 teaspoons baking powder
3 cans evaporated milk	7 1/2 teaspoons salt
9 teaspoons nutmeg	

Cream sugar and lard together.
Beat eggs.
Add milk and water.
Add liquid to cream mixture.
Mix flour, baking powder, salt, and nutmeg in large sieve and sift
    into other mixture.
Add enough flour to make stiff.
Roll and cut.
5 pounds lard to fry. Makes about 250 doughnuts.

30. Excerpt from Frank Weirauch, "A History of Maxwell Field's Bands, 1 October 1941 to 1 February 1944," in Edward F. Polic, *The Glenn Miller Army Air Force Band*, 2 vols. (Metuchen, N.J.: Scarecrow Press, 1989), 1:6. Miller was assigned to Maxwell Field immediately upon his induction into the Army. Captain Miller created his famous Army Air Force Band in early 1943 after being transferred to Atlantic City and later to Yale University.

31. WSFA, *Letters from Home*, ADAH.

32. Wesley P. Newton, interview with author, Montgomery, 12 March 1992.

33. McGee, *Origins of Fort Rucker*, 143.

34. Haygood Patterson, "Report of Alabama War Chest, Incorporated," 20 December 1946, Alabama Governor (1943–1947: Chauncey Sparks), Administrative Files (hereinafter cited as Sparks files): Alabama War Chest, ADAH.

35. Ed Leigh McMillan to Governor Sparks, 27 July 1945, Sparks files: War Bond Drives.

36. Elizabeth Lynne Anderson, "Improving Rural Life in Alabama: The Home Demonstration Program, 1911–1972" (Master's thesis, Auburn University, 1984), 83–84.

37. Record, *Dream Come True*, 2:254.

38. "World War II Scrapbooks," vol. 8.

39. *Birmingham News–Age-Herald*, 10 October 1943.

40. On the role of war bonds in reducing inflationary pressures, see Ed Leigh McMillan to Governor Sparks, 29 August 1945, and Fred Vinson to Governor Sparks, September 1945, Sparks files: War Bond Drives.

41. For the state's allotment of automobile tires, see Dixon files: Governor's Speeches, 1942.

42. *Montgomery Advertiser*, 25 January 1942.

43. Ibid., 26 December 1941.

44. Vehicle registration in the state of Alabama reached 300,000 cars and trucks in 1937

for the first time since 1928. By 1941, 368,000 vehicles traveled on Alabama highways. *Montgomery Advertiser*, 4 January 1942.

45. *Mobile Press Register*, 15 May 1942.

46. Allen Cronenberg, "U-Boats in the Gulf: The Undersea War in 1942," *Gulf Coast Historical Review* 5 (Spring 1990): 167.

47. Kennett, *For the Duration*, 138.

48. *Birmingham News*, 17 May 1942.

49. Susan M. Hartmann, *The Homefront and Beyond: American Women in the 1940s* (Boston: Twayne Publishers, 1982), 82–83; Karen Anderson, *Wartime Women: Sex Roles, Family Relations, and the Status of Women during World War II* (Westport, Conn.: Greenwood Press, 1981), 49–50, 84.

50. See the brief summary of rationing in John Riley Craf, *A Survey of the American Economy, 1940–1946* (New York: North River Press, 1947), especially 71–73.

51. Axford, *Limestone County*, 31.

52. Edwina Mitchell, "Crime and Delinquency," in Farmer, *War Comes to Alabama*, 31–35. The author of this article was a member of the State Board of Paroles and Pardons and one of the few women in state government at the time.

53. Doris Weatherford, *American Women and World War II* (New York: Facts on File, 1990), 203.

54. Ibid., 201.

55. See the many advertisements placed in newspapers by local defense councils. A good example was one entitled "The Home Front Pledge" placed by the Dallas County Defense Council in the *Selma Times-Journal*, 12 July 1943.

4. Alabama's Military Camps

1. Wesley Frank Craven and James Lea Cate, *Men and Planes*, vol. 6 of *The Army Air Forces in World War II* (Chicago: University of Chicago Press, 1955), 457.

2. *Montgomery Salutes Maxwell and Gunter*, 5.

3. Air University, *Fifty Years*, 38.

4. Craven and Cates, *Men and Planes*, 546–50.

5. Jimmy Stewart passed through Maxwell Field in early 1942 en route to Washington, where he took part in a birthday party for President Roosevelt and a fund raiser for infantile paralysis at the White House. See *Montgomery Advertiser*, 28 January 1942.

6. Dixon files: Lord Halifax Visit (8–9 April 1943).

7. Carl C. Morgan, Jr., "Craig Air Force Base: Its Effect on Selma, 1940–1977," *Alabama Review* 42 (April 1989): 83–96.

8. Davis, *Autobiography*, 98.

9. Ibid., 118.

10. Dixon files: Negro Airport and Negro Waacs at Tuskegee. This file contains reports about various incidents at Tuskegee and Maxwell by, among others, Alabama State Guard Inspector General Virgil Peterson and William Hastie, civilian aide to Secretary of War Henry L. Stimson.

11. Dixon to Senator Lister Hill, 12 May 1942, in ibid.

12. Major General John P. Smith to Governor Frank M. Dixon, 26 February 1942, in ibid.

13. Eugene Connor to President Franklin D. Roosevelt, 30 August 1942, Sparks files: Race-Military Order-Maxwell Field.

14. Davis, *Autobiography*, 84, 92.
15. *Mobile Press Register*, 19 June 1955.
16. Thomas, *Riveting and Rationing*, 25.
17. Ibid.
18. Ibid., 30.
19. *Birmingham News*, 14 June 1944.
20. For the history of Fort McClellan during wartime, see Lane, "History of Fort McClellan," 23–29.
21. Ibid., 23–24.
22. Ibid., 24–25.
23. On the role of Camp Rucker in World War II, see Val L. McGee, *Claybank Memories: A History of Dale County, Alabama* (Ozark, Ala.: Dale County Historical Society, 1989), 132–38; idem, *Origins of Fort Rucker*.
24. McGee, *Origins of Fort Rucker*, 118, 138.
25. Leo P. Brophy and George J. B. Fisher, *The Chemical Warfare Service: Organizing for War*, vol. 6, pt. 7:1, of *U.S. Army in World War II: The Technical Services* (Washington, D.C.: Office of the Chief of Military History, Department of the Army, 1959), 57, 125; also see photo-illustrated booklet prepared by the Public Relations Office at Camp Sibert, *This is Camp Sibert, Alabama: Chemical Warfare Service* (Brooklyn: Ullmann, n.d.).
26. David T. Childress, "The Impact of World War II in Northeast Alabama" (paper presented at the Alabama Studies Symposium, ADAH, Montgomery, 7 August 1992).
27. Brophy and Fisher, *Organizing for War*, 291.

5. Producing for Victory

1. Harry C. Thomson and Lida Mayo, *The Ordnance Department: Procurement and Supply*, vol. 6, pt. 3:2 of *U.S. Army in World War II: The Technical Services* (Washington, D.C.: Office of the Chief of Military History, Department of the Army, 1960), 5.
2. Ibid., 43.
3. Hallie Farmer, "Postwar Prospects," in idem, *War Comes to Alabama*, 132.
4. Thomson and Mayo, *Procurement and Supply*, 111; *Alabama* 6 (15 September 1941): 8–14.
5. Marjorie Longenecker White, *The Birmingham District: An Industrial History* (Birmingham: Birmingham Historical Society, 1981), 166; "O'Neal Steel," *Journal of the Birmingham Historical Society* 7 (June 1981): 32; Atkins, *Valley and the Hills*, 211; Malcolm McMillan, *Yesterday's Birmingham*, Seemann's Historic Cities Series no. 18 (Miami: E. A. Seemann, 1975), 150.
6. Douglas A. Fisher, *Steel in the War* (New York: United States Steel, 1946), 62–66.
7. Childress, "Impact of World War II," 4. Because the Anniston depot shipped ordnance to the Soviet Union through the Lend-Lease program, two Russian officers were stationed at the facility to ensure that crates and other supplies were properly labeled in the Cyrillic alphabet.
8. Stephens, *Historic Huntsville*, 91.
9. Ibid., 112.
10. On the history of the Huntsville and Redstone arsenals, see ibid., 107–9; Cason and Stroup, "Redstone Arsenal," 29–43; Dave Dooling and Sharon Dooling, *Huntsville: A Pictorial History* (Virginia Beach, Va.: Donning, 1980); Nancy Dickson, "Huntsville, the Arsenal, and Miss Susie," *Historic Huntsville Quarterly* 17 (Winter–Spring 1991): 23–41;

Kaylene Hughes, "Two 'Arsenals of Democracy,'" *Historic Huntsville Quarterly* 17 (Winter–Spring 1991): 48–66; John L. McDaniel, "The Memoirs of John L. McDaniel," *Historic Huntsville Quarterly* 17 (Winter–Spring 1991): 73–91; and "Redstone Arsenal Celebrates 50 Years," in *Huntsville Times*, 9 June 1991, sec. J, which contains articles on Huntsville during World War II.

11. *Huntsville Times*, 9 June 1991. The only accredited high school for blacks in Madison County in 1940 was private Oakwood School in Huntsville. See Bureau of Business Research, School of Commerce and Business Administration, University of Alabama, *Alabama County Statistical Abstracts*, Multilithed Series no. 4 (University, 1944), 199. Brophy and Fisher, *Organizing for War*, 122.

12. Brophy and Fisher, *Organizing for War*, 122.

13. Cason and Stroup, "Redstone Arsenal," 34–36.

14. Brophy and Fisher, *Organizing for War*, 121.

15. Leo P. Brophy, Wyndham D. Miles, and Rexmond C. Cochrane, *The Chemical Warfare Service: From Laboratory to Field*, vol. 6, pt. 7:2, of *U.S. Army in World War II: The Technical Services* (Washington, D.C.: Office of the Chief of Military History, Department of the Army, 1959), 64. Also see McDaniel, "Memoirs," 81.

16. Brophy, Miles, and Cochrane, *Laboratory to Field*, 51–54, 68.

17. Ibid., 372–74.

18. McDaniel, "Memoirs," 84, 81.

19. Stephens, *Historic Huntsville*, 107.

20. Ibid., 113.

21. Michael E. Baker and Kaylene Hughes, eds., *Redstone Arsenal Complex Chronology*, pt. 1, *The Pre-Missile Era (1941–1949)* (Redstone Arsenal, Ala.: Historical Division, U.S. Army Missile Command, 1991), 42. The name "Fred Project" apparently derived from Frederick Bellinger, an engineer who worked on the project. See letter from Frederick Bellinger to Bob Ward of the *Huntsville Times*, 6 July 1966, in the Historical Division's archives at Redstone Arsenal; also "'Fred's Folly' Becomes Important Test Apparatus," *Redstone Rocket*, 5 March 1957.

22. In October 1948 the Ordnance Department announced that Redstone Arsenal would be reactivated for rocket research. Too small for the military's rocket research needs, the Redstone Arsenal was enlarged with land from the idle Huntsville Arsenal. The Ordnance Rocket Center opened on 1 June 1949. Four months later the guided missile research group, which included Wernher von Braun and other top German rocket scientists, was transferred from Fort Bliss, Texas, to Huntsville. On the transition from ordnance to rocketry, see Cason and Stroup, "Redstone Arsenal," 41–43; Martin Burkey, "39,000-Acre Site Grew to Shape History," *Huntsville Times*, 9 June 1991, sec. J.

23. Childress, "Impact of World War II," 5; on the Childersburg and Talladega ordnance plants, also see Thomas, *Riveting and Rationing*, 15–16, 48–49. For a discussion of DuPont's P-9 project for manufacturing heavy water at the Alabama Ordnance Works and at two other plants in the United States between September 1943 and April 1945, see Anthony Cave Brown and Charles B. MacDonald, eds., *The Secret History of the Atomic Bomb* (New York: Dial Press, 1977), 142–46. Ultimately, the heavy water manufactured at the Childersburg plant was not necessary for the production of plutonium. Instead, a graphite process proved successful. Heavy water research was nonetheless of vital interest. It was known that German scientists were conducting experiments of their own using heavy water from Norway.

24. On conditions in Childersburg, see the study done by rural sociologists at Alabama

Polytechnic Institute, B. F. Alvord, H. E. Klontz, and S. C. McIntyre, eds., *Childersburg Pilot Study: A Survey of the Impact of Rapid Industrial Development in a Southern Community* (Auburn: Alabama Polytechnic Institute, Auburn Research Foundation, 1953), 3–7; also Thomas, *Riveting and Rationing*, 15–16; and Wayne Flynt, *Poor but Proud: Alabama's Poor Whites* (Tuscaloosa: University of Alabama Press, 1989), 333–35.

25. For personal reminiscences about Childersburg during and after the war, see Annie Louise Ryder-Bush, *Memoirs of Childersburg* (Alexander City, Ala.: Bama Printing, 1976).

26. Douglas A. Fisher, *Steel Serves the Nation, 1901–1951: The Fifty Year Story of United States Steel* (New York: Lind Brothers, 1951), 56.

27. Alabama Power Company, *Annual Report of Alabama Power Company for 1942* (Birmingham: Alabama Power Company, 1943), 5–6.

28. Earle L. Rauber, *The Alabama State Docks: A Case Study in State Development* (Atlanta: Federal Reserve Bank of Atlanta, 1945), 44; First National Bank of Mobile, *Highlights of 100 Years in Mobile* (Mobile: N.p., 1965), 115; *Alabama* 6 (15 September 1941): 8–14.

29. Thomas, *Riveting and Rationing*, 10; McMillan, *Yesterday's Birmingham*, 168.

30. ADDSCO launched its first Liberty ship, *J. L. M. Curry,* on 31 January 1942. A year later, 13 January 1943, the twentieth and final Liberty ship, *Lawton B. Evans,* slid from the ways on Pinto Island. Descriptions and photos of some of the Liberty ships are contained in the ADDSCO photograph collection in the University of South Alabama Archives, Mobile.

31. Cathalynn Donelson, *Mobile: Sunbelt Center of Opportunity* (Northridge, Calif.: Windsor Publications, 1986), 40–41.

32. McLaurin and Thomason, *Mobile*, 124.

33. Jane Faulkner, ed., *The Story of Stockham: Links to Better Living, 1903–1953—50 Golden Years—Stockham Valves and Fittings* (Birmingham: Stockham, 1953).

34. "O'Neal Steel," 32.

35. Atkins, *Valley and the Hills*, 200.

36. Donelson, *Mobile*, 33.

37. Campbell's World War I experiences included bitter fighting in the Argonne-Meuse offensive, which earned him the Croix de Guerre, the Distinguished Service Cross, and the Navy Cross. See Roy S. Simmonds, *The Two Worlds of William March* (University: University of Alabama Press, 1984), 17.

38. *Alabama* 6 (15 September 1941): 9.

39. *Montgomery Advertiser*, 25 January 1942.

40. Alabama Department of Agriculture and Industries, *Alabama Agricultural Statistics Service News*, 7 April 1990.

41. *Montgomery Advertiser*, 25 January 1942. Radio provided an especially informative medium for agricultural and homemaking advice. Nearly half of the 670,000 families in Alabama owned radios in 1940. Weekday programs on rural living originated at Alabama Polytechnic Institute. Tuskegee Institute produced programs on the last Saturday of the month featuring black farming households. On the use of radio by rural agricultural extension and home demonstration services, see Anderson, "Home Demonstration Program," 90–92.

42. *Montgomery Advertiser*, 6 January 1942.

43. Axford, *Limestone County*, 23, 113, 117.

44. Norwood Allen Kerr, *A History of the Alabama Agricultural Experiment Station,*

1883–1983 (Auburn University: Alabama Agricultural Experiment Station, 1985), 77.

45. Ibid., 76; Guzman, *Negro Year Book*, 182–83.

46. F. A. Kummer, "A History of Agricultural Engineering at Auburn University," *Highlights of Agricultural Research:* (Agricultural Experiment Station, Auburn University) 16 (Summer 1969): 11.

47. James E. Fickle and Donald W. Ellis, "POWs in the Piney Woods: German Prisoners of War in the Southern Lumber Industry, 1943–1945," *Journal of Southern History* 56 (November 1990): 699.

48. Marion H. Hawley, *Employment and Wage Payments in Alabama in Firms Covered by Unemployment Compensation, 1939–1946*, University of Alabama Bureau of Business Research, Mimeographed Series no. 10 (University: Bureau of Business Research, 1947), 22–23.

6. Governing Alabama

1. William D. Barnard, *Dixiecrats and Democrats: Alabama Politics, 1942–1950* (University: University of Alabama Press, 1974), 2–4.

2. The Dixon and Sparks files in ADAH contain letters or memos of phone calls in state and national Democratic party circles dealing with racial matters and issues of state sovereignty. See, for example, Dixon files: Negro Airport and Negro Waacs at Tuskegee; Race Problems, Race Riot; also Sparks files: Race-Military Order-Maxwell Field; Race Riots; Race-Segregation; Segregation Laws in Alabama; Boswell Amendment; Race Problems; Race Relations. For a thorough analysis of Dixon's career as governor, see John David Bevis, "Frank M. Dixon: Alabama's Reform Governor" (Master's thesis, Samford University, 1968).

3. Bevis, "Frank M. Dixon," 8–9.

4. Ibid., 16.

5. John David Bevis, "The 1938 Democratic Gubernatorial Contest," in *The Public Life of Frank M. Dixon: Sketches and Speeches*, Alabama State Department of Archives and History, Historical and Patriotic Series no. 18 (Montgomery: Skinner Printing, 1979), 6.

6. For a detailed analysis of the 1938 primary and general election, see Bevis, "Frank M. Dixon," 78–116; idem, "1938 Democratic Gubernatorial Contest," 1–14.

7. William H. Stewart, Jr., "Governor Frank Murray Dixon and Reform of State Administration in Alabama," in *Public Life of Dixon*, 15–30; Earl McGowin, "Frank M. Dixon and the Reorganization of State Government: A Reminiscence," in ibid., 31–32.

8. John M. Collier, *Earl McGowin of Alabama: A Portrait* (New Orleans: Faust, 1986), 32.

9. Frank M. Dixon, "The Moving Destiny of the Southland," in *Public Life of Dixon*, 33–52.

10. Frank M. Dixon, "Crossroads of Democracy," speech delivered to the New York Southern Society on 11 December 1942, reprinted in *Public Life of Dixon*, 53–65. Dixon had earlier, in a speech to the Governors' Conference at Asheville, North Carolina, decried the concentration of powers in the hands of the federal government. A copy of this speech of 23 June 1942 can be found in the Dixon files. Also see Raymond Jackson, "The Dixiecrats: Rumblings of an Impending Storm," manuscript in author's possession. Jackson demonstrates how the wartime experiences led Dixon to advocate a break with the national Democratic party and to participate in the founding of the Dixiecrat movement.

11. Bevis, "Frank M. Dixon," 4.

12. Neil Davis, interview with author, 1992. Davis and his wife Henrietta edited the *Lee County Bulletin*, a progressive weekly that Davis founded in 1937.

13. Barnard, *Dixiecrats and Democrats*, 97.

14. Dixon, "Crossroads of Democracy," 59.

15. Robert J. Norrell, *Reaping the Whirlwind: The Civil Rights Movement in Tuskegee* (New York: Alfred A. Knopf, 1985), 55–56.

16. On the disgruntlement with the national Democratic party in 1944, see Allen Woodrow Jones, "Republicanism in Jefferson County, Alabama, 1952–1958," *Alabama Historical Quarterly* 22 (Spring and Summer 1960): 104–5; Carl Grafton and Anne Permaloff, *Big Mules and Branchheads: James E. Folsom and Political Power in Alabama* (Athens: University of Georgia Press, 1985), 27–33.

17. William D. Barnard, "The Old Order Changes: Graves, Sparks, Folsom, and the Gubernatorial Election of 1942," *Alabama Review* 28 (July 1975): 163. The description of the 1942 gubernatorial campaign is drawn largely from this article. Also see Barnard, *Dixiecrats and Democrats*, 17–22.

18. Barnard, "Old Order Changes," 170.

19. Ibid., 173.

20. For a description of Folsom's early life, see Grafton and Permaloff, *Big Mules and Branchheads*, 1–36.

21. Key, "Steagall," 198–209; and Carl Grafton, "James E. Folsom's First Four Election Campaigns: Learning to Win by Losing," *Alabama Review* 34 (July 1981): 163–83.

22. Barnard, *Dixiecrats and Democrats*, 18–19.

23. Ibid., 22.

24. John Craig Stewart, *The Governors of Alabama* (Gretna, La.: Pelican, 1975), 190–93.

25. *A Report from the Governor (Chauncey Sparks) to the People of Alabama: October 1, 1943, through September 30, 1944* (Montgomery, 1944), copy in Sparks files.

26. Record, *Dream Come True*, 2:256, 262.

27. H. G. Dowling (State Commissioner of Revenue) and Hayse Tucker (State Director of Finance), "State Finance," in Farmer, *War Comes to Alabama*, 99–108.

28. Norrell, *Reaping the Whirlwind*, 55; Barnard, *Dixiecrats and Democrats*, 59.

29. Barnard, *Dixiecrats and Democrats*, 59–71; Guzman, *Negro Year Book*, 267–68.

30. Key, "Steagall," 198–209.

31. Virginia Van der Veer Hamilton, *Lister Hill: Statesman from the South* (Chapel Hill: University of North Carolina Press, 1987), 92–94.

32. Studs Terkel, *The Good War* (New York: Pantheon Books, 1984), 333–37; talk by Virginia Durr at Pebble Hill (Auburn University Center for the Arts and Humanities), 27 February 1991; see also Virginia Durr, *Outside the Magic Circle: The Autobiography of Virginia Foster Durr*, ed. Hollinger F. Barnard (University: University of Alabama Press, 1985).

33. Morgan, "Craig Air Force Base," 87.

34. Boykin, *Everything's Made for Love*, 102–3, 111.

35. U.S. House of Representatives and Senate, *Memorial Services . . . George W. Andrews*, 92d Congress, 2d sess. (Washington, D.C.: Government Printing Office, 1972).

7. The War and Society

1. Alabama Department of Public Health, *Alabama's Population, 1930–1976* (Montgomery: Alabama Department of Public Health, Division of Vital Statistics, 1977), 35.

2. Guzman, *Negro Year Book*, 1–3; Department of Public Health, *Alabama's Population*, 8–9, 12–13.

3. Bureau of Business Research, *Statistical Abstracts*, 2.

4. W. O. Dobbins, "Planning," in Farmer, *War Comes to Alabama*, 117.

5. Bureau of Business Research, *Statistical Abstracts*, 200, Stephens, *Historic Huntsville*, 112.

6. Hawley, *Employment and Wage Payments*, 10–12.

7. Flynt, *Poor but Proud*, 334.

8. Dos Passos, *State of the Nation*, 94.

9. Mary Martha Thomas, "The Mobile Homefront during the Second World War," *Gulf Coast Historical Review* 1 (Spring 1986): 61.

10. Department of Public Health, *Alabama's Population*, 65.

11. Guzman, *Negro Year Book*, 56.

12. Ibid., 61.

13. Ibid., 66; Patricia G. Harrison, "Riveters, Volunteers and WACS: Women in Mobile during World War II," *Gulf Coast Historical Review* 1 (Spring 1986): 43, 49; Thomas, *Riveting and Rationing*, 49.

14. John McDaniel, a high school science teacher in north Georgia where salaries were comparable to those in Alabama, decided, as he put it, "to get into defense work." His teaching salary was seventy dollars a month. With twenty-one dollars in his pocket, McDaniel drove to Huntsville and found a job making mustard gas at the arsenal. See McDaniel, "Memoirs," 79, 81; also Harrison, "Riveters," 43.

15. Guzman, *Negro Year Book*, 74.

16. Department of Public Health, *Alabama's Population*, 65.

17. Ralph Brown Draughon, *Alabama Polytechnic Institute* (New York: Newcomen Society in North America, 1954).

18. On the history of API during World War II, see David E. Alsobrook, "Auburn in the 'Good War,'" *Auburn Alumnews* 46 (July–August 1991): 6–7, and idem, "Boomtown on the Plains," *Auburn Alumnews* 46 (September 1991): 10–11. Also see Troy Teel, "The Busiest Village of the Plains: Alabama Polytechnic Institute during World War II" (manuscript, 13 August 1991, in author's possession).

19. Malcolm McMillan and Allen Jones, *Auburn University through the Years, 1856–1973*, Auburn University Bulletin 68:5 (Auburn: Auburn University, 1973), 24.

20. Joseph H. Parks and Oliver C. Weaver, Jr., *Birmingham-Southern College, 1856–1956* (Nashville: Parthenon Press, 1957), 204–5.

21. James G. Schneider, *The Navy V-12 Program: Leadership for a Lifetime* (Boston: Houghton Mifflin, 1987), 15, 437.

22. Suzanne Rau Wolfe, *The University of Alabama: A Pictorial History* (University: University of Alabama Press, 1983), 172–75.

23. Alsobrook, "Boomtown on the Plains," 10.

24. See Alabama State Department of Public Health, *Annual Report of the State Department of Public Health: 1940* (Wetumpka: Wetumpka Printing, 1941), and reports for the other war years that contain tables showing the incidence of communicable diseases reported in Alabama. See also B. F. Austin, "The Impact of the War on the Health Department," *Journal of the Medical Association of the State of Alabama* 15 (February 1946): 243–46; idem, "Public Health," in Farmer, *War Comes to Alabama*, 36–45.

25. State Department of Public Health, *Annual Report: 1940*, 161.

26. Axford, *Limestone County*, 10.

27. More than 200,000 selective service registrants agreed in 1940 to be tested for syphilis. By the end of that year 186,000 young men had been examined. Approximately 8.8 percent, or 16,447, tested positive. See State Department of Public Health, *Annual Report: 1940*, 37. In 1942 the Alabama legislature passed a law requiring all persons between the ages of fourteen and fifty to be tested for venereal diseases. Initial tests were done in Sumter, Wilcox, and Lee counties. For a brief analysis of the results of those tests, see W. H. Y. Smyth, D. G. Gill, and S. R. Damon, "A Preliminary Report of Blood Testing, As Required by Alabama Law, In the First Three Counties Surveyed," *Journal of the Medical Association of the State of Alabama* 14 (October 1944): 86–92.

28. This study continued until 1972 when public outrage forced the U.S. Public Health Service to abandon the project. See James H. Jones, *Bad Blood: The Tuskegee Syphilis Experiment* (New York: Free Press, 1981), 203–19; Alabama Committee to the United States Commission on Civil Rights, *The Tuskegee Study* (N.p., 1973).

29. Compared with the national average of one physician per 757 people, one physician served approximately 1,367 Alabamians. Dobbins, "Planning," 115–25.

30. Five Alabama doctors lost their lives during the conflict. Austin, "Impact of the War," 243–46.

31. *Birmingham Age-Herald*, 30 March 1943. According to this article, Alabama produced 109 percent of its quota for physicians, whereas New Mexico was 120 percent over its quota.

32. Seale Harris, "Medical Education in Alabama and Mississippi," *Journal of the Medical Association of the State of Alabama* 14 (October 1944): 93–96.

33. Axford, *Limestone County*, 82.

34. Grafton and Permaloff, *Big Mules and Branchheads*, 33.

35. Mitchell, "Crime and Delinquency," 32.

36. On conditions at Phenix City, see Survey of Commercialized Prostitution Conditions, February–March 1940, Dixon files: Law Enforcement—Phenix City; for a report on public safety in Childersburg, see Director of Public Safety J. F. Brawner to Governor Frank Dixon, 7 July 1941, Dixon files: Childersburg Operations.

37. Mitchell, "Crime and Delinquency," 34.

38. Jack House, "Alabama War Towns," *Birmingham News*, 28 March 1943.

39. Alabama Baptist State Convention, *Annual Report of the Alabama Baptist State Convention: 1942* (N.p., 1943), 107.

40. Ibid.

41. Board of Temperance and Social Service report, *Journal of the Alabama Conference, The Methodist Church*, 4th sess., Montgomery, 11–15 November 1942, 64.

42. "Resolution Concerning War," ibid., 55.

43. Ernest Trice Thompson, *Presbyterians in the South*, vol. 3, *1890–1972* (Richmond: John Knox Press, 1973), 521–22.

44. Ibid., 523.

45. David O'Brien, *Public Catholicism* (New York: Macmillan, 1989), 198–99.

46. Letter from Archbishop Oscar Lipscomb of Mobile to author, 1 December 1991.

47. On the reaction of Pentecostalism to World War II, see the study by Mickey Crews, *The Church of God: A Social History* (Knoxville: University of Tennessee Press, 1990), 128–37.

48. Ibid., 134.

49. Mark H. Elovitz, *A Century of Jewish Life in Dixie: The Birmingham Experience* (University: University of Alabama Press, 1974), 140–41.

50. On Pizitz and Birmingham's Jewish community, see ibid., 125–28.

51. Department of Public Health, *Alabama's Population*, 3, 23, 69.

52. Guzman, *Negro Year Book*, 9–11.

53. Gerald D. Nash, *World War II and the West: Reshaping the Economy* (Lincoln: University of Nebraska Press, 1990), 59–61, 76–77.

54. *The Alabama Negro, 1863–1946* (Mobile: Gulf Informer Publishing, 1946).

55. Ellen Sullivan and Marie Stokes Jamison, *An Alabama Scrapbook: 32 Alabamians Remember Growing Up* (Huntsville: Honeysuckle Imprint, 1988), 34; on Richard Arrington's childhood in Birmingham, see the biography by Jimmie Lewis Franklin, *Back to Birmingham: Richard Arrington, Jr., and His Times* (Tuscaloosa: University of Alabama Press, 1989), 3–35.

56. In general, anecdotal evidence suggests that World War II had a profound impact on the role of women in society. Recent scholarship, however, offers a more cautious and qualified assessment. The ground-breaking scholarly study of World War II's impact on women was William Chafe, *The American Woman: Her Changing Social, Economic and Political Roles, 1920–1970* (New York: Oxford University Press, 1972). Subsequent studies tended to stress continuity and deemphasized the war years in transforming women's roles in drastic and lasting ways. See Hartmann, *Homefront and Beyond*; D'Ann Campbell, *Women at War with America: Private Lives in a Patriotic Era* (Cambridge: Harvard University Press, 1984); Maureen Honey, *Creating Rosie the Riveter: Class, Gender and Propaganda during World War II* (Amherst: University of Massachusetts Press, 1984); and Weatherford, *American Women*.

57. On the impact of the war on women in Alabama, see the pioneering studies of Mary Martha Thomas ("Alabama Women on the Home Front, World War II," *Alabama Heritage* 19 [Winter 1991]: 55–75; "Rosie the Alabama Riveter," *Alabama Review* 39 [July 1986]: 196–212; and *Riveting and Rationing,* and Patricia G. Harrison ["Riveters"]).

58. A cover photograph of Nancy Batson appeared on the Army Air Forces' service journal, which ran a story about women pilots. See Charlotte Knight, "Our Women Pilots," *Air Force* 26 (September 1943): 10–12. Also *Birmingham Post*, 3 June 1944; *Birmingham News*, 11 May 1944; and Wolfe, *University of Alabama*, 175. On the history of the Women's Airforce Service Pilots during World War II, see Jean Hascall Cole, *Women Pilots of World War II* (Salt Lake City: University of Utah Press, 1992); Adela Riek Scharr, *Sisters in the Sky*, 2 vols. (Saint Louis: Patrice Press, 1986–88); Marianne Verges, *On Silver Wings: The Women Airforce Service Pilots of World War II, 1942–1944* (New York: Ballantine Books, 1991); Nancy Batson Crews, telephone interview with author, 20 August 1991.

59. John McCollister and Dianne Ramsden, *The Sky Is Home: The Story of Embry-Riddle Aeronautical University, 1926–1986* (Middle Village, N.Y.: Jonathan David, 1986), 63.

60. Jacqueline Cochran had been born in the Florida panhandle, moved first to Columbus, Georgia, and later to Montgomery, where she lived on Ann Street. Jackie Cochran and Maryann Bucknum Brinley, *Jackie Cochran: The Autobiography of the Greatest Woman Pilot in Aviation History* (New York: Bantam Books, 1987), 32–46, 204–7.

61. *Birmingham Age-Herald*, 22 August 1944.

62. The Eighty-eighth Station Hospital Group was the first group of volunteer nurses

to train at Fort McClellan. See clipping from unknown newspaper, "World War II Scrapbooks," vol. 3.

63. Thomas, *Riveting and Rationing*, 36–41; Harrison, "Riveters," 44–46.

64. Thomas, *Riveting and Rationing*, 40.

65. Thomas, "Rosie the Alabama Riveter," 198.

66. Thomas, *Riveting and Rationing*, 41–45.

67. Ibid., 49–50; Cason and Stroup, "Redstone Arsenal," 36.

68. Thomas, *Riveting and Rationing*, 48–49.

69. C. F. Anderson, "Manpower," in Farmer, *War Comes to Alabama*, 82–92.

70. Anderson, *Wartime Women*, 26.

71. Record, *Dream Come True*, 2:255.

72. Joanne Varner Hawks, "A Select Few: Alabama's Women Legislators, 1922–1983," *Alabama Review* 38 (July 1985): 178–79.

73. *Alabama News Magazine*, November 1973.

74. Guzman, *Negro Year Book*, 278.

75. McLaurin and Thomason, *Mobile*, 128.

76. Guzman, *Negro Year Book*, 233–34.

77. Sheriff W. H. Holcombe to Governor Sparks, 3 June 1943, Sparks files: Race Riots.

78. Brophy and Fisher, *Organizing for War*, 166.

8. Prisoners of War

1. Ted Spears, telephone conversation with author, 21 April 1992.

2. Arnold P. Krammer, "German Prisoners of War in the United States," *Military Affairs* 40 (April 1976): 71; Frederick J. Doyle, "German Prisoners of War in the Southwest United States during World War II: An Oral History" (Ph.D. diss., University of Denver, 1978), 178–82; Judith M. Gansberg, *Stalag, U.S.A.: The Remarkable Story of German POWs in America* (New York: Thomas Y. Crowell, 1977), 47–60, 132–33.

3. I. S. O. Playfair and C. J. C. Molony, *The Mediterranean and Middle East*, vol. 4, *The Destruction of the Axis Forces in Africa* (London: Her Majesty's Stationery Office, 1966), 449–62.

4. George G. Lewis and John Mewha, *History of Prisoner of War Utilization by the United States Army, 1776–1945*, Center for Military History Publication 104–11 (Washington, D.C.: Office of the Chief of Military History, Department of the Army, 1988), 125–26. This is a reprint of the original 1955 Department of the Army pamphlet 20-213 of the same title.

5. Arnold P. Krammer, *Nazi Prisoners of War in America* (New York: Stein and Day, 1979), vii, 3, 256. For a discussion of the sources for a study of POW camps in the United States, see Jake W. Spidle, Jr., "Axis Prisoners of War in the United States, 1942–1946: A Bibliographical Essay," *Military Affairs* 39 (April 1975): 61–66. Also Krammer, "German Prisoners of War," 68–73.

6. Randy Wall, "Inside the Wire: Aliceville and the Afrika Korps," *Alabama Heritage* 7 (Winter 1988): 2–29; W. Stanley Hoole, "Alabama's World War II Prisoner of War Camps," *Alabama Review* 20 (April 1967): 83–114; Chip Walker, "German Creative Activities in Camp Aliceville, 1943–1946," *Alabama Review* 38 (January 1985): 19–37; Fickle and Ellis, "POWs in the Piney Woods," 695–724; Public Information Subject Files—General, SG6979, Folder 1280: "Aliceville, Alabama, Camp," and SG6993, Folder

1654: "War Prisoners Camp," ADAH. The Aliceville Public Library and ADAH also have collections of photographs of the Aliceville camp.

7. *Birmingham World*, 10 June 1943.

8. Wall, "Inside the Wire," 15–16; *Birmingham Age-Herald*, 27 August 1943, 28 March 1945. In 1,880 escapes made by German and Italian war prisoners throughout the United States, only twenty-four POWs remained at large as of October 1946, and by 1953 there were only four. See Pluth, "German Prisoner of War Camps," 178–79. In the 1980s, Georg Gärtner claimed to be the last POW escapee still at large. Fearful of being returned to the Russian zone of occupation in Germany, twenty-five-year-old Gärtner had escaped from Camp Deming, New Mexico, by jumping a train. Eluding the FBI for forty years, he assumed a new identity in California. See his *Hitler's Last Soldier in America* (New York: Stein and Day, 1985), 61, which provides a detailed picture of the attitudes of German POWs and their personal reactions to their captivity.

9. Maxine Marlett was a young Opelika native who witnessed the arrival of the German POWs. "At the first trainload," she recounted, "Opelika turned out like it thought the president or Jesus was coming. I don't know what we expected—two-headed monsters!" Quoted in Pam Jones, "Opelika Residents Remember POW Camp," *Montgomery Review*, 13 April 1988. Maxine married a young soldier from Pennsylvania who arrived in Opelika in July 1944 to guard the Germans, whom he had recently fought in North Africa.

10. Hoole, "Prisoner of War Camps," 90–93; Lane, "History of Fort McClellan," 28–29.

11. Krammer, *Nazi Prisoners of War*, 28; Hoole, "Prisoner of War Camps," 85; also see articles about POW camps in other southern states, including Robert D. Billinger, Jr., "With the Wehrmacht in Florida: The German POW Facility at Camp Blanding, 1942–1946," *Florida Historical Quarterly* 58 (October 1979): 160–73; Merrill R. Pritchett and William L. Shea, "The Enemy in Mississippi (1943–1946)," *Journal of Mississippi History* 41 (November 1979): 351–71; and William L. Shea and Merrill R. Pritchett, "The *Wehrmacht* in Louisiana," *Louisiana History* 23 (Winter 1982): 5–19.

12. Side camps were located at the following Alabama towns: Abbeville, Andalusia, Chapman, Chatom, Clanton, Clio, Dothan, Dublin, Elba, Evergreen, Foley, Geneva, Greenville, Huntsville, Jackson, Linden, Loxley, Luverne, Montgomery, Camp Sibert, Troy, and Tuscaloosa.

13. Hoole, "Prisoner of War Camps," 94. See various newspaper clippings from 1943 about Aliceville and other POW camps in "World War II Scrapbooks," vol. 2. Some authorities, such as Krammer, describe Camp Sibert as a fifth base camp. See his *Nazi Prisoners of War*, 268–70. Also see Public Information Subject Files—General, SG6993, Folder 1654: "War Prisoner Camps," and SG6979, Folder 1280: "Aliceville, Alabama, Camp," ADAH.

14. Taped statement by Mary Louise Caton Weed to Wesley P. Newton, Montgomery, January 1992.

15. Krammer, *Nazi Prisoners of War,* 43–78; Gansberg, *Stalag, U.S.A.*, 22–42, 89–119; Pluth, "German Prisoner of War Camps," 202–36; Doyle, "German Prisoners of War," 82.

16. Walker, "German Creative Activities," 30–31.

17. Aliceville Prisoner of War Camp Collection, ADAH; see also Aliceville Prisoner of War Camp Collection, Aliceville Public Library, Aliceville.

18. Hoole, "Prisoner of War Camps," 97–98, 105–8.

19. Krammer, *Nazi Prisoners of War*, 51.

20. Ibid., 244.

21. See the chapter "Treatment of Prisoners" in Pluth, "German Prisoner of War Camps," 202–36.

22. Lewis and Mewha, *Prisoner of War Utilization*, 101–14.

23. *Birmingham News*, 1 October 1944.

24. The daily allowance of eighty cents was roughly equivalent to the twenty-one dollars monthly wages of privates in the U.S. Army. See Lewis and Mewha, *Prisoner of War Utilization*, 77.

25. Ibid., 125–26.

26. Fickle and Ellis, "POWs in the Piney Woods," 699.

27. Hoole, "Prisoner of War Camps," 103–4; Wall, "Inside the Wire," 22; Pluth, "German Prisoner of War Camps," 354.

28. Pluth, "German Prisoner of War Camps," 343; Krammer, *Nazi Prisoners of War*, 178; Gansberg, *Stalag, U.S.A.*, 60.

29. Krammer, *Nazi Prisoners of War*, 240–43.

30. Lewis and Mewha, *Prisoner of War Utilization*, 93–100.

31. Alfred Klein to Arnold P. Krammer in Krammer, *Nazi Prisoners of War*, 74.

32. Ibid.

33. Ibid., 261, photo 264–65; Lane, "History of Fort McClellan," 28.

34. Bernard M. Cohen and Maurice Z. Cooper, *A Follow-Up Study of World War II Prisoners of War* (Washington, D.C.: Veterans Administration, 1954), 15; John W. Dower claims that 4 percent of all Allied POWs died while under German control and that about 25 percent of those in Japanese hands succumbed. See his *War without Mercy: Race and Power in the Pacific War* (New York: Pantheon Books, 1986), 48.

35. "World War II Scrapbooks," vol. 1.

36. Wesley P. Newton address to Montgomery chapter of the Retired Officers' Association, 9 January 1992.

37. D. Clayton James, ed., *South to Bataan/North to Mukden: The Prison Diary of Brigadier General W. E. Brougher* (Athens: University of Georgia Press, 1971). After being reunited with his family in September 1945, Brougher served for two years as commanding general of Fort McClellan.

38. McGee, *Claybank Memories*, 138; on Ann Mealer, see *Birmingham News*, 22 March 1945, copy in "World War II Scrapbooks," vol 8.

39. Bert Bank, *Back from the Living Dead: An Original Story Describing the Infamous March of Death—33 Months in a Japanese Prison and Liberation by the Rangers* (Tuscaloosa: N.p., 1945), 73.

40. Lee Kennett, *G.I.: The American Soldier in World War II* (New York: Charles Scribner's Sons, 1987), 185.

9. Liberating Europe

1. Kennett, *G.I.*, 34–39.

2. Mattie Treadwell, *The Women's Army Corps*, vol. 2, pt. 2, of *U.S. Army in World War II: Special Studies* (Washington, D.C.: Office of the Chief of Military History, Department of the Army, 1954), app. A, table 1.

3. Ibid., 444, 752.

4. Eisenhower defended the North African invasion for its psychological impact rather than for military reasons. Its effect would be a gamble, he thought, rather like

Napoleon's return from Elba. Dwight David Eisenhower, *The Eisenhower Diaries* (New York: W. W. Norton, 1981), 76–78. On Eisenhower's appointment and the goals of Operation Torch, see his *At Ease: Stories I Tell to Friends* (Garden City, N.Y.: Doubleday, 1967), 252; Ed Cray, *General of the Army: George C. Marshall, Soldier and Statesman* (New York: W. W. Norton, 1990), 334; Stephen F. Ambrose, *Eisenhower*, vol. 1, *Soldier, General of the Army, President Elect* (New York: Simon and Schuster, 1983), 182; Eric Larrabee, *Commander in Chief: Franklin Delano Roosevelt, His Lieutenants, and Their War* (New York: Harper and Row, 1987), 138–40.

5. On the Allied decision to abandon hopes for an early landing in Europe in favor of an invasion of North Africa, see Winston S. Churchill, *The Hinge of Fate*, vol. 4 of *The Second World War* (Boston: Houghton Mifflin, 1950), 441–502. Wrangling between the Americans and the British over whether it would be feasible to invade Europe in 1942 or 1943 ended when President Roosevelt opted for landings in North Africa. General Dwight Eisenhower immediately began planning Operation Torch. In August Churchill went to Moscow to reveal Allied plans for Operation Torch to Stalin, who was delighted by the news. On Stalin's reaction to Churchill's summary of the objectives of Operation Torch, see Churchill to Roosevelt, 13 August 1942, in Francis L. Loewenheim, Harold D. Langley, and Manfred Jonas, eds., *Roosevelt and Churchill: Their Secret Wartime Correspondence* (New York: Saturday Review Press, 1975), 234–36.

6. Robert P. Fogerty, *Biographical Study of USAF General Officers, 1917–1952*, 2 vols. (Manhattan, Kans.: MA/AH Publishing, 1980), vol. 1; Wesley Frank Craven and James Lea Cate, eds., *Plans and Early Operations, January 1939–August 1942* vol. 1 of *The Army Air Forces in World War II* (Chicago: University of Chicago Press, 1948), 614; Roger A. Freeman, *The Mighty Eighth: Units, Men and Machines* (Garden City, N.Y.: Doubleday, 1970), 4.

7. Craven and Cate, *Plans and Early Operations*, 614.

8. Ibid., 612.

9. R. J. Overy, *The Air War, 1939–1945* (New York: Stein and Day, 1981), 131–52.

10. Freeman, *Mighty Eighth*, 12–13.

11. "World War II Scrapbooks," vol. 10; *Birmingham Post*, 19 August 1942.

12. H. M. Locker, "Hell over Bizerte," *Air Force* 26 (August 1943): 11, 44.

13. *Birmingham News*, 26 November 1942.

14. *Birmingham Age-Herald*, 17 October 1943.

15. "World War II Scrapbooks," vol. 6.

16. Leah Rawls Atkins, "Shug Jordan: Civil Engineer & Soldier," *Civil Engineering Newsletter* (Auburn University, Department of Civil Engineering), Spring 1988, 2–3.

17. *Birmingham Age-Herald*, 18 June 1943.

18. Roger A. Freeman, *Mighty Eighth War Diary* (London: Jane's, 1981), 35.

19. Ibid., 105, 247.

20. *Montgomery Advertiser*, 24 June 1945.

21. Grover C. Hall, Jr., *1000 Destroyed: The Life and Times of the 4th Fighter Group* (Montgomery: Brown Printing, 1946), 287.

22. Wolfe, *University of Alabama*, 173. At least ten Alabama pilots were recognized as "aces" for shooting down five or more enemy aircraft in World War II: Henry L. Condon II (Opelika), Jack S. Daniell (Birmingham), Elliot E. Dent, Jr. (Birmingham), Hoyt A. Eason (Eclectic), Andrew J. Evans (Montgomery), Samuel W. Forrer (Fitzpatrick), Paul G. McArthur (Reform), Leslie D. Minchew (Montgomery), John T. Moore (Montgomery), and Franklin W. Troup (Decatur). See Raymond F. Toliver and Trevor J. Constable,

Fighter Aces of the U.S.A. (Fallbrook, Calif.: Aero Publishers, 1979), 370–90. Several other aces—including Patrick D. Fleming, Noel Gayler, and David McCampbell—were born in Alabama but entered service elsewhere and are credited to other states.

23. Eddy Gilmore, *Me and My Russian Wife* (New York: Doubleday, 1954), 9; also idem, *After the Cossacks Burned Down the "Y"* (New York, Farrar, Straus, 1964), 1, 5, 23.

24. G. A. Shepperd, *The Italian Campaign, 1943–1945: A Political and Military Reassessment* (London: Arthur Baker, 1968), 3–16, 39–54.

25. On the Ninety-ninth Pursuit Squadron in southern Italy, see Davis, *Autobiography*, 98–101.

26. Rose, *Lonely Eagles*, 58. In his excitement when returning to his North African base, Campbell taxied accidentally, and with no great harm, into an unseen bomb crater.

27. Davis, *Autobiography*, 100.

28. Letter from Colonel Herbert E. Carter to the author, 12 June 1992. Relations between white and black pilots were professional and collegial. Pilots of the Seventy-ninth, who had more combat experience, willingly shared tactics and techniques with the pilots of the Ninety-ninth. According to Major George S. Roberts, who commanded the Ninety-ninth after the departure of Colonel Davis, this cooperation enabled his outfit to gain confidence rapidly. See Rose, *Lonely Eagles*, 63.

29. Rose, *Lonely Eagles*, 64.

30. Colonel Herbert E. Carter to the author, 12 June 1992.

31. Hardesty and Pisano, *Black Wings*, 53.

32. Stephen L. McFarland and Wesley P. Newton, *To Command the Sky: The Battle for Air Superiority over Germany, 1942–1944* (Washington, D.C.: Smithsonian Institution Press, 1991), 160–61. The authors contend that in early 1944 Major General Jimmy Doolittle—who had recently taken command of the Eighth Air Force—ordered a fundamental shift in fighter objectives. Earlier the mission of fighters had been to defend the bombers. In 1944 Doolittle decided the principal responsibility of fighters was to down German fighters and thus gain air superiority over Europe. According to McFarland and Newton, under Doolittle's new tactics the bombers were "used mainly as bait to lure German fighters into combat" (p. 161).

33. Ibid., 178–79.

34. Warren, *Spy in the Sky*, 137–39.

35. Diary entry for 6 June 1944, Isham "Ike" Dorsey papers, Record Group 832, Auburn University Archives, Auburn.

36. *Birmingham Age-Herald*, 2 July 1945.

37. *Montgomery Advertiser*, 13 April 1957.

38. Tom Ivie, *Aerial Reconnaissance: The 10th Photo Recon Group in World War II* (Fallbrook, Calif.: Aero Publishers, 1981), 139, 141, 161, 189.

39. *Montgomery Advertiser*, 28 January 1945; also see Robert S. Allen, *Lucky Forward: The History of Patton's Third Army* (New York: Vanguard Press, 1947), 181–84.

40. *Birmingham Age-Herald*, 25 August 1945.

41. George S. Patton, Jr., *War as I Knew It* (Boston: Houghton Mifflin, 1947), 114.

42. For an account of Miles Copeland's CIC activities in England and France, see his *The Game Player: Confessions of the CIA's Original Political Operative* (London: Aurum Press, 1989), 15–66.

43. U.S. House of Representatives and Senate, *Memorial Services . . . William F. Nichols*, 101st Congress, 1st sess. (Washington, D.C.: Government Printing Office, 1990). Nichols was born in Mississippi, but his family soon moved to Sylacauga, Alabama. Nichols

attended Alabama Polytechnic Institute in Auburn and earned two degrees in five years. He lettered in football and captained the team when he was completing his M.S. degree in agronomy in 1940. He turned down an opportunity to play professional football and instead worked as an assistant county farm agent in Autauga County. In 1942, as an ROTC graduate, he received his commission and was assigned to the Eighth Infantry Division. Nichols was also a longtime member of the Board of Trustees of Auburn University, where the ROTC building is named for him.

44. James E. Thompson, "A Journal of 'Papa T's' Army Days in World War II Europe ... As Viewed Forty Years Later" (manuscript, 1985, in possession of James E. Thompson, Jasper, Alabama), 9.

45. Russell F. Weigley, *Eisenhower's Lieutenants: The Campaign of France and Germany, 1944–1945* (Bloomington: Indiana University Press, 1981), 623–33.

46. Thompson, "'Papa T's' Army Days," 28.

10. Alabama and the War at Sea

1. Steve Ewing, *American Cruisers of World War II: A Pictorial Encyclopedia* (Missoula, Mont.: Pictorial Histories, 1984), 38–39; Public Information Subject Files—General, SG6939, Folder 88: USS *Alabama,* ADAH.

2. Naval Historical Center, Ships' History Branch (NHC/SHB), "*Tuscaloosa.*"

3. Morison, *Battle of the Atlantic,* 358–60.

4. Samuel Eliot Morison, *Operations in North African Waters, October 1942–June 1943* (Boston: Little, Brown, 1947), 36, 43, 91–114.

5. Samuel Eliot Morison, *The Invasion of France and Germany, 1944–1945* (Boston: Little, Brown, 1975), 86, 157, 161, 195–218, 271–76; idem, *Victory in the Pacific, 1945* (Boston: Little, Brown, 1961), 27, 30.

6. Ewing, *American Cruisers,* 109–10; Public Information Subject Files—General, SG6939, Folder 88: USS *Alabama,* ADAH; also see "War Record of the USS *Birmingham,*" in NHC/SHB; *Birmingham News,* 29 August 1945.

7. Samuel Eliot Morison, *Leyte: June 1944–January 1945* (Boston: Little, Brown, 1961), 86–109.

8. "War Record of the USS *Birmingham,*" in NHC/SHB; Morison, *Victory in the Pacific,* 148, 267; on Cabannis's role at Okinawa, see *Birmingham News,* 30 August 1945.

9. Ewing, *American Cruisers,* 111; Public Information Subject Files—General, SG6939, Folder 88: USS *Alabama,* ADAH; also see "War Record and Ship's History of the USS *Mobile,*" 26 September 1945, in NHC/SHB. The only major action that *Mobile* missed was at Iwo Jima when the cruiser was undergoing repairs in California.

10. Public Information Subject Files—General, SG6939, Folder 88: USS *Alabama,* ADAH. Semmes, a Navy pilot, subsequently flew seaplanes off USS *Alabama* as well as from USS *North Dakota* before becoming squadron commander on *Lunga Point* in waters near Okinawa later in the war. See Raphael Semmes, "Wildcat—The First Navy Cat," *Aerospace Historian* 28 (Spring 1981): 2–9.

11. Scott Orley, telephone conversation with author, 5 June 1992. Orley served as an antiaircraft gunner on USS *Alabama* from 1942 to 1946. Although the archives of the USS *Alabama* Battleship Memorial shed little light on the claim about the ship's early groundings, they do indicate that the ship spent a month in drydock for unspecified repairs before sailing for combat duty in Europe.

12. "Summary History of BB 60 (*Alabama*) prepared by the Office of Public Informa-

tion, Navy Department," Public Information Subject Files—General, SG6939, Folder 88: USS *Alabama*, ADAH; "History of USS *Alabama*," in NHC/SHB; Samuel Eliot Morison, *The Atlantic Battle Won, May 1943–May 1945* (Boston: Little, Brown, 1956), 229–31.

13. Samuel Eliot Morison, *The Two Ocean War: A Short History of the United States Navy in the Second World War* (Boston: Little, Brown, 1963), 343.

14. Harris, "Battle of Cape Esperance," 14–21.

15. On McMorris and Atkeson in the Aleutians, see John A. Lorelli, *The Battle of the Komandorski Islands, March 1943* (Annapolis: Naval Institute Press, 1984), 50–51, 140–41.

16. Spector, *Eagle against the Sun*, 180.

17. Jones, "Brain Center," 10–11, 38–39.

18. Thew, "America's Most Successful Submarine," 28–31; Blair, *Silent Victory*, 83, 99; Roscoe, *Submarine Operations*, 8–10; Samuel Eliot Morison, *The Rising Sun in the Pacific, 1931–April 1942* (Boston: Little, Brown, 1948), 213, n. 11.

19. On Charles and Richard Crommelin, see Barrett Tillman, *The Wildcat in WWII* (Annapolis: Nautical and Aviation Publishing, 1983), 14, 40, 49; idem, *Hellcat: The F6F in World War II* (Annapolis: Naval Institute Press, 1979), 30–33, 222.

20. *Montgomery Advertiser*, 8 August 1945; *New York Times*, 9 August 1945.

21. Edward P. Stafford, "Action Off Santa Cruz," in S. E. Smith, ed., *The United States Navy in World War II* (New York: William Morrow, 1966), 359–88.

22. Edward P. Stafford, *The Big E: The Story of the USS Enterprise* (New York: Random House, 1962), 403.

23. Edwin B. Hoyt, *The Men of the Gambier Bay* (Middlebury, Vt.: Paul S. Eriksson, 1979), 85.

24. John Beecher, *All Brave Sailors: The Story of the SS Booker T. Washington* (New York: L.B. Fischer, 1945), 87–88.

25. *Montgomery Advertiser*, 23 October 1944.

26. Schneider, *Navy V-12 Program*, xi–xii, 15, 437.

27. *Selma Times-Journal*, 16 May 1943.

11. Capturing the Pacific

1. D. M. Horner, *High Command: Australia and Allied Strategy, 1939–1945* (Sydney: George Allen and Unwin, 1982), 41–50, 65–128.

2. Robert Bain, telephone interview with author, 24 October 1991.

3. Thomas H. Moorer, "Routine Patrol out of Port Arthur," *Harper's Magazine* 185 (August 1942): 308–11; *Montgomery Advertiser*, 29 March 1942; "Three Hats for a Hero," *Time* 85 (26 February 1965): 21; Joel P. Smith, "WWII Heroics Launched Moorer's Naval Career," *Eufaula Tribune*, 13 December 1992.

4. John Miller, Jr., *Guadalcanal: The First Offensive*, vol. 2, pt. 3, of *U.S. Army in World War II: The War in the Pacific* (Washington, D.C.: Office of the Chief of Military History, Department of the Army, 1949), 2–3.

5. On the breaking of Japanese codes, see Edwin T. Layton, Roger Pineau, and John Costello, *"And I Was There"—Pearl Harbor and Midway—Breaking the Secrets* (New York: William Morrow, 1985).

6. John Costello, *The Pacific War* (New York: Rawson, Wade, 1981), 249–63.

7. Tillman, *Wildcat*, 31.

8. A. H. Hoehling, *The Lexington Goes Down* (Englewood Cliffs, N.J.: Prentice-Hall,

1971), 31; Spector, *Eagle against the Sun*, 150–51.

9. Howard Mingos, *American Heroes of the War in the Air* (New York: Lanciar, 1943), 106.

10. Costello, *Pacific War*, 263.

11. Tillman, *Wildcat*, 49.

12. Hoehling, *Lexington Goes Down*, 64.

13. Stanley Johnson, *Queen of the Flat-Tops: The USS Lexington and the Coral Sea Battle* (New York: E. P. Dutton, 1942), 237.

14. Record, *Dream Come True,* 2:252.

15. Costello, *Pacific War*, 399–400; for the war in the Aleutians, see Donald Goldstein and Katherine Dillon, *The Willawaw War: The Arkansas National Guard in the Aleutians in World War II* (Fayetteville: University of Arkansas Press, 1992).

16. Mitsuo Fuchida and Masatake Okumiya, *Midway: The Battle That Doomed Japan* (New York: Ballantine Books, 1958), 78–82.

17. Layton, Pineau, and Costello, *"And I Was There,"* 408–48.

18. Gordon W. Prange, *Miracle at Midway* (New York: McGraw-Hill, 1982), 397.

19. Robert Lee Sherrod, *History of Marine Corps Aviation in World War II* (Washington, D.C.: Combat Forces Press, 1952), 90.

20. *Birmingham Age-Herald*, 24 January 1944.

21. In 1936 the Alabama legislature created the Naval Militia, which consisted of naval reservists. Inducted into federal service, the reservists were sent to Norfolk for further training and most shipped out on the *Long Island*. Originally a C-3 cargo ship, the *Mormacmail*, was converted into a small, escort carrier—also known as a "Jeep carrier" or "Woolworth carrier"—and entered service in 1941 as the *Long Island*. On the role of the "Jeep carriers" in the war, see Samuel Eliot Morison, *The Struggle for Guadalcanal, August 1942–February 1943* (Boston: Little, Brown, 1950), 73–74.

22. See John Howard McEniry, *A Marine Dive-Bomber Pilot at Guadalcanal* (Tuscaloosa: University of Alabama Press, 1987).

23. Miller, *Guadalcanal*, 349–50.

24. *Birmingham News*, 10 April 1944.

25. Norman V. Cooper, *A Fighting General: Biography of Holland M. "Howlin Mad" Smith* (Quantico, Va.: Marine Corps Association, 1987), 2; Ralph B. Draughon, Jr., "General Holland M. Smith, U.S.M.C.," *Alabama Review* 21 (January 1968): 64–76; Harry A. Gailey, *Howlin' Mad vs. The Army: Conflict in Command, Saipan 1944* (Novato, Calif.: Presidio Press, 1986). Also see Holland Smith's autobiography written with Percy Finch, *Coral and Brass* (New York: Charles Scribner's Sons, 1949).

26. On the career of Higgins, see Michael Jernigan, "Andrew Jackson Higgins: Southern Entrepreneur" (Master's thesis, Auburn University, 1986); also John A. Heitmann, "Demagogue and Industrialist: Andrew Jackson Higgins and Higgins Industries," *Gulf Coast Historical Review* 5 (Spring 1990): 152–62; and Gailey, *Howlin' Mad*, 25.

27. Cooper, *Fighting General*, 103.

28. See "A Brief Resume of the Saipan Incident," in Love, *27th Infantry Division*, app. 1; also Gailey, *Howlin' Mad*, 1–19.

29. *Birmingham News*, 19 April 1953.

30. *Mobile Register*, 5 December 1945; William S. Coker, *The Mobile Cadets, 1845–1945: A Century of Honor and Fidelity* (Bagdad, Fla.: Patagonia Press, 1993), 177–93.

31. On General John Persons, see the brief but excellent biography by Margaret England Armbrester, *John C. Persons: Citizen-Soldier* (Birmingham: Oxmoor Press, 1974);

John C. Persons, "The 31st Infantry (Dixie) Division in World War II" (paper read before the Alabama Historical Association, sixth annual meeting, Mobile, 24 April 1953); and George C. Hinckley, "John Cecil Persons: Southern Businessman and Military Leader" (Master's thesis, Samford University, 1975). The John C. Persons Collection at ADAH consists of scrapbooks containing correspondence, photographs, and other personal items.

32. Armbrester, *Persons*, 71–72. By some accounts, Persons formed a rather unflattering view of Patton at the Carolina maneuvers. Persons came to regard his junior as slipshod with respect to security and reconnaissance, and unmindful of orders. See Hinckley, "Persons," 106. A story told very proudly by E. B. Peebles of Mobile about Patton during Louisiana maneuvers lends some credence to this assessment. According to Peebles, his Thirty-first Cavalry Reconnaissance unit infiltrated Patton's headquarters in a schoolhouse. To prove it had been there, his unit set off smokebombs. "Patton was mad as hell," Peebles said, "and I kept getting the bill for damages for years afterward. But, of course, I never paid anything." E. B. Peebles, telephone interview with author, 14 April 1992.

33. Coker, *Mobile Cadets*, 181.

34. Armbrester, *Persons*, 76–77.

35. On the Thirty-first Division in combat in the Pacific, see *History of the 31st Infantry Division in the Pacific* (Baton Rouge: Army and Navy Publishing, 1946) and *167th Infantry* (Baton Rouge: Army and Navy Publishing, 1951).

36. On the Aitape operation, see Walter Krueger's account, *From Down Under to Nippon: The Story of the Sixth Army in World War II* (Nashville: Battery Classics, 1989), 69–78; Robert Ross Smith, *The Approach to the Philippines*, vol. 2, pt. 12, of *U.S. Army in World War II: The War in the Pacific* (Washington, D.C.: Office of the Chief of Military History, Department of the Army, 1953), 103–205.

37. Persons, "31st Infantry Division," 17.

38. *Alabama Guardsman* 2 (August 1982): 4. Ten years later Lieutenant General Hanna commanded National Guard forces sent to maintain order in Phenix City following the assassination of Alabama attorney general Albert J. Patterson.

39. *History of the 31st Division*, 20; Armbrester, *Persons*, 77, 86; Smith, *Approach to the Philippines*, 277; and *167th Infantry*.

40. On the Morotai operation, see Krueger, *From Down Under*, 122–32; *History of the 31st Division*, 20–22; Smith, *Approach to the Philippines*, 275–493; Collier, *War in the Far East*, 395.

41. Krueger, *From Down Under*, 122–32.

42. Smith, *Approach to the Philippines*, 483.

43. Krueger, *From Down Under*, 129.

44. Armbrester, *Persons*, 88–90.

45. Colonel W. J. Hanna to Wallace Houston, New Guinea, 27 July 1944, Persons Collection.

46. Joseph Langan, telephone interview with author, 3 January 1992. E. B. Peebles of Mobile, provost marshal of the Thirty-first Division at the end of the war, shares Langan's opinion. In a telephone interview with the author, 14 April 1992, Peebles expressed the view that tensions between National Guard and regular Army officers, plus the disappointment over failing to make lieutenant general and corps commander, led Persons to request permission to return to Birmingham.

47. See correspondence, including MacArthur's 22 September 1944 approval of Persons's request for a leave of absence, in Persons Collection (scrapbook), vol. 4.

48. Eugene B. Sledge, *With the Old Breed at Peleliu and Okinawa* (Novato, Calif.: Presidio Press, 1981; reprint, New York: Oxford University Press, 1990).

49. Paul Fussell, *Wartime: Understanding and Behavior in the Second World War* (New York: Oxford University, 1989), 292.

50. Sledge, *With the Old Breed*, 55–56.

51. Ibid., 218, 156.

52. For a vivid description of the battle at Peleliu, see Harry A. Gailey, *Peleliu 1944* (Annapolis: Nautical and Aviation Publishing, 1983).

53. *Birmingham Age-Herald*, 30 November 1944.

54. Sledge, *With the Old Breed*, 267.

55. Ibid., 268, n. 312.

56. William Slim, *Defeat into Victory* (New York: David McKay, 1961), 140–41; Collier, *War in the Far East*, 400–401; Ronald Lewin, *Slim: The Standardbearer* (London: Archon Books, 1976), 138.

57. See Leslie Anders, *The Ledo Road: General Joseph W. Stilwell's Highway to China* (Norman: University of Oklahoma Press, 1965); Don Moser, *China-Burma-India* (Alexandria, Va.: Time-Life Books, 1978), 194–203.

58. Anders, *Ledo Road*, 213.

59. "History of the Dixie Division," in *167th Infantry*; Smith, *Approach to the Philippines*, 450, n. 1.

60. United States Senate, Committee on Veterans' Affairs, *Medal of Honor Recipients, 1863–1978* (Washington, D.C.: Government Printing Office, 1979), 571.

61. *Birmingham Age-Herald*, 22 March 1945.

62. Costello, *Pacific War*, 547–53.

63. Baker and Hughes, *Redstone Arsenal Complex Chronology*, pt. 1: *Pre-Missile Era*, 37. On the effectiveness of the M-69 napalm bombs, see Spector, *Eagle against the Sun*, 491–92.

64. Ben Johnson, telephone interview with author, 15 August 1991.

65. Sledge, *With the Old Breed*, 253.

66. Roy Edgar Appleman, James M. Burns, Russel A. Gugeler, and John Stevens, *Okinawa: The Last Battle*, vol. 2, pt. 11, of *U.S. Army in World War II: The War in the Pacific* (Washington, D.C.: Office of the Chief of Military History, Department of the Army, 1948), 461; George Feifer, *Tennozan: The Battle of Okinawa and the Atomic Bomb* (New York: Ticknor and Fields, 1992), 502–4.

67. One important figure, General Holland Smith, was not present at the surrender ceremony. For the former commander of the Fifth Amphibious Corps, which had taken one Japanese-held island after another in the central Pacific, this snub was the most bitter pill in his career as a Marine Corps officer.

12. The End of the War

1. Leah Rawls Atkins with Flora Jones Beavers, *The Jones Family of Huntsville Road* (Birmingham: Privately printed, 1981), 150.

2. *Birmingham World*, 15 May 1945.

3. *Montgomery Advertiser*, 15 August 1945; *Birmingham News*, 16 August 1945.

4. For a summary of the costs of the war, see John Keegan, *The Second World War* (New York: Penguin Books, 1989), 588–95.

5. War Department, *Honor List*; United States Navy Department, Office of Informa-

tion, *Combat Connected Naval Casualties, World War, by States,* vol. 1: *Alabama through Missouri* (Washington, D.C.: Government Printing Office, 1946).

6. *Birmingham News,* 20 July 1946.

7. War Production Board, *Summary of War Supply and Facility Contracts by State, Industrial Area and County: Cumulative through June 1944,* copy in Sparks files: Henry S. Geismer.

8. Bruce Joseph Schulman, "From Cotton Belt to Sunbelt: Federal Policy and Southern Economic Development, 1933–1980" (Ph.D. diss., Stanford University, 1987), 156–59.

9. Department of Public Health, *Alabama's Population,* 65–68.

Appendix: Alabama's War Heroes

1. *Montgomery Advertiser,* 24 January 1943.

2. *Birmingham News,* 14 March 1944.

3. Senate Committee on Veterans' Affairs, *Medal of Honor Recipients,* 532–33.

4. Ibid., 500; for an account of the Battle of the Dikes and the crossing of the Mark, see Leo A. Hoegh and Howard J. Doyle, *Timberwolf Tracks: The History of the 104th Infantry Division, 1942–1945* (Washington, D.C.: Infantry Journal Press, 1946), 75–93; *Birmingham News,* 24, 29, and 30 August 1945.

5. *Birmingham News,* 29 and 30 August 1945.

6. Senate Committee on Veterans' Affairs, *Medal of Honor Recipients,* 499.

7. Sledge, *With the Old Breed,* 55; Senate Committee on Veterans' Affairs, *Medal of Honor Recipients,* 641–42; on the role of the First Marine Division on Peleliu, see Gailey, *Peleliu 1944.*

8. Senate Committee on Veterans' Affairs, *Medal of Honor Recipients,* 564; *Birmingham Age-Herald,* 17 April 1946.

9. Senate Committee on Veterans' Affairs, *Medal of Honor Recipients,* 601–2; *Birmingham Age-Herald,* 15 August 1944; *Birmingham News,* 31 August 1945.

10. Senate Committee on Veterans' Affairs, *Medal of Honor Recipients,* 545–46; *Birmingham Age-Herald,* 25 April 1945; Sidney Shallett, "Above and Beyond the Call of Duty," *New York Times Magazine,* 17 June 1945, sec. 6, 10, 35–36; *Birmingham News,* 31 August 1945.

11. Karl Schuon, *U.S. Navy Biographical Dictionary* (New York: Franklin Watts, 1964), 155–56; Edwin P. Hoyt, *McCampbell's Heroes: The Story of the U.S. Navy's Most Celebrated Carrier Fighters of the Pacific War,* with introduction by Captain David McCampbell (New York: Van Nostrand Reinhold, 1983), 51–60, 140–52; Tillman, *Hellcat,* 77–84, 139–41; *Birmingham News,* 23 August 1945; also see entry on McCampbell in Senate Committee on Veterans' Affairs, *Medal of Honor Recipients,* 617–18.

12. Senate Committee on Veterans' Affairs, *Medal of Honor Recipients,* 605–6.

13. A monument at the USS *Alabama* Battleship Memorial Park in Mobile commemorates Howard Walter Gilmore and the *Growler.* For a brief sketch of his career and the *Growler's* fourth war patrol, see Blair, *Silent Victory,* 269–70, 373–75; Edwin P. Hoyt, *Submarines at War: The History of the American Silent Service* (New York: Stein and Day, 1983), 144, 183–86.

14. *Birmingham Post,* 21 August 1942; *Birmingham News,* 25 August 1942.

15. *Birmingham World,* 15 May 1945.

Bibliography

Primary Sources

Archives

Alabama Department of Archives and History, Montgomery, Alabama.
    Alabama Governor (1939–1943: Frank Murray Dixon), Administrative Files.
    Alabama Governor (1943–1947: Chauncey Sparks), Administrative Files.
    Aliceville Prisoner of War Camp Collection.
    Frank Boykin Collection.
    John C. Persons Collection.
    Vera Ruth "Millie" (Gomillion) Prentiss Collection.
    Public Information Subject Files.
    WSFA (radio station, Montgomery), *Letters from Home*.
Aliceville Public Library, Aliceville, Alabama.
    Aliceville Prisoner of War Camp Collection.
Auburn University Archives, Auburn, Alabama.
    Isham "Ike" Dorsey papers. Record Group 832.
    Franklin A. Hart papers. Record Group 25.
    Holland M. Smith papers. Record Group 41.
    Joseph Stewart papers. Record Group 45.
Birmingham Public Library, Tutwiler Collection of Southern History, Birmingham, Alabama.
    "World War II Scrapbooks, 1939–1945." 11 vols.
National Archives and Records Administration, Washington, D.C.
    Records Relating to U-Boat Warfare, 1939–1945. Record Group 242.
United States Navy. Naval Historical Center, Ships' History Branch, Washington, D.C.
    War records and ships' histories of *Alabama* (BB-60), *Birmingham* (CL-62), *Mobile* (CL-63), *Tuscaloosa* (CA-37).
University of South Alabama Archives. Mobile, Alabama.
    Alabama Drydock and Shipbuilding Company (ADDSCO) collection.

Periodicals

Alabama, 1941–42.
Birmingham Age-Herald, 1940–45.
Birmingham News, 1940–46.
Birmingham Post, 1941–45.
Birmingham World, 1941, 1943, 1945.
Harper's Magazine, 1942.
Mobile Press Register, 1941–42.
Montgomery Advertiser, 1941–45.
New York Times, 1941, 1945.
Selma Times-Journal, 1941, 1943.

Reports, Memoirs, and Personal Accounts

Alabama Baptist State Convention. *Annual Report of the Alabama Baptist State Convention: 1942*. N.p., 1943.

Alabama Department of Agriculture and Industries. *Alabama Agricultural Statistics Service News*, 7 April 1990.

Alabama Department of Public Health. *Alabama's Population, 1930–1976*. Montgomery: Alabama Department of Public Health, Division of Vital Statistics, 1977.

Alabama Power Company. *Annual Report of Alabama Power Company for 1942*. Birmingham: Alabama Power Company, 1943.

Alabama State Department of Public Health. *Annual Report of the State Department of Public Health of Alabama: 1940*. Wetumpka: Wetumpka Printing, 1941.

———. *Annual Report of the State Department of Public Health of Alabama: 1942*. Wetumpka: Wetumpka Printing, 1943.

———. *Annual Report of the State Department of Public Health of Alabama: 1953*. Wetumpka: Wetumpka Printing, 1954.

Alabama State Military Department. Office of the Adjutant General. *Quadrennial Report of the Adjutant General for the Four Year Period Ending September 30, 1942*. N.p., n.d.

Atkins, Leah Rawls, with Flora Jones Beavers. *The Jones Family of Huntsville Road*. Birmingham: Privately printed, 1981.

Austin, B. F. "The Impact of the War on the Health Department." *Journal of the Medical Association of the State of Alabama* 15 (February 1946): 243–46.

Bank, Bert. *Back from the Living Dead: An Original Story Describing the Infamous March of Death—33 Months in a Japanese Prison and Liberation by the Rangers*. Tuscaloosa: N.p., 1945.

Beecher, John. *All Brave Sailors: The Story of the SS Booker T. Washington*. New York: L. B. Fischer, 1945.

Bennett-Wright, Lucille. "Army Memories." Manuscript in possession of James E. Thompson, Jasper, Alabama.

Bureau of Business Research. School of Commerce and Business Administration. University of Alabama. *Alabama County Statistical Abstracts*. Multilithed Series no. 4. University, 1944.

Cason, Cleo, and Winona Stroup. "The Early Years of Redstone Arsenal." *Huntsville Historical Review* 1 (July 1971): 29–43.

Chestnut, J. L., Jr., and Julia Cass. *Black in Selma: The Uncommon Life of J. L. Chestnut, Jr.* New York: Farrar, Straus and Giroux, 1990.

Churchill, Winston S. *The Hinge of Fate*. Vol. 4 of *The Second World War*. Boston: Houghton Mifflin, 1950.

Cochran, Jackie, and Maryann Bucknum Brinley. *Jackie Cochran: The Autobiography of the Greatest Woman Pilot in Aviation History*. New York: Bantam Books, 1987.

Cohen, Bernard M., and Maurice Z. Cooper. *A Follow-Up Study of World War II Prisoners of War*. Washington, D.C.: Veterans Administration, 1954.

Copeland, Miles. *The Game Player: Confessions of the CIA's Original Political Operative*. London: Aurum Press, 1989.

Davis, Benjamin O., Jr. *Benjamin O. Davis, Jr., American: An Autobiography*. Washington, D.C.: Smithsonian Institution Press, 1991.

Doenitz, Karl. *Memoirs: Ten Years and Twenty Days*. Annapolis: Naval Institute Press, 1990.

Dos Passos, John. *State of the Nation*. Boston: Houghton Mifflin, 1944.

Draughon, Ralph Brown. *Alabama Polytechnic Institute*. New York: Newcomen Society in North America, 1954.

Durr, Virginia. *Outside the Magic Circle: The Autobiography of Virginia Foster Durr*. Edited by Hollinger F. Barnard. University: University of Alabama Press, 1985.

Egger, Bruce, and Lee MacMillan Otts. *G Company's War: Two Personal Accounts of the Campaign in Europe, 1944–1945*. Edited and with commentary by Paul Roley. Tuscaloosa: University of Alabama Press, 1992.

Eisenhower, Dwight David. *At Ease: Stories I Tell to Friends*. Garden City, N.Y.: Doubleday, 1967.

———. *The Eisenhower Diaries*. New York: W. W. Norton, 1981.

Farmer, Hallie, ed. *War Comes to Alabama*. University: Bureau of Public Administration, University of Alabama, 1943.

First National Bank of Mobile. *Highlights of 100 Years in Mobile*. Mobile: N.p., 1965.

Fisher, Douglas A. *Steel in the War*. New York: United States Steel, 1946.

Fuchida, Mitsuo, and Masatake Okumiya. *Midway: The Battle That Doomed Japan*. New York: Ballantine Books, 1958.

Gärtner, Georg. *Hitler's Last Soldier in America*. New York: Stein and Day, 1985.

Gilmore, Eddy. *After the Cossacks Burned Down the "Y."* New York: Farrar, Straus, 1964.

———. *Me and My Russian Wife*. New York: Doubleday, 1954.

Guzman, Jessie Parkhurst, ed. *Negro Year Book: A Review of Events Affecting Negro Life, 1941–1946*. Tuskegee Institute: Department of Records and Research, 1947.

Hall, Grover C., Jr. *1000 Destroyed: The Life and Times of the 4th Fighter Group*. Montgomery: Brown Printing, 1946.

Harris, Seale. "Medical Education in Alabama and Mississippi." *Journal of the Medical Association of the State of Alabama* 14 (October 1944): 93–96.

Hawley, Marion H. *Employment and Wage Payments in Alabama in Firms Covered by Unemployment Compensation, 1939–1946*. University of Alabama Bureau of Business Research, Mimeographed Series no. 10. University: Bureau of Business Research, 1947.

History of the 31st Infantry Division in the Pacific. Baton Rouge: Army and Navy Publishing, 1946.

James, D. Clayton, ed. *South to Bataan/North to Mukden: The Prison Diary of Brigadier General W. E. Brougher*. Athens: University of Georgia Press, 1971.

Jefferson County Chapter, American Red Cross. *World War II History of Jefferson County Chapter American Red Cross: A Report to the Membership . . . September 1, 1939–December 31, 1945*. Birmingham: [Jefferson County Chapter, American Red Cross], 1946.

Jones, George E. "Brain Center of the Pacific War." *New York Times Magazine*, 8 April 1945, sec. 6, 10–11, 38–39.

Krueger, Walter. *From Down Under to Nippon: The Story of the Sixth Army in World War II*. Nashville: Battery Classics, 1989.

Layton, Edwin T., Roger Pineau, and John Costello. *"And I Was There"—Pearl Harbor and Midway—Breaking the Secrets*. New York: William Morrow, 1985.

Locker, H. M. "Hell over Bizerte." *Air Force* 26 (August 1943): 11, 44.

Loewenheim, Francis L., Harold D. Langley, and Manfred Jonas, eds. *Roosevelt and Churchill: Their Secret Wartime Correspondence*. New York: Saturday Review Press, 1975.

Love, Edmund G. *The 27th Infantry Division in World War II.* Washington, D.C.: Infantry Journal Press, 1949

McDaniel, John L. "The Memoirs of John L. McDaniel." *Historic Huntsville Quarterly* 17 (Winter–Spring 1991): 73–91.

McEniry, John Howard. *A Marine Dive-Bomber Pilot at Guadalcanal.* Tuscaloosa: University of Alabama Press, 1987.

Moorer, Thomas H. "Routine Patrol out of Port Arthur." *Harper's Magazine* 185 (August 1942): 308–11.

167th Infantry. Baton Rouge: Army and Navy Publishing, 1951.

Patton, George S., Jr. *War as I Knew It.* Boston: Houghton Mifflin, 1947.

Persons, John C. "The 31st Infantry (Dixie) Division in World War II." Paper read before the Alabama Historical Association, sixth annual meeting, Mobile, 24 April 1953.

Pictorial History: Twenty-Seventh Division, United States Army, 1940–1941. Atlanta: Army-Navy Publishers, 1941.

Public Life of Frank M. Dixon: Sketches and Speeches. Alabama Department of Archives and History, Historical and Patriotic Series no. 18. Montgomery: Skinner Printing, 1979.

Rauber, Earle L. *The Alabama State Docks: A Case Study in State Development.* Atlanta: Federal Reserve Bank of Atlanta, 1945.

"Resolution Concerning War." *Journal of the Alabama Conference, The Methodist Church.* 4th sess. Montgomery, 11–15 November 1942, 55.

Ryder-Bush, Annie Louise. *Memoirs of Childersburg.* Alexander City, Ala.: Bama Printing, 1976.

Shallett, Sidney. "Above and Beyond the Call of Duty." *New York Times Magazine,* 17 June 1945, sec. 6, 10, 35–36.

Sledge, Eugene B. *With the Old Breed at Peleliu and Okinawa.* Novato, Calif.: Presidio Press, 1981. Reprint. New York: Oxford University Press, 1990.

Slim, William. *Defeat Into Victory.* New York: David McKay, 1961.

Smith, Holland M., and Percy Finch. *Coral and Brass.* New York: Charles Scribner's Sons, 1949.

Smyth, W. H. Y., D. G. Gill, and S. R. Damon. "A Preliminary Report of Blood Testing, As Required by Alabama Law, In the First Three Counties Surveyed." *Journal of the Medical Association of the State of Alabama* 14 (October 1944): 86–92.

Sullivan, Ellen, and Marie Stokes Jamison. *An Alabama Scrapbook: 32 Alabamians Remember Growing Up.* Huntsville: Honeysuckle Imprint, 1988.

This is Camp Sibert, Alabama: Chemical Warfare Service. Brooklyn: Ullmann, n.d.

Thompson, James E. "A Journal of 'Papa T's' Army Days in World War II Europe . . . As Viewed Forty Years Later." Manuscript, 1985, in possession of James E. Thompson, Jasper, Alabama.

United States Navy Department. Office of Information. *Combat Connected Naval Casualties, World War, by States.* Vol. 1: *Alabama through Missouri.* Washington, D.C.: Government Printing Office, 1946.

United States Senate. Committee on Veterans' Affairs. *Medal of Honor Recipients, 1863–1978.* Washington, D.C.: Government Printing Office, 1979.

United States War Department. Bureau of Public Relations. *World War II Honor List of Dead and Missing: State of Alabama.* Washington, D.C.: N.p., 1946.

Warren, Hoyt M. *The Making of a Spy in the Sky: A Story of a World War II Pilot.* Abbeville, Ala.: Henry County Historical Society, 1982.

Secondary Sources

Alabama Committee to the United States Commission on Civil Rights. *The Tuskegee Study*. N.p., 1973.

The Alabama Negro, 1863–1946. Mobile. Gulf Informer Publishing, 1946.

Allen, Robert S. *Lucky Forward: The History of Patton's Third Army*. New York: Vanguard Press, 1947.

Alsobrook, David E. "Auburn in The 'Good War.'" *Auburn Alumnews* 46 (July–August 1991): 6–7.

———. "Boomtown on the Plains." *Auburn Alumnews* 46 (September 1991): 10–11.

Alvord, B. F., H. E. Klontz, and S. C. McIntyre, eds. *Childersburg Pilot Study: A Survey of the Impact of Rapid Industrial Development in a Southern Community*. Auburn: Alabama Polytechnic Institute, Auburn Research Foundation, 1953.

Ambrose, Stephen F. *Eisenhower*. Vol. 1, *Soldier, General of the Army, President Elect*. New York: Simon and Schuster, 1983.

Anders, Leslie. *The Ledo Road: General Joseph W. Stilwell's Highway to China*. Norman: University of Oklahoma Press, 1965.

Anderson, Elizabeth Lynne. "Improving Rural Life in Alabama: The Home Demonstration Program, 1911–1972." Master's thesis, Auburn University, 1984.

Anderson, Karen. *Wartime Women: Sex Roles, Family Relations, and the Status of Women during World War II*. Westport, Conn.: Greenwood Press, 1981.

Appleman, Roy Edgar, James M. Burns, Russel A. Gugeler, and John Stevens. *Okinawa: The Last Battle*. Vol. 2, pt. 11, of *U.S. Army in World War II: The War in the Pacific*. Washington, D.C.: Office of the Chief of Military History, Department of the Army, 1948.

Armbrester, Margaret England. *John C. Persons: Citizen-Soldier*. Birmingham: Oxmoor Press, 1974.

Atkins, Leah Rawls. "Shug Jordan: Civil Engineer & Soldier." *Civil Engineering Newsletter* (Auburn University, Department of Civil Engineering), Spring 1988, 2–3.

———. *The Valley and the Hills: An Illustrated History of Birmingham and Jefferson County*. Woodland Hills, Calif.: Windsor Publications, 1981.

Axford, Faye A. *Limestone County during World War II*. Athens, Ala.: Limestone County Historical Society, 1983.

Baker, Michael E., and Kaylene Hughes, eds. *Redstone Arsenal Complex Chronology*. Pt. 1, *The Pre-Missile Era (1941–1949)*. Redstone Arsenal, Ala.: Historical Division, U.S. Army Missile Command, 1991.

Barnard, William D. *Dixiecrats and Democrats: Alabama Politics, 1942–1950*. University: University of Alabama Press, 1974.

———. "The Old Order Changes: Graves, Sparks, Folsom, and the Gubernatorial Election of 1942." *Alabama Review* 28 (July 1975): 163–84.

Barrett, Kayla. "Auburn's Soldier Statesman." *Auburn Alumnews* 47 (January–February 1993): 6–8.

Bevis, John David. "Frank M. Dixon: Alabama's Reform Governor." Master's thesis, Samford University, 1968.

Billinger, Robert D., Jr. "With the Wehrmacht in Florida: The German POW Facility at Camp Blanding, 1942–1946." *Florida Historical Quarterly* 58 (October 1979): 160–73.

Blair, Clay, Jr. *Silent Victory: The U.S. Submarine War against Japan*. Philadelphia: J. B. Lippincott, 1975.

Boykin, Edward. *Everything's Made for Love in this Man's World: Vignettes from the Life of Frank W. Boykin*. Mobile: Privately printed, 1973.

Brophy, Leo P., and George J. B. Fisher. *The Chemical Warfare Service: Organizing for War*. Vol. 6, pt. 7:1, of *U.S. Army in World War II: The Technical Services*. Washington, D.C.: Office of the Chief of Military History, Department of the Army, 1959.

Brophy, Leo P., Wyndham D. Miles, and Rexmond C. Cochrane. *The Chemical Warfare Service: From Laboratory to Field*. Vol. 6, pt. 7:2, of *U.S. Army in World War II: The Technical Services*. Washington, D.C.: Office of the Chief of Military History, Department of the Army, 1959.

Brown, Anthony Cave, and Charles B. MacDonald, eds. *The Secret History of the Atomic Bomb*. New York: Dial Press, 1977.

Campbell, D'Ann. *Women at War with America: Private Lives in a Patriotic Era*. Cambridge: Harvard University Press, 1984.

Carter, Kit. *The Army Air Forces in World War II: Combat Chronology, 1941–1945*. New York: Arno Press, 1980.

Chafe, William. *The American Woman: Her Changing Social, Economic and Political Roles, 1920–1970*. New York: Oxford University Press, 1972.

Childress, David T. "The Impact of World War II on Northeast Alabama." Paper presented at the Alabama Studies Symposium, Alabama Department of Archives and History, Montgomery, 7 August 1992.

Cobb, James C. *The Selling of the South: The Southern Crusade for Industrial Development, 1936–1980*. Baton Rouge: Louisiana State University Press, 1982.

Coker, William S., ed. *The Mobile Cadets, 1845–1945: A Century of Honor and Fidelity*. Bagdad, Fla.: Patagonia Press, 1993.

Cole, Jean Hascall. *Women Pilots of World War II*. Salt Lake City: University of Utah Press, 1992.

Collier, Basil. *The War in the Far East, 1941–1945: A Military History*. London: Heinemann, 1969.

Collier, John M. *Earl McGowin of Alabama: A Portrait*. New Orleans: Faust, 1986.

Cooper, Norman V. *A Fighting General: Biography of Holland M. "Howlin Mad" Smith*. Quantico, Va.: Marine Corps Association, 1987.

Costello, John. *The Pacific War*. New York: Rawson, Wade, 1981.

Craf, John Riley. *A Survey of the American Economy, 1940–1946*. New York: North River Press, 1947.

Craven, Wesley Frank, and James Lea Cate, eds. *Men and Planes*. Vol. 6 of *The Army Air Forces in World War II*. Chicago: University of Chicago Press, 1955.

——. *Plans and Early Operations, January 1939–August 1942*. Vol. 1 of *The Army Air Forces in World War II*. Chicago: University of Chicago Press, 1948.

Cray, Ed. *General of the Army: George C. Marshall, Soldier and Statesman*. New York: W. W. Norton, 1990.

Crews, Mickey. *The Church of God: A Social History*. Knoxville: University of Tennessee Press, 1990.

Cronenberg, Allen. "U-Boats in the Gulf: The Undersea War in 1942." *Gulf Coast Historical Review* 5 (Spring 1990): 163–78.

Dickson, Nancy. "Huntsville, the Arsenal, and Miss Susie." *Historic Huntsville Quarterly* 17 (Winter–Spring 1991): 23–41.

Donelson, Cathalynn. *Mobile: Sunbelt Center of Opportunity*. Northridge, Calif.: Windsor Publications, 1986.

Dooling, Dave, and Sharon Dooling. *Huntsville: A Pictorial History*. Virginia Beach, Va.: Donning, 1980.

Dower, John W. *War without Mercy: Race and Power in the Pacific War*. New York: Pantheon Books, 1986.

Doyle, Frederick J. "German Prisoners of War in the Southwest United States during World War II: An Oral History." Ph.D. diss., University of Denver, 1978.

Draughon, Ralph Brown, Jr. "General Holland M. Smith, U.S.M.C." *Alabama Review* 21 (January 1968): 64–76.

Elovitz, Mark H. *A Century of Jewish Life in Dixie: The Birmingham Experience*. University: University of Alabama Press, 1974.

Ewing, Steve. *American Cruisers of World War II: A Pictorial Encyclopedia*. Missoula, Mont.: Pictorial Histories, 1984.

Faulkner, Jane, ed. *The Story of Stockham: Links to Better Living, 1903–1953—50 Golden Years—Stockham Valves and Fittings*. Birmingham: Stockham, 1953.

Feifer, George. *Tennozan: The Battle of Okinawa and the Atomic Bomb*. New York: Ticknor and Fields, 1992.

Ferguson, William C. *Black Flyers in World War II*. Cleveland: W. C. Ferguson, 1987.

Fickle, James E., and Donald W. Ellis. "POWs in the Piney Woods: German Prisoners of War in the Southern Lumber Industry, 1943–1945." *Journal of Southern History* 56 (November 1990): 695–724.

Fisher, Douglas A. *Steel Serves the Nation, 1901–1951: The Fifty Year Story of United States Steel*. New York: Lind Brothers, 1951.

Flynt, Wayne. *Poor but Proud: Alabama's Poor Whites*. Tuscaloosa: University of Alabama Press, 1989.

Fogerty, Robert P. *Biographical Study of USAF General Officers, 1917–1952*. 2 vols. Manhattan, Kans.: MA/AH Publishing, 1980.

Foscue, Virginia O. *Place Names in Alabama*. Tuscaloosa: University of Alabama Press, 1989.

Francis, Charles E. *The Tuskegee Airmen: The Story of the Negro in the U.S. Air Force*. Boston: Bruce Humphries, 1955.

Franklin, Jimmie Lewis. *Back to Birmingham: Richard Arrington, Jr., and His Times*. Tuscaloosa: University of Alabama Press, 1989.

Freeman, Roger A. *The Mighty Eighth: Units, Men and Machines*. Garden City, N.Y.: Doubleday, 1970.

———. *Mighty Eighth War Diary*. London: Jane's, 1981.

Fussell, Paul. *Wartime: Understanding and Behavior in the Second World War*. New York: Oxford University Press, 1989.

Gailey, Harry A. *Howlin' Mad vs. The Army: Conflict in Command, Saipan 1944*. Novato, Calif.: Presidio Press, 1986.

———. *Peleliu 1944*. Annapolis: Nautical and Aviation Publishing, 1983.

Gannon, Michael. *Operation Drumbeat: The Dramatic True Story of Germany's First U-Boat Attacks along the American Coast in World War II*. New York: Harper and Row, 1990.

Gansberg, Judith M. *Stalag, U.S.A.: The Remarkable Story of German POWs in America*. New York: Thomas Y. Crowell, 1977.

Goldstein, Donald, and Katherine Dillon. *The Willawaw War: The Arkansas National*

Guard in the Aleutians in World War II. Fayetteville: University of Arkansas Press, 1992.

Grafton, Carl. "James E. Folsom's First Four Election Campaigns: Learning to Win by Losing." *Alabama Review* 34 (July 1981): 163–83.

Grafton, Carl, and Anne Permaloff. *Big Mules and Branchheads: James E. Folsom and Political Power in Alabama.* Athens: University of Georgia Press, 1985.

Hamilton, Virginia Van der Veer. *Lister Hill: Statesman from the South.* Chapel Hill: University of North Carolina Press, 1987.

Hardesty, Von, and Dominick Pisano. *Black Wings: The American Black in Aviation.* Washington, D.C.: Smithsonian Institution Press, 1983.

Harris, Russell. "Battle of Cape Esperance." *Sea Classics* 23 (April 1990): 14–21.

Harrison, Patricia G. "Riveters, Volunteers and WACS: Women in Mobile during World War II." *Gulf Coast Historical Review* 1 (Spring 1986): 33–54.

Hartmann, Susan M. *The Homefront and Beyond: American Women in the 1940s.* Boston: Twayne Publishers, 1982.

Hawks, Joanne Varner. "A Select Few: Alabama's Women Legislators, 1922–1983." *Alabama Review* 38 (July 1985): 175–201.

Heitmann, John A. "Demagogue and Industrialist: Andrew Jackson Higgins and Higgins Industries." *Gulf Coast Historical Review* 5 (Spring 1990): 152–62.

Hinckley, George C. "John Cecil Persons: Southern Businessman and Military Leader." Master's thesis, Samford University, 1975.

Hoegh, Leo A., and Howard J. Doyle. *Timberwolf Tracks: The History of the 104th Infantry Division, 1942–1945.* Washington, D.C.: Infantry Journal Press, 1946.

Hoehling, A. A. *The Lexington Goes Down.* Englewood Cliffs, N.J.: Prentice-Hall, 1971.

Honey, Maureen. *Creating Rosie the Riveter: Class, Gender and Propaganda during World War II.* Amherst: University of Massachusetts Press, 1984.

Hoole, W. Stanley. "Alabama's World War II Prisoner of War Camps." *Alabama Review* 20 (April 1967): 83–114.

Horner, D. M. *High Command: Australia and Allied Strategy, 1939–1945.* Sydney: George Allen and Unwin, 1982.

Hoyt, Edwin P. *McCampbell's Heroes: The Story of the U.S. Navy's Most Celebrated Carrier Fighters of the Pacific War.* Introduction by Captain David McCampbell. New York: Van Nostrand Reinhold, 1983.

———. *The Men of the Gambier Bay.* Middlebury, Vt.: Paul S. Eriksson, 1979.

———. *Submarines at War: The History of the American Silent Service.* New York: Stein and Day, 1983.

Hughes, Kaylene. "Two 'Arsenals of Democracy.'" *Historic Huntsville Quarterly* 17 (Winter–Spring 1991): 48–66.

Ivie, Tom. *Aerial Reconnaissance: The 10th Photo Recon Group in World War II.* Fallbrook, Calif.: Aero Publishers, 1981.

Jackson, Raymond. "The Dixiecrats: Rumblings of an Impending Storm." Manuscript in author's possession.

Jakeman, Robert J. *The Divided Skies: Establishing Segregated Flight Training at Tuskegee, Alabama, 1934–1942.* Tuscaloosa: University of Alabama Press, 1992.

———. "Jim Crow Earns His Wings: The Establishment of Segregated Flight Training at Tuskegee, Alabama, 1934–1942." Ph.D. diss., Auburn University, 1988.

Jernigan, Michael. "Andrew Jackson Higgins: Southern Entrepreneur." Master's thesis, Auburn University, 1986.

Johnson, Stanley. *Queen of the Flat-Tops: The USS Lexington and the Coral Sea Battle*. New York: E. P. Dutton, 1942.

Jones, Allen Woodrow. "Republicanism in Jefferson County, Alabama, 1952–1958." *Alabama Historical Quarterly* 22 (Spring and Summer 1960): 103–32.

Jones, Hank. "50 Years of Civilian Air Patrol." *Retired Officer Magazine*, January 1992, 38–42.

Jones, James H. *Bad Blood: The Tuskegee Syphilis Experiment*. New York: Free Press, 1981.

Jones, Maxine D., and Joe M. Richardson. *Talladega College: The First Century*. Tuscaloosa: University of Alabama Press, 1990.

Keegan, John. *The Second World War*. New York: Penguin Books, 1989.

Kennett, Lee. *For the Duration: The United States Goes to War, Pearl Harbor—1942*. New York: Charles Scribner's Sons, 1985.

———. *G.I.: The American Soldier in World War II*. New York: Charles Scribner's Sons, 1987.

Kerkvliet, Benedict John. *The Huk Rebellion: A Study of Peasant Revolt in the Philippines*. Berkeley and Los Angeles: University of California Press, 1977.

Kerr, Norwood Allen. *A History of the Alabama Agricultural Experiment Station, 1883–1983*. Auburn University: Alabama Agricultural Experiment Station, 1985.

Key, Jack Brien. "Henry B. Steagall: The Conservative as a Reformer." *Alabama Review* 17 (July 1964): 198–209.

Krammer, Arnold P. "German Prisoners of War in the United States." *Military Affairs* 40 (April 1976): 68–73.

———. *Nazi Prisoners of War in America*. New York: Stein and Day, 1979.

Kummer, F. A. "A History of Agricultural Engineering at Auburn University." *Highlights of Agricultural Research* (Agricultural Experiment Station, Auburn University) 16 (Summer 1969): 11.

Lane, Mary C., ed. "The History of Fort McClellan." Manuscript, Fisher Library, U.S. Army Chemical School, Fort McClellan, 1955. Revised 1958.

Larrabee, Eric. *Commander in Chief: Franklin Delano Roosevelt, His Lieutenants, and Their War*. New York: Harper and Row, 1987.

Lax, Roger, and Frederick Smith. *The Great Song Thesaurus*. 2d ed. New York: Oxford University Press, 1989.

Lazenby, Marion Elias. *History of Methodism in Alabama and West Florida*. N.p., 1960.

Lewin, Ronald. *Slim: The Standardbearer*. London: Archon Books, 1976.

Lewis, George G., and John Mewha. *History of Prisoner of War Utilization by the United States Army, 1776–1945*. Center for Military History Publication 104–11. Washington, D.C.: Office of the Chief of Military History, Department of the Army, 1988.

Lorelli, John A. *The Battle of the Komandorski Islands, March 1943*. Annapolis: Naval Institute Press, 1984.

McCollister, John, and Dianne Ramsden. *The Sky Is Home: The Story of Embry-Riddle Aeronautical University, 1926–1986*. Middle Village, N.Y.: Jonathan David, 1986.

McFarland, Stephen L., and Wesley P. Newton. *To Command the Sky: The Battle for Air Superiority over Germany, 1942–1944*. Washington, D.C.: Smithsonian Institution Press, 1991.

McGee, Val L. *Claybank Memories: A History of Dale County, Alabama*. Ozark, Ala.: Dale County Historical Society, 1989.

———. *The Origins of Fort Rucker*. Ozark, Ala.: Dale County Historical Society, 1987.

McGovern, James R. *Black Eagle: General Daniel 'Chappie' James, Jr.* University: University of Alabama Press, 1985.

McLaurin, Melton, and Michael Thomason. *Mobile: The Life and Times of a Great Southern City*. Woodland Hills, Calif.: Windsor Publications, 1981.

McMillan, Malcolm. *Yesterday's Birmingham*. Seemann's Historic Cities Series no. 18. Miami: E. A. Seemann, 1975.

McMillan, Malcolm, and Allen Jones. *Auburn University through the Years, 1856–1973*. Auburn University Bulletin 68:5. Auburn: Auburn University, 1973.

Matloff, Maurice, ed. *American Military History*. Rev. ed. Army Historical Series. Washington, D.C.: Office of the Chief of Military History, Department of the Army, 1973.

Mellor, William B., Jr. *Sank Same*. New York: Howell, Soskin, 1944.

Miller, John, Jr. *Guadalcanal: The First Offensive*. Vol. 2, pt. 3, of *U.S. Army in World War II: The War in the Pacific*. Washington, D.C.: Office of the Chief of Military History, Department of the Army, 1949.

Mingos, Howard. *American Heroes of the War in the Air*. New York: Lanciar, 1943.

Montgomery Salutes Maxwell and Gunter. El Cajon, Calif.: National Military Publications, 1985.

Morgan, Carl C., Jr. "Craig Air Force Base: Its Effect on Selma, 1940–1977." *Alabama Review* 42 (April 1989): 83–96.

Morison, Samuel Eliot. *History of U.S. Naval Operations in World War II*. 15 vols. Boston: Little, Brown, 1947–62.

———. *The Two Ocean War: A Short History of the United States Navy in the Second World War*. Boston: Little, Brown, 1963.

Moser, Don. *China-Burma-India*. Alexandria, Va.: Time-Life Books, 1978.

Napier, John H., III. "The Military, Montgomery, and Maxwell." *Aerospace Historian* 24 (Winter 1977): 189–95.

Nash, Gerald D. *World War II and the West: Reshaping the Economy*. Lincoln: University of Nebraska Press, 1990.

Norrell, Robert J. *Reaping the Whirlwind: The Civil Rights Movement in Tuskegee*. New York: Alfred A. Knopf, 1985.

O'Brien, David. *Public Catholicism*. New York: Macmillan, 1989.

Office of Information. Air University. Maxwell Air Force Base. *Fifty Years of Aviation at Maxwell Air Force Base, 1910–1960*. Montgomery: Air University, Maxwell Air Force Base, 1960.

"O'Neal Steel." *Journal of the Birmingham Historical Society* 7 (June 1981): 32.

Parks, Joseph H., and Oliver C. Weaver, Jr. *Birmingham-Southern College, 1856–1956*. Nashville: Parthenon Press, 1957.

Playfair, I. S. O., and C. J. C. Molony. *The Mediterranean and Middle East*. Vol. 4, *The Destruction of the Axis Forces in Africa*. London: Her Majesty's Stationery Office, 1966.

Pluth, Edward John. "The Administration and Operation of German Prisoner of War Camps in the United States during World War II." Ph.D. diss., Ball State University, 1970.

Polic, Edward F. *The Glenn Miller Army Air Force Band*. 2 vols. Metuchen, N.J.: Scarecrow Press, 1989.

Prange, Gordon W. *At Dawn We Slept: The Untold Story of Pearl Harbor*. New York: Penguin Books, 1982.

———. *Miracle at Midway*. New York: McGraw-Hill, 1982.

Pritchett, Merrill R., and William L. Shea. "The Enemy in Mississippi (1943–1946)." *Journal of Mississippi History* 41 (November 1979): 351–71.

Record, James. *A Dream Come True: The Story of Madison County and Incidentally of Alabama and the United States*. 2 vols. Huntsville. N.p., 1970–78.

Roscoe, Theodore. *United States Submarine Operations in World War II*. Annapolis: United States Naval Institute, 1949.

Rose, Robert A. *Lonely Eagles: The Story of America's Black Air Force in World War II*. Los Angeles: Tuskegee Airmen, 1976.

Sandler, Stanley. *The Black Airmen of World War II*. Birmingham: Alabama Center for Higher Education, 1979.

Scharr, Adela Riek. *Sisters in the Sky*. 2 vols. Saint Louis: Patrice Press, 1986–88.

Schneider, James G. *The Navy V-12 Program: Leadership for a Lifetime*. Boston: Houghton Mifflin, 1987.

Schulman, Bruce Joseph. "From Cotton Belt to Sunbelt: Federal Policy and Southern Economic Development, 1933–1980." Ph.D. diss., Stanford University, 1987.

Schuon, Karl. *U.S. Navy Biographical Dictionary*. New York: Franklin Watts, 1964.

Semmes, Raphael. "Wildcat—The First Navy Cat." *Aerospace Historian* 28 (Spring 1981): 2–9.

Shea, William L., and Merrill R. Pritchett. "The *Wehrmacht* in Louisiana." *Louisiana History* 23 (Winter 1982): 5–19.

Shepperd, G. A. *The Italian Campaign, 1943–1945: A Political and Military Re-assessment*. London: Arthur Baker, 1968.

Sherrod, Robert Lee. *History of Marine Corps Aviation in World War II*. Washington, D.C.: Combat Forces Press, 1952.

Simmonds, Roy S. *The Two Worlds of William March*. University: University of Alabama Press, 1984.

Smith, Robert Ross. *The Approach to the Philippines*. Vol. 2, pt. 12, of *U.S. Army in World War II: The War in the Pacific*. Washington, D.C.: Office of the Chief of Military History, Department of the Army, 1953.

Smith, S. E., ed. *The United States Navy in World War II*. New York: William Morrow, 1966.

Spector, Ronald H. *Eagle against the Sun: The American War with Japan*. New York: Free Press, 1985.

Spidle, Jake W., Jr. "Axis Prisoners of War in the United States, 1942–1946: A Bibliographical Essay." *Military Affairs* 39 (April 1975): 61–66.

Stafford, Edward P. *The Big E: The Story of the USS Enterprise*. New York: Random House, 1962.

Stephens, Elise Hopkins. *Historic Huntsville: A City of New Beginnings*. Woodland Hills, Calif.: Windsor Publications, 1984.

Stewart, John Craig. *The Governors of Alabama*. Gretna, La.: Pelican, 1975.

Taruc, Louis. *Born of the People*. Westport, Conn.: Greenwood Press, 1973.

Teel, Troy. "The Busiest Village of the Plains: Alabama Polytechnic Institute during World War II." Manuscript, August 1991, in author's possession.

Terkel, Studs. *The Good War*. New York: Pantheon Books, 1984.

Thew, Robert. "America's Most Successful Submarine." *Sea Classics* 23 (April 1990): 28–31.

Thomas, Mary Martha. "Alabama Women on the Home Front, World War II." *Alabama Heritage* 19 (Winter 1991): 2–23.

———. "The Mobile Homefront during the Second World War." *Gulf Coast Historical Review* 1 (Spring 1986): 55–75.

———. *Riveting and Rationing in Dixie: Alabama Women and the Second World War*. Tuscaloosa: University of Alabama Press, 1987.

———. "Rosie the Alabama Riveter." *Alabama Review* 39 (July 1986): 196–212.

Thompson, Ernest Trice. *Presbyterians in the South*. Vol. 3, *1890–1972*. Richmond: John Knox Press, 1973.

Thomson, Harry C., and Lida Mayo. *The Ordnance Department: Procurement and Supply*. Vol. 6, pt. 3:2, of *U.S. Army in World War II: The Technical Services*. Washington, D.C.: Office of the Chief of Military History, Department of the Army, 1960.

Tillman, Barrett. *Hellcat: The F6F in World War II*. Annapolis: Naval Institute Press, 1979.

———. *The Wildcat in WWII*. Annapolis: Nautical and Aviation Publishing, 1983.

Toliver, Raymond F., and Trevor J. Constable. *Fighter Aces of the U.S.A.* Fallbrook, Calif.: Aero Publishers, 1979.

Treadwell, Mattie. *The Women's Army Corps*. Vol. 2, pt. 2, of *U.S. Army in World War II: Special Studies*. Washington, D.C.: Office of the Chief of Military History, Department of the Army, 1954.

U.S. House of Representatives and Senate. *Memorial Services Held in the House of Representatives and Senate of the United States, Together with Tributes Presented in Eulogy of George W. Andrews, Late a Representative from Alabama*. 92d Congress, 2d sess. Washington, D.C.: Government Printing Office, 1972.

———. *Memorial Services Held in the House of Representatives and Senate of the United States, Together with Tributes Presented in Eulogy of William F. Nichols, Late a Representative from Alabama*. 101st Congress, 1st sess. Washington, D.C.: Government Printing Office, 1990.

van der Vat, Dan. *The Atlantic Campaign: World War II's Great Struggle at Sea*. New York: Harper and Row, 1988.

Verges, Marianne. *On Silver Wings: The Women Airforce Service Pilots of World War II, 1942–1944*. New York: Ballantine Books, 1991.

Walker, Chip. "German Creative Activities in Camp Aliceville, 1943–1946." *Alabama Review* 38 (January 1985): 19–37.

Wall, Randy. "Inside the Wire: Aliceville and the Afrika Korps." *Alabama Heritage* 7 (Winter 1988): 2–29.

Weatherford, Doris. *American Women and World War II*. New York: Facts on File, 1990.

White, Marjorie Longenecker. *The Birmingham District: An Industrial History*. Birmingham: Birmingham Historical Society, 1981.

Whitten, Clinton William. "Alabama Editorial Opinion on American Entry Into World War II, 1939–1942." Master's thesis, Auburn University, 1961.

Williams, Mary H., ed. *U.S. Army in World War II: Chronology, 1941–1945*. Washington, D.C.: Office of the Chief of Military History, Department of the Army, 1960.

Wolfe, Suzanne Rau. *The University of Alabama: A Pictorial History*. University: University of Alabama Press, 1983.

Wright, Gavin. *Old South, New South: Revolutions in the Southern Economy Since the Civil War*. New York: Basic Books, 1986.

Index

Adams, Julius C., 121
Adamsville, 169
Adcock, K. D., 115
ADDSCO. *See* Alabama Drydock and Shipbuilding Company
African-Americans, 10, 12, 40; participation in aviation, 4; classroom expenditures on, 6, 176 (n. 27); reaction to war, 20; USO facilities, 27, 28; money for bombers, 30–31; training at Tuskegee Army Air Field, 38; Ninety-ninth Pursuit Squadron, 38; 332d Fighter Group, 38, 117–18; 477th Composite Group, 39; segregated training for blacks, 39; Ninety-second Division, 42–43; poll tax and, 66, 69; and all-white political primary, 69–70; migration patterns, 73, 84–85; war as catalyst for social change, 85–86; workers at Mobile shipyards, photo, 86; nurses, 88–89; women workers at Brookley Field and in ordnance works, 89, 90; opportunities in industry, 91–92; impact of war, 164, 165
Afrika Korps, 94, 95, 114
Agricultural chemicals, 57–58
Agriculture, 2, 56, 57; mechanization, 58
Alabama (battleship), 125, 128–31, 195 (nn. 10 and 11); in Tokyo Bay, 160
Alabama A & M, 49, 92
Alabama Byproducts Company, 53
Alabama Drydock and Shipbuilding Company (ADDSCO), 53; photo, 55; women workers, 89; integrated crew, 91; racial tension, 91–92; photos, 92, 163; Liberty ships, 184 (n. 30)
Alabama Extension Service, 30, 56, 57, 101; radio programs, 184 (n. 41)
Alabama Ordnance Works (Childersburg), 51–52; secret research into heavy water, 51–52, 183 (n. 23)
Alabama Polytechnic Institute (Auburn University), 11, 14, 111, 114, 136, 143, 194 (n. 43); photo, 14; tillage laboratory, 58; effects of war, 77, 78; educational program for POWs, 97; radio extension programs, 184 (n. 41)
Alabama Power Company, 53
Alabama Rammer Jammer (plane), 115
Alabama War Chest, 29
Alaska, 140

Alcohol, views of churches concerning, 80–81
Aliceville POW camp, 95–96, 101; camp orchestra and newspaper, 97; educational program, 97; segregation compound for troublemakers, 102; deactivation, 103, 104
Aliens, 20
Almond, Edward M., 43
Aluminum Ore Company, 2, 53
American Cast Iron Pipe Company (ACIPCO), 3, 53
Amphibious landings, 143
Anderson, Alfred, 4
Andrews, George W., 72
Anniston, 37, 87
Anniston Ordnance Depot, 48, 182 (n. 7)
Anniston USO, photo, 29
Anzio, Italy, 38
Arizona (battleship), 12
Arnold, Henry "Hap," 84
Arrington, Richard, Jr., 85
Arrington, Richard, Sr., 85
Athens, 20, 31
Atkeson, John C., 132
Atkins, Leah Rawls, 179 (n. 17)
Atomic bomb, 131, 160, 161
Attucks, Crispus, 177 (n. 18)
Australia, defense of, 137
Autauga County, 195 (n. 43)
Avondale Mills, 56

Bain, Robert, 137–38
Baldwin County, 103
Bank, Bert, 106–8
Bankhead, John, Jr., 25, 70
Bankhead, William, 65, 70
Baptists, 77; on alcohol, 81; 1942 convention, 81
Barbour County, 67
Barker, Joseph Rhett, 17–18
Batson, Nancy, 87–88
Bauxite, 2
Beavers, Charlie, 161
Beavers, Jack, 161
Bechtel-McCone-Parsons aircraft modification plant, 31, 53; women workers, 89
Beecher, John, 135
Bellinger, Fred, 183 (n. 21)
Berkowitz, Abe, 83

Bessemer, 142, 158, 170
Bibb County, 169
Big Mules, 60
Birmingham, 2–3, 10, 16, 18, 61, 81, 135, 146, 151, 173, 193 (n. 22); target for Axis attack, 21; antiterrorist exercise, 22; defense production, 48; V-J Day, 162
Birmingham (cruiser), 125, 127–28
Birmingham Age-Herald, 104
Birmingham Blitzkrieg (plane), 112–13
Birmingham Blitzkrieg II (plane), 113–14
Birmingham News, 42, 101
Birmingham Post, 172
Birmingham World, 12
Birmingham-Southern College, 77
Black, Hugo: ties to Ku Klux Klan, 71; christening of *Alabama*, 128
Blackburn, Cecil, 115
Black marketing, 34
Blackout, 22, 23
Blair, Algernon, 95–96
Blanding, Albert, 7; retirement as commander of Thirty-first "Dixie" Division, 146
Blood drives, 26
Bolden, Paul, 168
Bolton, Cecil, 168
Bomber modification plants, 2, 53
Booker T. Washington (Liberty ship), 135
Borders, Bob, 113–14
Borders, Tom, 112–13
Boswell amendment, 70
Bougainville Island, 139, 167, 171
Bowfin (submarine), 133
Boyd, Charles Andrew, 12
Boykin, Frank, 2, 25, 72, 175 (n. 6)
Brecon Loading Company, 5; explosives, 52; women workers, 90
Brewton, 63
Brookley Field (Mobile), 41–42; handicapped employees, 42; aircraft modification, 53; Frank Boykin and, 72; employment of women, 87, 89
Brougher, Edward, 106
Buckner, Simon, 159
Budget, 68–69
Burma-Ledo Road, 155–57, 159
Burns, Lucien, 28
Busby, Anna, 11
Butler County, 58

Cabannis, William Jelks, 128
Cabin in the Sky (plane), 169
Calhoun, Rod, 115

Camden, 11
Camp Blanding, 15, 109, 122
Camp Rucker, 3, 27, 46, 72; Eighty-first "Wildcat" Division, 43; Joe Louis exhibition, 43; POW camp, 96, 103, 104
Camp Sibert, 44–45, 46
Campbell, William, 117, 194 (n. 26)
Campbell, William March, 54, 184 (n. 37)
Carbon Hill, 154
Carter, Herbert, photo, 39
Carwile, Henry J., 67
Casualties, combat and civilian, 162–63; Alabamians, 163–64
Catholics, 82
Chamber of Commerce, 1, 52
Chambers County, 42, 43
Chapman, 58, 63
Chehaw, 4
Chemical warfare, 44–45, 47; mustard gas, phosgene and lewisite, 50; incendiary weapons, 50
Chestnut, J. L., 10
Childersburg, 5, 15, 74, 76, 80; ordnance plant, 51–52, 183 (n. 23); women workers, 87, 89
China, supplies to, 155–57
Choctaw County, 173
Churchill, Winston, 110, 115–16, 118, 193 (n. 5)
Church of God, 82–83
City of Los Angeles (plane), 170
Civil Air Patrol, 23
Civilian Pilot Training (CPT) program, 4, 78
Clark, Mark, 43
Clay, Theodore Roosevelt, 49
Clothing styles, 34–35
Coca-Cola, 52
Cochran, Jacqueline, 88, 189 (n. 60)
Codebreaking: Pearl Harbor attack, 12; Coral Sea, 138; Midway, 141
Coffee County, 67
Coffee rationing, 33
Colbert County, 111
Cole, Houston, 21
Colleges and universities, 76–78
Columbia, 132
Columbus (German merchant vessel), 125–26
Condon, Henry L., 193 (n. 22)
Conner, Eugene "Bull," 40
Conners Steel, 48
Conscientious objectors, 82–83
Continental Gin, 54
Cooper, Angus, 54
Cooper, Arthur W., 58
Coosa River, 51; ordnance plant (Talladega), 51

Copeland, Miles, 122–23
Coral Sea, battle of, 134, 138–40
Cotton, 2, 57, 73
Courtland Field (Lawrence County), 36
Craig Field (Selma), 11, 28, 36, 38, 71, 119
Crescent Towing and Salvage Company
   (Mobile), 54
Crommelin, Charles, 134
Crommelin, Henry, 134
Crommelin, John, 134–35
Crommelin, Quentin, 134
Crommelin, Richard, 134, 139, 140
Crommelin family, 173
Cullens, Jim, 106
Cullman, 67
Cundy, Arthur C., 115

D-Day, 109, 119, 121. *See also* Operation
   Overlord
Dale County, 3
Dallas County, 3, 28; Colored Community
   Center, 28
Daniel, Jack S., 193 (n. 22)
Davenport, William O., 121
Davis, Benjamin O., Jr.: Ninety-ninth Pursuit
   Squadron, 38, 39 (photo), 117; 332d Fighter
   Group, 38, 117; at Tuskegee, 40–41
Davis, Charles W., 167–68
Davis, Harwell, 77, 135–36
Davis, Henrietta, 186 (n. 12)
Davis, Neal, 186 (n. 12)
Davis, Paul O., 56
Day, Lorraine, 27
Daylight Savings Time, 35
Deason, Charity, 173
Decatur, 22, 56, 193 (n. 22)
Decter, Moses, 123
Defense investments and contracts, 1–2, 52–56,
   164
Dent, Elliot E., Jr., 193 (n. 22)
Dill, John, 37
Dixiecrats, 60; Frank Dixon and origins of, 66,
   185 (n. 2 and 10); opposition of Lister Hill
   and John Sparkman, 71; criticism of wartime
   expansion of federal power, 164
Dixon, Frank (Alabama governor, 1938–42), 6,
   20, 22, 76; founder of Alabama War Chest;
   and car pooling, 32; racial tension at
   Tuskegee, 40; and Democratic party, 60;
   early life, 60–62; first gubernatorial race, 62;
   elected governor, 62; reforms enacted by
   legislature, 62–63; philosophy of govern-
ment, 62, 63–65; supporter of poll tax, 66;
   christening of *Alabama*, 128–31
Doenitz, Karl, 124
Doolittle, Jimmy: raid on Japan, 18, 84; 8th Air
   Force, 194 (n. 32)
Dorsey, Isham "Ike," 119–21
Dos Passos, John, 75
Dothan, 12
Duncan, Asa North, 111, 112, death of, 113
Durr, Clifford, 71
Durr, Virginia, 71

Eaker, Ira, 111
Eason, Hoyt, 193 (n. 22)
Eclectic, 193 (n. 22)
Eden, Anthony, 37
Edmund Pettus Bridge (Selma), 38
Education: school year lengthened, 68–69, 76;
   school overcrowding, 75–76; classroom
   expenditures: 176 (n. 27)
Eight Ball (plane), 115
Eighth Air Force, 111–12, 114, 115; daylight
   bombing, 112; *Birmingham Blitzkrieg* and
   first raid on continental target, 112–13;
   Hell's Angels Bombardment Group, 115;
   Cabin in the Sky, 169
Eighty-first "Wildcat" Division, 43
Eisenhower, Dwight D., 95, 111, 118, 119, 121,
   122
Electricity, 53
Ellsberry, Julius, 12, 30
Enola Gay (plane), 160
Enterprise (carrier), 134, 170
Erwin, Henry, 169–70, photo, 171
Eufaula, 16
Evans, Andrew J., 193 (n. 22)

Farm agents, 25
Farmers Union, 70
Feller, Bob, 131
First Marine Division, 142, 152
Fleming, Patrick D., 194 (n. 22)
Fletcher, Frank Jack, 139, 140
Fletcher, Hattie B., 173
Florence, 54
Flowers, Emma P., 26
Flynt, Claude, 75
Foley, 103
Folsom, James E. ("Big Jim"), 80; 1942
   gubernatorial race, 67–68
Forestry industry, 2, 58; use of POW labor, 58,
   102
Forrer, Samuel W., 193 (n. 22)

Fort Benning, Georgia, 5
Fort McClellan (Anniston), 3, 15, 22, 46, 89, 104, 109; POW camp, 96, 103; education program for POWs, 97; POW cemetery, 104
Fort Payne, 67
Fred Project, 51, 183 (n. 21)
Freeman, James S., 135
Frisco City, 173
Fussell, Paul, 153

Gabilan (submarine), 133
Gadsden, 44; ordnance plant, 47
Gallup Poll, 6, 33
Gambier Bay (escort carrier), 135
Gambling, 5
Gardiner-Waring Company, 54–55
Gaston, Arthur G., 30–31, 173
Gayler, Noel, 139, 140, 194 (n. 22)
German POW camps, 105
German POWs. *See* POWs
GI Bill, 1, 78, 165
Gilmore, Eddy, 116, 194 (n. 22)
Gilmore, Howard, 133, 172–73
Goggins, William, 131
Goodyear Mills, 56
Gordo, 167
Goto, Aritomo, 132
Grady, Emma, 173
Graves, Bibb, 62, 67, 68
Gray, Ross Franklin, 169
Green, Cooper, 32, 127
Green, Hattie, 127
Green, Myrtle, 90
Greer (destroyer), 8
Grist, Paul, 28
Growler (submarine), 133, 172–73
Guadalcanal, 132, 134, 141, 142, 167
Gulf Chemical Warfare Depot, 49
Gulf of Mexico, 25; German U-boats, 23–24, 55, 111; escape of *Columbus*, 126; U-67, 179 (n. 11)
Gulf Shipbuilding, 52, 53; women workers, 89
Gunter Field (Montgomery), 3, 12, 36

Halifax, Lord, 38
Hall, Fitzgerald, 51
Hall, Grover, 115
Hall, Grover C., Jr., 115
Halsey, William, 13, 127, 133
Hanna, Walter J., 148, 152; occupation of Phenix City, 198 (n. 38)
Hardie-Tynes Manufacturing Company, 3, 54
Harr, Harry, 157

Harvest, Henry P., 121
Hastie, William, 181 (n. 10)
Heavy water research, 51–52, 183 (n. 23)
Heflin, Howell, 167, photo, 171
Higgins, Andrew Jackson, 24, 143
Hill, Hugh, 20
Hill, Lister, 3, 60; FDR's 1940 nominating speech, 70–71; interest in medicine, 80; christening of *Alabama*, 128
Hillis, Eugene, 80
Hirohito, Emperor, 160, 162
Hiroshima, 160, 163
Hitchhiking, 32
Hobbs, Sam, 3, 71
Hodges, Courtney Hicks, 123, 124
Holcombe, W. H., 91–92
Homma, Masaharu, 17
Hope, Bob, 27
"Hot beds," 75
Housing, wartime shortages of, 75
Houston, 8
Howard, Neal, 14, 177 (n. 24)
Howard College, 68, 77, 135
Huntsville, 5, 12, 76, 172; fear of sabotage, 21; arsenals and rapid growth of town, 48–51; air service, 49; population growth, 74, 75; women workers, 87, 89; Oakwood School, 183 (n. 11)
Huntsville Arsenal, 5, 44, 80, 187 (n. 14); chemical warfare production and storage, 44, 49–51; Fred Project, 51, 183 (n. 21); incendiary bombs, 158
Huntsville Chemical Warfare Depot, 49

Industry defense contracts and manufacturing, 51–56
Ingalls Iron Works, 52, 53–54
Isney, 173
Isom, Luther James, 12
Italian POWs. *See* POWs
Iwo Jima, 157–59

Japanese POW camps, 104, 105
Jefferson County, 12, 30, 53, 105, 169
Jews, 83–84
Johnson, Ben, 158
Jolly, Hoyt, 167
Jones, Mrs. James, 173
Jordan, Ralph, 114, 121
Julius Ellsberry (plane), 30

Kamikaze, 128, 131
Kearney (destroyer), 8

Kirtland, Fred D., 129, 131
Klein, Alfred, 99, 103–4
Krueger, Walter, 147, 148, 157
Ku Klux Klan, 65, 67, 82; Hugo Black's ties to, 71
Kudzu, 57
Kummer, F. A., 58

La Guardia, Fiorello, 21
Landsdowne Steel and Iron Company, 47
Langan, Joseph, 146, 152, 198 (n. 46)
Larsen, Harold H., 141
Lawley, William, 118, 169
Lawrence County, 36
Ledo Road, 156–57
Lee County Bulletin, 186 (n. 12)
LeFlore, John (Mobile), 91
Leighton (town), 111
LeMay, Curtis, 37
Lewis, W. C., 112
Lexington (carrier), 138, 139, 140
Limestone County, 80; defense council, 22; rationing, 31, 33
Lindsey, Jake, 173
Lipscomb, Oscar, 82
Liscome Bay (escort carrier), 134
Lively, William, 114
Lomax, 173
Lombardo, Guy, 27
Long Island (escort carrier), 141, 197 (n. 21)
Louis, Joe, 42, photo, 43

MacArthur, Douglas, 9, 15–18, 130, 135, 137, 138, 148, 150, 152, 159, 160; with John Persons, photo, 149
Madison County, 30, 90, 140, 168, 183 (n. 11)
Manhattan Project, 160
Manila, 9
Mann, Hoyt, 139
March, William (William March Campbell), 54, 184 (n. 37)
Marengo County, 90
Marianas Turkey Shoot, 130, 159
Marlett, George, 96, 191 (n. 9)
Marlett, Maxine, 191 (n. 9)
Marshall, George C., 111, 152; at Maxwell Field, 37
Marshall County, 68
Martin, Clarence E., 157
Marvel Valley, 169
Matsumoto, 20
Maxwell Field (Montgomery), 3, 12, 36, 97;

instructors' school, 37; Wacs, 37; B-29s, 37; racial tensions, 40, 65
McArthur, Paul G., 193 (n. 22)
McCampbell, David, 170–72
McDaniel, John L., 51, 187 (n. 14)
McDonald, Mrs. William B., 173
McEniry, John Howard, 142
McGhee, Thomas K., 114
McGowin, Earl, 58, 63
McKenzie, Frank, 140
McLemore brothers, 58
McMillan, Ed Leigh, 30
McMorris, Charles H., 12–13, 131, 132, 133
Mealer, Ann, 106
Mechanization of agriculture, 58
Medals of Honor, 167–73
Medical College of Alabama, 79
Methodists, 81; 1942 convention, 81
Midway, battle of, 140–41
Miller, Glenn, 27, 37, 180 (n. 30)
Mims, John L., 114
Minchew, Leslie D., 193 (n. 22)
Missouri (battleship), 160
Mitchell, Edwina, 181 (n. 52)
Mitchell, H. L., 70
Mobile, 2, 9, 22, 41, 52, 53, 76, 82, 91, 152, 169, 175 (n. 4 and n. 6); port of, 54; racial tensions in shipyard, 65; population growth, 74, 75; convoys to Russia, 116
Mobile (cruiser), 125, 128, 195 (n. 9)
Mobile Air Service Command, 41, 53, 89
Mobile Cadets (Thirty-first Signal Company), 146
Mobile Press Register, 21
Montevallo, 173
Montgomery, 3, 26, 36, 81, 167; USO, 26–27, 193 (n. 22); ordnance, 48; POWs, 104; V-J Day, 162. *See also* Maxwell Field
Montgomery Advertiser, 19, 31, 65, 67; Spangler cartoon, photo, 74
Montgomery, Bernard, 95, 116, 118
Moore, John T., 193 (n. 22)
Moorer, Thomas, 138
Morotai Island, 148–51
Morrow, Hugh, 61
Moton Field, 4
Movies, 10
Mullin, Atticus, 67
Mullinnix, H. M., 134
Munger T. Ball (tanker), 32
Murphy, Vincent R., 131
Muscle Shoals, 50
Myitkyina pipeline, 156

NAACP, 91
Nagasaki, 128, 160, 163
Napier Field, 4, 36
National Guard (Alabama), 3, 5, 6, 7, 14, 17, 21, 142, 145, 148; federalization, 146–47; maneuvers in Louisiana and Carolinas, 147
Negro County Farm Bureau, 26
Neosho (oiler), 139
New, John Henry, 169
New Guinea, photo, 149
Newton, Wesley P., 27, 105
Nicholas, Clarence, 154
Nichols, William F., 123, 194–95 (n. 43)
Nimitz, Chester, 137, 138, 141, 157
Ninety-ninth Pursuit Squadron (African-American), 4, 38, 41, 117–18, 194 (n. 28); photo, 39
Nist, Joan, 11
Normandy invasion. *See* Operation Overlord
Norred, William, 113
Nursing, 88–89

Office of Civilian Defense, 21
Office of Price Administration, 32–33
Okinawa, 127, 128, 155, 157, 159
Oklahoma (battleship), 12
O'Neal, Edward, 70
O'Neal, Kirkman, 48
O'Neal Steel Corporation, 3, 48, 54
104th Coast Artillery Battalion, 137–38
Opelika, 193 (n. 22)
Opelika POW camp, 94, 96; arrival of POWs, 191 (n. 9); education program for POWs, 97; deactivation, 103
Operation Anvil, 121
Operation Overlord: background, 110; planning, 118, 123; reconnaissance for, 118–19; postponed, 119; D-Day, 109, 119, 121; photo, 120; role of *Tuscaloosa*, 127
Operation Torch, 94–95, 111, 113, 126
Opp, 173
Ordnance plants, 47–48, 59
Orley, Scott, 195 (n. 11)
Otis, J. R., 56
Ozark, 27, 68

Palmer, Rhey, 121
Parham, William B., 133
Patch, Alexander M., 7, 121, 137
Patterson, Fred, 4
Patterson, Haygood, 29
Patterson, William B., 121–22

Patton, George, 114, 116, 119, 121, 122, 198 (n. 32)
Paty, Raymond, 78
Pearl Harbor, 9, 12, 13, 19, 125; and *Tautog*, 133
Peebles, E. B., 198 (nn. 32 and 46)
Peleliu, 43, 152, 154–55, 169
Pell City, 13
Penicillin, 79–80
Pentacostalism, 82–83
Persons, John C.: Commander of Thirty-first Division, 7, 17, 146–47, 148; photo, 149; commander of Operation Tradewind, 148–51; resignation of command, 151–52, 198 (n. 46); awarded Distinguished Service Medal, 152; opinion about George Patton, 198 (n. 32)
Peterson, Virgil, 181 (n. 10)
Phenix City, 5, 80, 198 (n. 38)
Philippines: Japanese conquest, 15–18, 130; liberation, 148, 150, 155, 157, 158
Philippine Sea, battle of, 127, 129, 170
Pick, Lewis A., 156–57
Pickens County, 95
Pine Apple Express (plane), 113
Pizitz, Louis, 83–84
Polio, 78
Poll tax, 65, 66, 69
Poole, Joe, 57
Poole, Sybil, 90–91
Porter, William N., 44
Port Moresby (New Guinea), 140
POWs (prisoners of war), 26, 94–108; location of POW camps, 95; Afrika Korps prisoners, 95; in lumber industry, 58, 102; SS prisoners, 96; layout of POW camps, 97; daily routine, 97; diversions, 97–99; religious services, 99; sports, 99; canteens, 99; treatment under Geneva Convention, 99, 100, 102; POWs in labor force, 100–102; 1944 peanut harvest, 101; Italian POWs, 102–3; Italian service units, 103; repatriation of POWs, 103; deactivation of camps, 103; wages, 192 (n. 24)
Prentiss, Vera Ruth Gomillion, 26
Presbyterians, 81–82; proclamations on racial justice, 82
Princeton (cruiser), 127
Prostitution, 5, 80
Public health, 78–80
Pullman-Standard Car Manufacturing Company, 52

Racial justice, 82
Radio, 10–11, 184 (n. 41)
Ragland, Elnora, 49

Rationing, 31, 32–34, 64; end of, 162
Recruits, 109
Red Cross, 25, 26, 29; and POWs, 98, 99, 100, 107
Redstone Ordnance Plant (Redstone Arsenal), 5, 50, 89–90, 183 (n. 22); Fred Project, 183 (n. 21)
Religion, 81–84; Christianity and war, 81
Republic Steel Company, 3, 52
Reuben James (destroyer), 9
Reynolds Metals, 52, 53
Richardson, R. H., 22
Roberts, George S., 194 (n. 28)
Robinson, William, 14, 177 (n. 24)
Rommel, Erwin, 94, 95, 114, 119
Roosevelt, Eleanor, 4
Roosevelt, Franklin D., 1, 5, 6, 8, 9, 14, 20, 32, 82; cruises on *Tuscaloosa*, 125, 126; created Office of Civilian Defense, 21; and Alabama voters, 60; 1940 presidential campaign, 65; and Alabama congressional delegation, 70; address to Congress after Pearl Harbor, 19; war goals, 110, 115–16; and Operation Torch, 193 (n. 5); and Operation Overlord, 118; death, 124, 160
Rural electrification, 73
Russell County, 143

Salvage drives, 26
Sanders, Verbon, 167
San Francisco (cruiser), 12, 131–32
Schmidt, Harry, 157–58
Schroer, John, 104
Seale, 143
Seals, Carl, 16, 105–6
Seals, Margaret, 17, 106
Selective Service and Training Act, 3, 6, 64, 87
Selma, 10, 11, 27–28, 71; housing shortages, 38
Semmes, Raphael (Confederate admiral), 128
Semmes, Raphael (descendant of Confederate admiral), 128, 195 (n. 10)
Sherlock, Chris, 67
Shipbuilding industry, 53–54, 59; Frank Boykin and, 71; women in, 89
Shoho (light carrier), 139
Shokaku (carrier), 139
Short, Walter C., 9
Sibert, William, 44. *See also* Camp Sibert
Sieglaff, Barney, 13
Simpson, James A., 60
Slater, Frank, 132
Sledge, Eugene, 152–55, 159, 169

Sloss-Sheffield Steel and Iron Company, 3
Smith, Ben M., 6
Smith, Holland McTyeire, 142–45, 157, 199 (n. 67); portrait, 144; spat with Army, 145, 151
Smith, John P., 40
Smith, Ralph, 151
Smith Lumber Company, 58
Smith v. *Allwright*, 69–70
Solomons, 132, 135
Southeast Air Corps Training Center, 3. *See also* Maxwell Field
Southeast Army Air Depot, 41, 89
Southern Tenant Farmers Union, 70, 101
Spaatz, Carl, 111, 112
Sparkman, John, 71, 123
Sparks, Chauncey, 30, 91; racial tensions at Maxwell Field, 40; and Democratic party, 60; first gubernatorial race (1938), 62; 1942 gubernatorial contest, 67
Spears, Ted, 94
Spirit of Tuskegee Institute (plane), 31
Spruance, Raymond A., 141, 157
Stalingrad, 116
Starnes, Joe, 25
Starr, Edward M., 148
State Defense Council, 21
State docks (Mobile), 2, 53, 54
State Guard (Alabama), 21, 64
States' rights issue, 60, 65
Steadman, W. A., 1. *See also* Defense investments and contracts
Steagall, Henry, 3, 68, 70
Steagall, James, 37, 181 (n. 5)
Stockham Valves and Fittings, 48, 54
Sugar hoarding, 33
Sumter County, 85
Sylacauga, 56, 94, 194 (n. 43)

Talladega, 5, 51
Talladega Student, 20
Tate, Glenn Howard, 140
Tautog (submarine), 13
Taxes, 68–69
Taylor brothers (Opp), 173
Telephones, 73
Tennessee Coal and Iron, 3, 48, 52
Theodore ordnance depot, 48
Thirty-first (Dixie) Division, 3, 7, 14, 145–52; arrival in Pacific, 147; Operation Tradewind, 148–51; Philippine campaign, 157
Thomas, Frank, 9
Thompson, James E., 123–24
Thorpe, Claude, 17

332d Fighter Group, 117–18
Tibbets, Paul, 112, 160
Tojo, Hideki, 145
Tokyo, fire bombing of, 158
Tombigbee River, 96
Touchet (Liberty ship), photo, 55
Traywick, J. T., 105–6
Treadwell, Jack, 172
Troup, Franklin W., 193 (n. 22)
Truman, Harry, 124, 160, 162
Tucker, Henry W., 139
Turner, R. Kelly, 157
Tuscaloosa, 36, 101
Tuscaloosa (cruiser), 125–27
Tuscaloosa News, 106
Tuscumbia, 172
Tuskegee Army Air Field, 4, 36, 176 (n. 16);
    Ninety-ninth Pursuit Squadron training, 38,
    117; 477th Composite Group, 39; racial
    tensions, 39–40, 65
Tuskegee Institute, 4, 26, 88; Orange Blossom
    Bowl, 9; agricultural extension programs, 56,
    57, 184 (n. 41)
Tuskegee VA hospital, 78–79
TVA (Tennessee Valley Authority), 49; Wilson
    Dam, 50
Twenty-seventh "Empire" Division (New
    York National Guard), 15, 178 (n. 27)

U-boats (German), 8, 111, 179 (n. 11); attacks in
    Atlantic, Gulf of Mexico and Caribbean, 23–
    25, 32, 55, 116; and coffee rationing, 33
Union Springs, 71
University of Alabama, 63, 68, 77–78, 87, 113,
    115, 136, 146, 168; education programs for
    POWs, 97
Urbanization, 74
USO (United Service Organizations), 26, 27;
    Montgomery, 27; Selma, 28; photo, 28

V-E Day, 123, 161; photo, 163
V-J Day, 160, 161–62
V-12 program, 77, 135–36
Vandergrift, Alexander, 141
Venereal diseases, 78, 80, 188 (n. 27)

Victory gardens, 34
Vogtle, Alvin W., 105

Waco, 37, 42, 110
Wade, Russell Burdick, 8
Wages, 73; rapid growth of industrial wages,
    75; teaching and industry, 76; women's
    wages, 90; impact of war, 164
Wainwright, Jonathan, 16–17, 18, 105–6, 137
Wallace, Henry A., 65
War bonds, 30
War Manpower Commission, 87, 90; and POW
    labor, 101
War prisoners. *See* POWs
Warren, Hoyt, 11, 119
Warrior River, 3
Washington, Booker T., 4
Waterman Steamship Line, 54
Watson, Wilson Douglas, 172
Weed, Mary Louise Caton, 97
West, Kent, 112–13
Wetumpka, 12, 133, 173
Wheeler Dam, 15
White, Francis S., 61
Williams, Aubrey, 70
Williams, Joe, 85
Williamson, Edward, 123
Willingham, J. R., 122
Willingham, Joseph H., 12, 13, 133
Winston County, 8
With the Old Breed at Peleliu and Okinawa, 153.
    See also Sledge, Eugene
Women, 85–91; women workers, 2, 41–42, 76,
    87, 89–90; War Manpower Commission and,
    87; industrial wages, 90; in politics, 90–91; in
    military service, 110; impact of war, 164;
    photo of welders, 56
Women's Airforce Service Pilots (WASPs), 87–
    88
Wright, J. T., 20
WSFA (Montgomery radio station), 27

Yamamoto, Isoroku, 14, 140, 141
Yorktown (carrier), 134, 138, 139, 140

Zaungast (Aliceville POW camp newspaper),
    98
Zuikaku (carrier), 139